# Narendra Modi

## Changing Direction of the Wind

## And Challenges Ahead

M.L. Gupta

# Dedication

This book is dedicated to the memory of my mother
and father

# Preface

Perhaps there is no other Indian politician who has braved the coordinated attack from the legislature, executive, judiciary and the media at the same time since 2002 when he was the Chief Minister of Gujarat. The worst thing was the attack from his own party seniors, who had used for long a rhetoric distinctly unwelcome to many in the civil society, in the name of Rajdharma. Objectivity was lost by many right thinking individuals under the media din against Narendra Modi. The international media too bought into motivated stories spun by the Indian media against Narendra Modi. Indian paid lobbies operating abroad went to the extent of requesting the USA not to give Visa to Narendra Modi, as if a visa to the US is a ticket to the heaven. How mischievous all those stories were has been proved by courts and the admirable record of service of Narendra Modi as Chief Minister of Gujarat for 12 years in a straight row. It has been appreciated by the people of India who chose him to be the Prime Minister of India in 2014. His service to the nation in these two years has won him all round appreciation. He has made India proud and earned her respect from all countries. It is a matter of great relief that he has given the country a strong and clean government. Time at his disposal is too short to fulfill the aspirations of 1.25 billion people. The people know it and may give him another term when the time to take that decision comes.

Meanwhile the world has seen too much of the reality since 2002. The values of the civilized world have come under attack from the same forces which created riotous situations in Gujarat, Mumbai, Jaipur, Delhi, Punjab and other places in India as they repeated their organized crimes in London, Paris, Brussels or Orlando. They have created fear and security concerns throughout the world, imposing terrible economic costs to the world. They have created a peculiar situation of mass exodus of people affected by ISIS and AQ to Europe. Terrorism is more than that: it is a new form of war the civilized world has never fought so far. How long shall the civilized world go on holding candle marches, laying wreaths  and saying prayers? That is not enough.

India has suffered the terrorist attacks the most in the world for more than 35 years now. The civilized world ignored the enormity of these crimes against Indians and humanity in general as they were the most inhuman methods adopted by a set of people with a medieval mindset. They forgot that India was being used as a test bed for the terror factories sponsored by those states which used terrorism as a state policy only to subdue the Western World ultimately. They have yet to connect the dots. Attack on India is an attack on democracy, liberal society, peace and non-violence. India is one of the few vibrant democracies in the region. Signs of weakening of the democratic structure were causing terrible worry to the masses. Narendra Modi held out hope to the 1.25 billion people of India against all the maligning by his opponents, who were very powerful indeed. The people adopted him as their leader and gave him a thumping majority in the Lok Sabha (The House of Representatives in the Indian Parliament) to form a strong and stable government. Modi has not disappointed them. Modi has also proved himself a statesman of a very high stature.

Modi has done the unimaginable by changing the direction of the wind taking the country from the disastrous path of mis-governance, corruption and calamity to transparency with a strong and stable good government; from dejection to hope; from shame to honor.

This book is an authentic account of the events of the last 3 years by a keen observer of political trends and developments in India for more than 50 years. A wider perspective is provided by significant world events and political trends affecting India and other countries. Readers will enjoy it if they temporarily move to the time mentioned in the chapters with the writer and feel themselves being in New Delhi from the second half of 2013 to date. India is a vast country. Its diversity of people, places, politics, culture, languages and religions may demand a little more reader attention to appreciate the evolution of Narendra Modi to the position of the Prime Minister of India.

Mahatma Gandhi, Martin Luther King and Nelson Mandela are not born every day. They are the products of the cumulative thinking of a society for decades and even centuries. Ignoring such leaders is no act of wisdom. Narendra Modi, Prime Minister of India, is a similar product of the past and present cumulative thinking of the people of India and their vision for the future, which has led to a strong, stable and forward looking government. Attempts to eliminate such leaders can cost heavily on internal security for the country concerned as also world peace. Maintaining world peace can't be the responsibility of the UNO alone; it is the collective responsibility of the member nations and their leadership. Member nations don't have first rate understanding of each other's social, political and cultural make. Lack of information and understanding creates huge gaps, wherein the press and media steps in. The media is known to be partisan. Instead of creating an atmosphere of understanding, it creates misunderstanding among nations or peoples. Negative coverage of the leaders and their work harms development of a nation, its internal security and world peace. Media has become an "industry" today, whose news products can be "injurious to health". News pushing is akin to drug pushing and news lords are as dangerous as drug lords. The world should not go by adulterated news about Narendra Modi but form its own independent opinion. In India, nobody can survive for long in politics unless he practices a clean & transparent public service career. The news industry can hardly make or mar a Prime Minister in India. Only writers can produce reliable critique. Such writers owe no allegiance to anybody but the truth. Truth reflects the values of its practitioner.

This book has not been written to cast Prime Minister Modi in the mold of the writer's idea of him but to evaluate the significant developments influenced by him or because of him. It may look at times repetition of the same theme, but the context change compels its subsequent inclusion to emphasize the point that it is no accidental assault on Modi but something well designed and intelligently timed.

Readers from all sections of the global community will find the book of great interest so long as they are interested in knowing India and Its Prime Minister Mr. Narendra Modi.

Readers interested in Indian politics, economic and developmental policies, business opportunities, academia, terrorist threats to its sovereignty and people, media working, world peace, non-violence, elections, democracy and administration of Justice would certainly find it worth the time spent on reading it.

Governments, NGOs, Charities and human rights organizations would get to know the true strengths of India and spend their time, effort and money on genuinely productive work which will earn them real appreciation.

Universities globally need such authentic books on current affairs of immense value as they change the course of history.

Well-wishers of India would undoubtedly read through its pages. All Indians, resident or non-resident and PIOs of all shades of opinion will have the opportunity of reading a different account of India and its Prime Minister Narendra Modi to weigh their own understanding of them both.

If the presentation succeeds in proving to be of interest to the readers, it would have achieved the goal of placing before them a piece of significant history of modern India, which is going to influence policies in the next few decades.

M.L. Gupta

New Delhi, June 2016

# CONTENTS

## Part I - Narendra Modi's March to the Parliament of India

## Part II - Election And After

## Part III – After Completion of First Year in Office

## Part IV – Obstacles Overcome During Second Year

## Part V – A Billion Hopes To Deliver In Only 36 Months

## Part VI – Challenges Ahead

# Part I

## Narendra Modi's March to the Parliament of India

# Why was Narendra Modi in the News?

Narendra Modi was in the news in the second half of 2013 for various reasons after his nomination as the candidate of the BJP for the position of the Prime Minister of India in the next General Elections. So why were people excited, agitated or neurotic? There were several reasons that have not been highlighted by the media, especially the dominant English channels. The journalists of these channels have often claimed to be secular, progressive and independent. These are some of the pet words that have been successfully exploited for more than 60 years by the elite class in India, who have thrived in politics and media like the Upper Castes in the socio-economic and power structure in the Indian society for centuries. How much progressive or regressive, secular or fundamentalist, independent or embedded they are, is not hidden from the eyes of the people of India, who are neither poor nor uneducated as they were 60 years ago. While the disadvantaged and disempowered groups of the population have progressed to a level where they can analyze issues for themselves, the media has refused to yield space to them. They disappoint by presenting political, social or economic issues in a colored manner. If they are out to damage the reputation and prospects of Narendra Modi, they are doing only what they are best at. Even if it were another person, the media would have been no less harsh, though the rhetoric would have been slightly different to suit the individual's personality as with any leader from the farming community or labour class.

Modi's critics are hiding behind words like "divisive", "polarization", "communal" etc. Let us subject these three

1

words to a bit of critical analysis. Have the political parties professing secularism already not divided society in to communal and caste enclaves? Have they not made it an almost a permanent divide? Are they thinking of further division of India, the Second Partition of India? Are they blind to the consequences of the divisive politics that had cut India in to 2 and the country lost its territory to the rabidly communal forces, who rather than becoming satisfied and friendly have turned into the worst enemy of India, bleeding the country by the day ? Are these politicians not playing a dangerous game in the name of secularism by promoting fundamentalist forces? Why are they talking all the time Hindu-Muslim? Why don't they talk of Indians? Why do they forget the Sikhs, Christians, Buddhists and all other religious groups while talking of secularism? Why don't they blame the forces that cut India in to two parts? Will these politicians agree for another partition? If India suffers the consequences of divisive politics, it will not be because of Narendra Modi but because of those politicians, who were party to the first partition of India and who are taking India to another partition.

What the country is looking for in any new leader is his capability to create a genuine communal harmony and fraternity among all sections of India. The real polarizing politicians and their parties fear the emergence of such a leadership in the country. They know that Narendra Modi has that capacity to promote harmony and unity, and that is what these political parties and their leaders fear the most. In spite of their sustained vilification campaign against Narendra Modi for more than a decade, Gujarat has been free from any communal riots, whereas there have been more than a hundred under the rule of the political parties shouting the loudest the Mantra of Secularism! If Narendra Modi succeeds in forging that kind of unity at the all India level, all such politicians and their parties will cease to be relevant in the country. Whether Narendra Modi or another leader achieves this goal, the results will be the same for these parties. The self-proclaimed "protectors of the minorities" forget that it was India 2013 and not 1947. The minorities, a euphemism for only the Muslim community in India excepting Jammu & Kashmir, are so learned, rich, powerful and superior that these politicians fear them to the extent of keeping them away from the spotlight in politics or the media. For them donning a Muslim cap or Kafia in the company of one religious leader (they fear even a group of 100 or 300 of such faces) and mouthing reservation or secularism in public is service to the community! They are charged with appeasement and playing vote bank politics. They forget that the Muslim community does not survive on their charity or mercies but on their own intelligence, hard work and contribution to the development in all walks of life. Highlighting such achievements of the Indian Muslims is heresy for the players of the secular politics in India. Even the much talked about Sachar Committee ignored to record and report these aspects. It is nothing more than contempt for a sizable section of the population. Who polarized? Who divided? Who is still pursuing these nefarious designs? The Muslim intellectuals must give these forces a cultured response, different from the kind their protégés have been giving to keep the society divided and polarized to serve their vested interests.

Narendra Modi or any other leader will encounter resistance from these well entrenched politicians, who change their views and parties more often when it suits them. It was known at that time that if Modi succeeded in making it to the prime minister, he would need to change and adapt faster than he had so far given evidence. One thing should be clear to every politician in India that there is not going to be another exchange of population ever again. It means all have to live in harmony. This will be possible if all sections of the society take active part in forging that kind of unity. People have changed, politicians have changed, political parties have changed and political ideologies have changed. It has taken more than 50 years for politicians to understand Mahatma Gandhi and adopt his ideology for peace, harmony and development of the country; it will not take much time for Narendra Modi or another leader to rise above communal or caste considerations. The hyped Atal Bihari Vajpayee evolved from a Jansanghi to a Janata Party politician after working and learning the ropes as the Minister for Foreign Affairs. L.K.Advani, under the influence of the fake secularists, eulogized Jinnah, miscalculating it to yield rich dividends in the form of support of the Muslim community. It never happened. In the process, he has lost so much on 13th September 2013 that he will not have time even to regret it. He should have instead ensured that the emerging leadership of the party learnt the lessons in good governance, giving them the benefit of his experience as the Home Minister and the Deputy Prime Minister for full 5 years. Instead Advani chose to make public his frustration with the working of the party, forgetting that Vajpayee kept Advani in check so that he did not grow in stature to challenge his leadership.

There is another angle to Narendra Modi's bad press and livid TV channels: it is taking away the Delhi power center outside the National Capital Region or NCR. Whenever

4

Delhi is threatened by regional leadership, it reacts exactly like this. There is so much business and trade of politics in Delhi that no political party thinks of it ever shifting out of Delhi. One reason why the BJP failed to win the 2004 General Elections was its war cry against corruption. Compare the failure or success of the government in 2004-2013 period with that preceding it immediately. The "personally honest" prime minister sees no corruption in scams like the CWG, Coalgate, 2G & dozen others. What level of tolerance? Had the BJP or LK Advani shown that kind of a tolerance and worked out proper "adjustment" (!!!) with corruption, they would have been ruling even now! They are again raising the hackles of the corrupt by their chorus against corruption, and they will pay for it in due course. Running a government at the center requires millions of committed party workers of high integrity and public servants of caliber, capabilities, integrity and vision. The BJP or any other party has no such means at their disposal. You may talk against corruption to the fullest satisfaction to your heart, but can't remove or "root out" corruption without the services of that kind of party workers and public servants. Alas! There is a famine of such people in the contemporary scenario of ubiquitous corruption. When Indira Gandhi stated that corruption was a global phenomenon, she was not wrong. Consider it: can any political party ensure recruitment of 100,000 honest police personnel to run the police stations? Can any political party recruit honest officers to run the revenue, education, health, welfare and other schemes to deliver public services in a short tenure of 5 years?

The mass bribing of the voters has corrupted the whole society. The public perception is that all political parties are corrupt. Experiments of the past 10 years have not changed such a perception even though new leadership was entrusted the responsibility of governance in several states. The regional leadership has only displayed traits of autocracy, favoritism, pettiness, inequity and personal goals. They were all busy projecting themselves as the messiah of secularism, development and progressivism. The manner in which Narendra Modi has raced to the highest political position even before election results has shattered the dreams of these leaders. Why they are always issuing certificates to Vajpayee is because Vajpayee allowed them to exercise power as minister in his cabinet at the cost of the party interests, so much so that he did not allow even L.K. Advani to act as bold and independent as the allies! They were dreaming of swallowing the BJP vote bank by constantly harping on the 2002 riots in Godhara to malign Narendra Modi, turning a blind eye to their own record in engineering riots in several parts in the country or patronizing rioters for political dividends. The BJP has seen through this game and freed itself in time from the predators. These political elements failed to capitalize on L.K. Advani's ambition for the Prime Minister's position when the party anointed Narendra Modi ignoring the resistance from LK Advani.

There is yet another enigma hidden in these outbursts. Narendra Modi was reported to be a Chaiwallah (term of contempt from the neo-rich and politically corrupt class and their acolytes), who used to work at a stall run by his father, serving tea and snacks in Ahmedabad. Instead of celebrating it as an achievement for an ordinary Indian to rise to such wonderful heights, the neo-feudal political masters of the poor in India were calling it a shortcoming or disqualification for Narendra Modi. These rich and powerful

6

can only visualize themselves as benefactors of the poor/minorities/women/children/scheduled castes/scheduled tribes/backward classes etc but abhor the idea of any one from these segments ever reaching the level of the Prime Minister of India. They are educated, rich and minting money as any knowledgeable person can do, but they effectively block the entry of anybody outside their own elite circle, impede his progress, frustrate his achievements, down play his qualities and over play perceived shortcomings, indulge in vilification and even work for his elimination through fair or foul means. It is not "motiveless malignity". It is a fight, a struggle for existence, a war for the survival of the fittest. They have no qualms of conscience in approaching foreign countries to support them in their designs by material help and non-stop propaganda. The foreign policy interests of these countries match the domestic interests of the Indian politicians. A weak India is a market forever for goods and services exported by the world's super-powers. They protect regimes of their choosing and the illegal wealth of these corrupt politicians kept in tax havens or foreign banks. Narendra Modis challenge them, their operations and their goals. Neither the domestic nor foreign groups tolerate such leadership or political thoughts. They use the local political bombs to explode such leadership. Communalism, secularism, polarization, divisiveness, riots etc are only some of these political weapons over ground but there are many more political bombs underground. It will be a daunting task for any leader to maneuver such dangerous traps and lead the country to a stable and strong democracy. It needs to be emphasized that even Late Jawahar Lal Nehru too was under attack from the incumbent leadership of the proponents of neo-liberalism.

Whether the voter gave the mandate to the BJP or Narendra Modi was too early to speculate about. The elections were still more than 6 months away. Any development could have taken place. The much talked about third front might have taken birth. But Modi sharpened the competition. Every party was compelled to declare its PM candidate. Whether the third front would have been able to do so was always doubtful. The Congress was certain to shy away. The people were extremely angry with the Man Mohan Singh government, holding it responsible for unprecedented corruption, inflation, price rise, unemployment, non-working government etc. They were desperate for a change. For half the population Narendra Modi was the choice. The remaining half had enough time to think coolly. They were expected to contribute significantly in bringing in any emerging leadership to forge the traditional fraternity among all communities, castes and creeds in the country. The failed leadership of the forces of institutionalized corruption needed to be voted out in the common interests of the masses. They should build inter community trust in place of the suspicions created by exploiters of the poor people. The leadership shoulders the greatest responsibility in this regard.

There should be total elimination of acts which create suspicions even remotely. The people needed to restore the authority of the society, which practices values unlike the government and bureaucracy at the grass root level, over the authority of the plethora of government agencies out to harass them. Their credo is to ensure faithful implementation of the Constitutional provisions in all

8

respects. Nothing less than that is acceptable to anyone of them. A people friendly leadership can make India a united, integrated and strong country. People had seen failed leadership in the last 10 years. They had no stomach for more. Narendra Modi should remember that. Unless the new leadership is open-minded, receptive, flexible and liberal, it will fail to win hearts. Narendra Modi has raised hopes of the people for a stable, strong, transparent, fair, just, respectable good government, which can promote national unity, integrity and development of all. In poverty the masses are only one community. In development too they shall be one community. A leader, who can promote people's participation in good governance, alone can discharge the responsibilities of a good government (*sushaashan*).

Who was that leader going to be? Till his opponents named a viable alternative, it was to be Narendra Modi.

# Modi in Top Gear

Election 2014 India. Narendra Modi increasing his lead over his rivals day by day. Congress has no match against him and is dependent on all other "secular" forces, meaning all anti-Hindu outfits indulging freely in spreading their religion under its overt and covert patronage. Hindus have no objection to other religions spreading their spiritual wisdom - it is the essence of Sanatan Dharma. But the Congress has given it a malicious twist for vote bank politics. They have inflicted untold social, cultural, economic, political and spiritual misery on a nation of peace loving people, who respect others and expect the others to do the same thing. Indulging in obnoxiously disgusting abuse of religion ad nauseam election after election by the self-proclaimed secular forces led by the Congress has divided India more in just 67 years than the British could achieve in 200 years! They have stoked repeatedly communal violence, caste strife, regional conflicts, political rivalries, industrial disturbances, snapped supplies, impeded development, substituted rule of law by the rule of the jungle and have even started bullying the judiciary. They have actively promoted corruption. They have monopolized agriculture, trade, industry and almost every means of production and income. They control everything. They can't be ignored, even if you despise to see them. They have grown arrogant, turned autocratic and conduct themselves as the Most Privileged MPs/MLAs and Netas (politicians) in the belief that there is nobody to challenge them, to de-throne them, to oust them. They think themselves the superman, treating others nothing more than insects. They got a rude shock in December last year when the ordinary voter in Delhi showed them the might of the vote and the power of the common man. Since then, they are shaking in uncertainty and fear of the electoral verdict this May 16.It is in this context that an ordinary man like Narendra Modi is making  them to lose their sleep.

What is so remarkable about such an ordinary man? Nothing excepting what the Indian voter wants from its Prime Minister: honesty, character, resoluteness. The last ten years have witnessed corruption and lack of lawful governance. The sturdy organizational infrastructure for lawful governance in the country bequeathed by the British has been undermined by the incumbent government. The politicians still think the people don't understand the methods of governance or the machinations of the corrupt. That is where they err. The old generation which has been witness to the success of the old communal exploitation or caste divide mechanism of the Congress is incapable of seeing the India that rejects their methods outright. It is a generational gap that the old politicians refuse to accept. It is Vaanprastha (retirement) time for them, but they refuse to vacate and make room for the youth to move in. The result is policy paralysis. The post Emergency born are now 35 plus, highly qualified, global citizens, capable of introducing change for the better. They are genuinely concerned and want to transform governance in the country to subserve the common good of the people without discrimination of caste, creed, community, region or gender. They have done it in their specific fields as professionals in India and abroad. They are financially sound. They have seen abundance in the country unlike us who had suffered situations like wheat imports under PL-480 to feed the hungry mouths. Modi has been particularly addressing this new generation, which has approved him for the highest job on the basis of his governance record in Gujarat.

Modi is being opposed by all those who are the beneficiaries of the status quo. But things have changed- Congress is going to be the biggest loser in this election. In Delhi election last year, the anti-Congress vote went to the newbie, which secured 28 seats. Its captain is openly asking for instability, an "unstable" government. He had given the people of Delhi a taste of his anarchy and unstable government. It would be too daunting for anybody to consider the wise Indian voter so immature as to secure an unstable government at the center. The people have decided in favor of Modi. They know Modi is a changed man, the BJP is a changed party and the political environment is changed. The vilification campaign against Modi by overplaying something that happened more than 12 years ago and underplaying communal riots in Muzaffarnagar as recently as 6 months ago has exposed these elements, which have successfully fooled the minorities for so long. Their old trick to use the influence of the religious leaders also appears to be ineffective. There lies the secret of Modi's gains and frustrations of his opponents, within and outside his own party. What the Hindu-bashers were attacking so far was the BJP leadership, which was generally in the hands of the upper castes. Modi belongs to "other backward class" (OBC). A polity, a secular brigade, an anti-caste intellectual liberal minded modern society has consistently refused to

12

acknowledge the perpetual social divide caused in post-independence India by legalizing the social stratification in the name of reservation for government jobs. It was supposed to be a temporary measure to uplift the disadvantaged sections of the society. Congress converted it in to a convenient method to create loyal vote banks. It was bound to make others see the game and pay the Congress in its own coin. The emergence of the BSP (Bahujan Samaj Party) was but a natural growth in the caste politics of the Congress, because the beneficiaries understood the politics and asserted their vote power by first constituting a new political party and then forming a government. This development undercut the Congress, which would have been archived by now but for the life support granted to it by the BSP in the last 10 years. Even if the Congress managed to stitch a majority, it suffered the real loss in terms of no scion of the Gandhi-Nehru family becoming the PM in the past more than 25 years. Its loss this election will make it 30 long years. Unbiased political observers would show due prescience for evolving democratic trends in the next 20 years. My hunch is that the thinking of the ordinary people in India would be completely different from what it is today-they would think beyond caste and creed; they would think of living standards; they would fight for development. Modi has struck the right cord. The cry for development rises from across all religious denominations- it is not as if the poor and the marginalized among the Muslims and the Christians are better served either by their political leaders or religious leaders. They know the difference in the living standards, social standing and opportunities monopolized by the upper strata in these two communities. They know the reasons for their own backwardness. They want to break free of the choking grip of their religious leaders, using them as vote banks they barter away every election for their own aggrandizement and treating them as slaves of the medieval times. The condition of the poor in these communities is as worse or better as in other communities, excepting where democracy has freed them of the fear of the religious and economic masters. The greatest gift of Gandhi is his exhortation to the people to become fearless. This was a message delivered to the awfully frightened people of India in the last century and Gandhi proved that it could win them freedom if they challenged their tormentor. The exploited in the two communities have been demanding such a freedom, which the Congress has been suppressing by promoting the interests of the lobbies controlling the poor in these communities in the name of minority concerns. The reservation granted to the Schedule castes and tribes among the Hindu community has been thwarted for the Muslim and Christian communities. It is these segments who see in Modi a ray of hope: they have rejected the communal appeals made in the name of secularism. They know that the Hindu society is very liberal. But the secularists led by Congress have been demanding and promising 5% reservation for the Muslims. Think for a moment the availability of same rights as for the Hindu SC/ST to the exploited in these 2 communities and effect on the composition of the government it will have. It will change the composition of religious communities forever. But will the upper caste among these 2 communities ever allow the lower castes to share equally the community wealth and other privileges? For that the composition of the government has to undergo change. At the moment it looks these people are going to favor Modi. This is in spite of the media, which is in the hands of the upper castes so far. They have exploited foreign media also to block Modi's advance without much success, the Economist magazine becoming the latest journalistic buffoon of the century.

I consider trends more valuable than individuals. It is the job of historians to deliver the verdict whether the individual brought about the change or the change propped up the right kind of the individual at the right time. At this critical juncture of the country Narendra Modi has succeeded in winning the hearts of the masses and may be handed a powerful mandate to prove himself worthy of their trust. The American Congress is acting ridiculous by talking colonial rhetoric without even knowing simple facts about the country, misled by the likes of John Dayals and Katrina Swett. There has been an active lobby in America to ensure that relations between India and America always remain fragile. What has America achieved or lost due to such propagandists? Has it forgotten 9/11 so soon? Do these American lobbies believe that the CIA did not know where Osama was living while the whole world was made to suffer the consequences of a shadow counter terrorism operation led by America? The Americans will only harm their interests by indulging in silly interference in the Indian elections or mounting any absurd campaign against Narendra Modi or any other emerging Indian leader, who might not serve their diktats. The change is imminent. It would be in the interests of everyone to accept the reality and welcome it. A strong India is an example of strong democracy; a prosperous India is a sign of democratic dividends; a glorious India is proof of peaceful co-existence of all of us on planet Earth!

# Modi's Biggest Achievement

I had eagerly awaited the outcome of the 2009 elections thinking that it might throw up a leader who could take the country forward expeditiously towards a prosperous and strong nation, overcoming all the challenges before him. It didn't happen. Hence the election 2014 gained significance. Narendra Modi was one of the several contestants for the Prime Minister position. His main opponent was Rahul Gandhi, son of Sonia Gandhi (Vice President & President respectively of the Congress Party). Any scion of the Nehru Gandhi family (the dynasty in media & political glossary) is projected as the only rightful claimant to the office of the Prime Minister of India. It matters little if the person is prime ministerial material or not; it is more than enough that he or she is a descendant of the dynasty. It is propounded on the strength of the contribution of late Jawahar Lal Nehru, who was the first prime minister of India and who is rightly credited with laying solid foundations of democratic India. Nehru was a socialist, rather a Fabian socialist. He became PM of a poor, largely illiterate, underdeveloped country. He became PM just after the end of the WW-II. The world was suffering the miseries of the power blocks. Globally, the poor and under-developed countries, largely colonies of the imperial powers, numbered many times more than the developed countries. These super-powers were directly and indirectly controlling or regulating development in the poor countries and they were making use of international institutions also to further their strategic interests. In such an environment, the government under Nehru marched with great caution without aligning with any power block. For the socialist Nehru, a tilt against the rich nations and towards the USSR was somewhat natural. Unfortunately, it got mixed up with the traditional Indian anti-wealth thought, which for centuries condemned money or wealth or richness or prosperity as an illusion impeding spiritual growth. Poverty has been raised to the level of a great virtue under such a dispensation. Without going in to the merits of the issue, it needs to be stressed that the second half of the 20th Century was witnessing very fast unprecedented change in all spheres due to advancements in science and technology. Nehru & his government got stuck in socialist rhetoric, which proved costly later on. It drove India in to what came to be known as the license raj. Government and bureaucratic grip on all levers of development retarded development, leading to virtual stalling of new investments in industry or the farm sector. The world was experiencing intense competition while India was unwittingly walking in to a strange kind of protectionism. The results are visible even today in the form of negligible exports of manufactured goods, few brands, not many patents, hardly any inventions or discoveries. It was all due to the attitude born out of the license & subsidy regime.

We have no instruments to take measurements of this attitude. Nehru could succeed because of the nationalist fervor of the freedom movement, the constructive & positive attitudes of the leaders of that time and the faith of the people in the honesty and integrity of Nehru and other illustrated leaders of the time. India of the first 15 years was a country to whom leaders could sell any dreams- dreams of a bright and prosperous future (tryst with destiny) and demand the maximum sacrifice from the masses. This the people gave in abundance, only to be cheated by successors to Nehru. Indira Gandhi, who became Prime Minister after the mysterious death of Lal Bahadur Shastri in Tashkent (USSR), tilted to the left to consolidate her position. It meant a stronger anti-business, anti-industry and anti-rich attitude to rule the country. She promoted her own kind of leftist ideology by forming a group known as the Young Turks. The choice of the word "Turk" reveals all about the attitude of the new regime. It inflicted greater economic misery on the country in the form of a still stronger license regime. Setting up industries became almost impossible, unless the middlemen were duly satisfied and rewarded. It was the beginning of the parallel economy, black money generation and flight of capital to Swiss banks or other tax havens from a country facing terrible scarcity of capital for its own developmental needs. Indira Gandhi imposed the first Emergency on the country soon. That act of hers jolted the sleeping giant India. The people started thinking of alternative leadership to govern the country. Experiments half succeeded but the process was set in motion.

Corruption, crony capitalism, black money, tax default, sickness in industry, growth of poverty, public discontent, crowd influence on government were some of the traits which emerged out of a failed leadership that could win elections at home but had no influence in the comity of nations. Any visionary leadership should have jettisoned the baggage of socialism to be able to march in tandem with changes occurring in advanced countries.

Even the USSR and China have adopted the capitalist models of economic growth, but India proclaims to be a socialist republic even today. The results are before us all: India is considered a corruption infested country where it is very difficult to do business. It means neither capital nor technology is allowed to enter the country. One of the reasons for such a poor showing is the poor quality of leadership in India. The Congress Party President, Ms. Sonia Gandhi, hardly fulfills the requirements of a Leader for a continent size country that India is. Her son is too young to understand the complexities of Indian politics: he asks village children what is "toffee" forgetting that the poor children don't understand what toffee is as they only know what "Laddoo" is. His sister, who has come out in his support quotes Garcia to the same lot, who know Tulsidas' epic the Ramcharitmanas by heart but not Garcia. They all talk the royal jargon of aid, subsidy or freebies. They don't understand the value of the wise saying that if you feed a man a fish you feed him for a day, but if you teach him how to fish you feed him for life. But that kind of jargon flows from scions of any dynasty, who are air dropped as leaders but do not work hard to win the trust of the masses as a leader. And here comes the difference between the Congress leader and his rival Narendra Modi.

Narendra Modi has built his political career by working with and for the people. He demonstrates his success in Gujarat to justify his claim. The Congress is a victim of autocratic aggression and autocratic submission, extracting submission from others. Its ministers have hurt the masses so much that they are highly despised. They have been carrying empty propaganda against Narendra Modi, extracting submission from the print and electronic media to aid in their efforts to malign Narendra Modi. What mean things have not been said by some newspapers, their columnists, their group television channels and their anchors shouting hoarse against Narendra Modi and giving him a hostile coverage in the media?

In spite of all this Modi has made wonderful strides and now these same media Moguls and their intellectual journalists are publishing exclusive interviews running into more than 2 full pages without a single advertisement inserted and TV interviews. The power of the social media and the internet has exposed all of them so badly in the reprehensible submission of the National Television, the Doordarshan, which edited out more than 30 minutes of the content from his interview. Nobody knows who ordered such a criminal act. But it has proved that the government is not run by Dr. Manmohan Singh but others, who try to operate from behind dark curtains.

The Congress has survived on manipulation of the press and electronic media for long. It got over the crime of cash for vote in the confidence vote and also succeeded in penalizing the Members of Parliament who exposed this crime. It had tasted blood during the black Emergency of 1975, when excepting for the Ramnath Goenka owned Indian Express newspaper, all others meekly submitted to the autocracy of Congress aggression. The film, Aandhi, boldy captured the situation and mood of the nation. The Congress forgot that we were no longer living in the 1975, but 2014 and could humbly claim to belong to the knowledge society. The full text of the Narendra Modi interview to Doordarshan (DD) was put on the social media the next day, leaving the so called "autonomous" Prasar Bharati (PB) pale faced. In this age of the internet the media cannot deliver victory to the Congress as it had so far done successfully. It has lost that kind of power. It has lost its credibility so much that excepting for the social media nobody wastes time on reading newspapers or watching TV for news or views. The crowd anger against these evil elements (ministers/media) is costing Rahul Gandhi dearly. Since Rahul could do nothing against his own ministers, Narendra Modi has succeeded in winning the trust of the people as a leader who will deliver on his promises. The more Rahul allows; the more Sonia reads without understanding the implications of speeches put in to her hands and the more Priyanka attacks Modi, he ends up gathering more strength. Why?

Modi has filled the crucial gap of "Leadership" and "Leader". The diarchy of Manmohan Singh as de jure Prime Minister & Sonia Gandhi as de facto PM has instilled in the public mind the image of an extremely poor leadership of the government, which has caused price rise, inflation, scams and destruction of all institutions of governance. It has established the existence of extra-constitutional centers of power, outside the Constitutional frame of scheme of governance, hijacking of the government by the outsourced agents who are extracting submission of lawful functionaries by complete lawlessness on the strength of autocracy of attitude towards law, citizens, government, parliament and state. India, that is Bharat, has not been in the safest hands.

Modi promises to India, which is a Union of States, a government as by law established. Modi promises a government that will engage on programs of growth that will create quality jobs. Modi understands what people want and he is committed to deliver that to them to the best of his ability. How much he would succeed, if he gets the opportunity to serve India, is to be seen.

Modi's best achievement is the emergence of a Leader. As the Emergency proved to be a turning point in the political history of modern India, so was the economic liberalization initiated by Rajiv Gandhi (for which credit has wrongly been given to Manmohan Singh & PVN Rao), carried forward by PVN Rao as well as AB Vajpayee. It is in succession of this approach to the developments of the 21st Century and equipping the country to get an honorable place in the comity of advanced nations that Narendra Modi seems to be focused. Modi possesses many traits to meet those requirements of a leader and has the potential to learn the remaining. Attempts continue to be made under the "Mission Contain Modi" to erect barriers to his march to the highest office, but it is bound to fail, for the bar for leadership has been raised very high this time. It will not be possible for the Congress or other self-styled secular forces (comprising extremist communal and caste forces whose only aim is to capture power so as to loot as much wealth of the nation as is possible, transport it to some tax haven and migrate to such haven to enjoy a good life) to thrust on the masses another disaster of a PM as was done by them exactly 5 years ago on May 16, 2009. It is bound to be different this coming May 16, 2014 as the country is going to have a true and genuine Leader this time.

# Not Minority but Scare-Mongers Afraid of Modi

Who is afraid of Narendra Modi? The scare mongers say the minority community is afraid of Modi. They are focused on only one community, forgetting others. It is neither their love for the community nor concern for their safety but rabid political trade-off. Had the community not been a solid vote bank, all these political leaders would have left them to fend for themselves, as they have done to other minority communities. The genuine minority in the "minority community" ruled state had been driven away from their habitats or states under the active connivance of the very same politicians. They don't even remember how many such victims have come to suffer inhuman atrocities in states like Jammu & Kashmir. Because of the social organization of the religious minority communities, they continue to be swayed by their religious leaders. These leaders are in cahoots with politicians, who encourage them to live feudal in the name of religion and "govern" their flock. Democracy is a big threat to them. Politicians encouraging them to come out of the influence of such forces and participate in the democratic process like others are viewed as dangerous people. It is these worried people who don't want to free their followers to actively participate in the democratic process. They fear Modi, who appeals to the ordinary hard working masses instantly with his sincerity. They communalize the atmosphere, knowing it well that second exchange of population is simply out of question. Those who live in India will live in India. It is better to forge fraternity among different communities and make India a strong, prosperous and great nation.

Besides political power that these politicians have enjoyed rather undeservedly for so long, they are minting money like never before. Take the classic case of Jammu & Kashmir-the Sheikh Abdulla family has ruled for the third generation. It fears Modi and threatens all kinds of silly consequences. The other beneficiary is the Nehru family, which is in the fifth generation. Like them Mulayam Singh, Lalu Yadav, Karunanidhi and several other politicians have usurped democratic power by rigging the voting process or sucking the gullible masses. They do fear Narendra Modi as he is bound to affect their style of politics.

Then there are criminals, who are a dread in their areas. Varanasi provides a glimpse. Rae Bareli, Agra, Indore, Neemuch, Bombay, Dubai, London, New York- the travelling route of opium and other drugs is known to national and international agencies. Such trades need the services of hardened criminals. Earlier they were supporting political parties but now political parties support them. They are members of state assemblies and parliament. Some of them are charged with heinous crimes. But they win elections, applying their skills of gun running and other arms operations expertise, to rule the territory they call their own. Modi (or anybody professing clean government) holds a potential threat to their very survival and trade and hence they fear him. The terrorists fear him, without whose valuable contribution the arms manufacturers will starve and thousands of jobs will be lost. They fear Modi becoming

Prime Minister of India. Modi threatens black money owners, but the whole parallel economy runs on black money. Where from the capital will come without black money hidden in India or abroad? The world might have suffered some meltdown in 2008 but it hardly had any effect on such operators in India, excepting reduction in exports (but India hardly exports manufactures- it is largely commodities or talent).

More than anything else Modi is feared for not being corruptible. So long as one is corruptible, there is no reason to fear: only the price tag may be different. The problem arises when someone refuses to price-tag himself/herself.

Modi is the change that the masses want. Modi has got the approval from the common man- the man on the streets, the man who has been fooled, starved and humiliated. The fall to street urchins language by college principal of a well-known institution in Mumbai, an intellectual in Kolkata, politicians, media wedded to them, mercenaries, ISI Agents called sleeper cells, foreign trade or policy interests, international business groups and elements hostile to India betray their anxiety and fear about Modi. These elements know neither India nor Modi. They are thriving on the doles from foreign countries under the garb of charity. Some are basking in the reflected glory of Anna Hazare, having no luster of their own. For them, propaganda against Modi is the free publicity. They too fear Modi only because the money coming to NGOs (Non-Government Organizations) is a windfall of unearned money, fame, awards, foreign junkets and trading influence for power without accountability.

Rest of India fears neither Modi nor anybody else. We are a nation of skilled people who love to earn their bread and butter through hard work. We are feared by those who try to interrupt it or impede it. Modi is one of us. If he slips, we have the option to replace him. But scare mongers have no business to create fear of Modi. Let them note that Modi shall unite, integrate and strengthen India; pull it out of the doldrums into which it has been thrown in the past 10 years; retrieve its honor and dignity which has been compromised by forces inimical to India through the operation of diarchy-an extra-constitutional mechanism. If Modi comes to power, nobody shall dare again to belittle Indian democracy so much. The Indian Prime Minister is not a titular head of government, whose executive authority can be exercised by any Tom, Dick or Harry or their combination.

Indian election 2014 calls for in depth analysis by political psychologists!

# The Congressmen's Sudden Love for L.K. Advani

Ever since the BJP announced its decision about their nominee for the Prime Minister in September 2013, the hearts of every Congressman started overflowing with love, respect and sadness for Mr. Lal Krishna Advani, former Deputy Prime Minister and the PM nominee of the party for the 2004 elections. The Congress Party, as also various other parties, had been ridiculing L.K.Advani, even forgetting common courtesies. They made fun of his "ambition" to become the Prime Minister and the Rath (chariot) campaign undertaken by him in the past to facilitate the party to come to power at the center. As the BJP (Bhartiya Janata Party) proved to be no match for the guile and machination of the Congress Party and its allies, the BJP lost to the UPA (United Progressive Alliance) in 2004. How "progressive" was such an alliance has been proved by the historic scams, non-governance, debilitated economy, unconstitutional centers of executive power in contravention of the constitution of India and several of its ministers being jailed for corruption. The UPA were living under the illusion that the BJP, which they pejoratively termed "Hindutvawadi" and "communal", is a rigid political party that will show no flexibility and continue with its grandstanding in a system corrupted by the UPA beyond redemption. In L.K.Advani they imagined only such a politician, who would cause easy defeat to his party's dreams to come to power at the center. They were, perhaps, not too wrong. L.K.Advani is a man of impeccable integrity. He is a nationalist. He does not practice caste or regionalism like most UPA politicians. He is educated, intelligent, erudite and sensitive to public needs. He is widely travelled in India. His value system brooks no compromise for political gain. These are no virtues for the pragmatic politicians that the political spectrum in India witnesses as ministers today. In fact, these are shortcomings which limit the maneuverability of the politician who loves slithering. The doctrine of "Aya Ram, Gaya Ram" is in wide practice in the country (revolving door policy). With all the pragmatic types united, they saw an easy victory in L.K.Advani being their rival in election 2014. Unfortunately for them, the BJP outsmarted them this time by nominating Narendra Modi as the party's PM candidate. This upset the strategy of the Congress and its allies.

They had long over-played the communalism card, which they labored hard to cash once Narendra Modi was declared the prime ministerial nominee by the BJP. They advertised the Gujarat riots like the refrain of a song without mentioning even once the burning of 49 innocent Hindu pilgrims in a railway coach at Godhara in Gujarat. For the Congress and other self-certified secular forces, it was not inhuman or criminal or communal or dastardly. In the process, these parties brought down the public discourse to a very low level and hate speech became their forte. It proved to be counterproductive as the election proceeded with each day ringing the death knell for the UPA with the motor mouths of the Congress Party indulging in license to say whatever came to their mind or tongue. They started displaying sudden liking, love, respect and admiration for L.K.Advani, fighting a kind of a battle for him in the

Bhartiya Janata Party. What crocodile tears? The other group that was playing politics in the name of Advani was that of Nitish Kumar, Chief Minister of Bihar, who expressed intense hatred for Narendra Modi and hardly ever accepted him as the PM nominee of the NDA (National Democratic Alliance). He and his party, Janata Dal (U), were equally nursing secret ambition to become Prime Minister of the NDA. The flexibility shown by the BJP in making adjustments with all kinds of allies and Narendra Modi displaying prowess to successfully work with a team as diverse as the NDA, the UPA's apple cart was upturned. The defeat of the forces of corruption represented by the UPA-I & II, numbed the Congress Party for almost a month. Other parties like the SP, BSP etc. took time to gather their wits to come to terms with the debacle faced by them.

The Congress Party continued with its special affection for L.K.Advani. They took upon themselves the onerous responsibility of portraying him as a victim of the intra -party feud between the Advani and Narendra Modi groups. Their followers in the media started writing special editorials to drive a wedge between the two camps. Great dissemblers! They shed tears feeling sorry for the treatment the party was giving to L.K.Advani. They mischievously started comparing him with Bhishma Pitahmah in the Mahabharat. They failed in their efforts as there was nothing like that in the prevailing dynamic political situation.

Had the BJP not shown flexibility or had they not opted for Narendra Modi at that critical juncture, UPA-III would have been ruling us in oppression even today. It is Modi alone who has routed not only the Congress Party but several others and got for the BJP an absolute majority on its own for the first time in independent India, so that it can't be blackmailed by supporters or allies. It is Modi again who has given the party an opportunity to be generous to the NDA partners. This partnership has satisfied the people as a government, representative of all interest groups in the country. Attempts to create a "Mahabharat" (Great War) in the ruling party led by Narendra Modi were bound to prove sour grapes for them.

The commiseration brigade took to indulging in the futile exercise, like those columnists, who wrote in the newspapers long sentimental articles on the plight of the domestic servants ignoring crucial issues demanding urgent attention. These columnists had so many demands from the government and the people on humanitarian grounds, but hardly ever paid them even the prescribed minimum wages under the law. One woman had written about her three maid servants (just note the designation), complaining in a typical sophisticated way about the two of the elderly maids and grudgingly complimenting the third one, who appeared to be a minor by the description of her adolescent behavior. You underpay, violate the law, breach all norms of human consideration and also make big issue about their plight because of the government or the people? Same is the prescription of a few popular fiction writers/ novelist turned columnist. One of them was too vexatious about the plight of these maid servants that he even prescribed norms (sanskars) to treat them humanely. My question to all such writers is: are you paying your maidservants the prescribed minimum wages and other facilities? The unfortunate truth is that the higher strata of Indian society treats domestic helps worse than slaves torturing them in the worst possible manner, inflicting injuries on them and in a few cases even murdered them. Starting such debates even before Narendra Modi had settled down in his new position as the Prime Minister was less than well intentioned. Preaching is easier than practicing. Dissemblers do more harm than the perpetrators.

In the name of modernity, all good norms (sanskars) have been jettisoned in the last 50 years in India. Maltreatment of domestic helps or children or women or elderly are new vices afflicting the Indian society. When the individuals choose to violate social or family rules, which are not law as passed by any legislature, they express contempt for "society" or "morals" and profess not to care for the society. Their logic is confounding as they demand to know what the society gives to them. But when crimes, especially those against women, take place the same people complain of public apathy as nobody from the crowd comes to help them. Once human kindness dries up because of curtness or cussedness of members of the society or the family, the results can be disastrous. One big epidemic that has gripped the Indian society is the neglect of the aged parents/grandparents or even siblings by sons/daughters/daughters-in-law staying in the traditional joint family. It has crossed the limits of decency as the son/daughter/daughter-in-law are frequently accused of "abusing" their father/mother/grandfather/grandmother etc. physically and verbally. The Government has been compelled to take notice of the problem and a law was put on the statute book in 2007, giving the parents legal rights to claim maintenance from their children. It does put some sense in the swollen heads of the children, but is really no solution to my mind. I have been watching the developments in this area since such a law made by the government of Himachal Pradesh came to my notice sometime in 1996. The parental need, especially a widowed mother/father, is much more than mere maintenance. Old age can be painful without the loving care of the family members. One becomes emotionally, financially, socially, medically dependent on others in old age. I have seen from close quarter scores of persons who survived the trauma only because of the care provided by the family members. We have been trained from early childhood to treat our parents like God. The story of Shrawan Kumar, who carried his blind parents on his shoulders to all places of pilgrimage, is ingrained in our minds. It is shocking for us to read in the newspapers the stories of physical and verbal abuse of the aged parents. They are no poor sons or daughters or daughters-in-law. They are rich, highly educated and well placed members of the society. What kind of humanity do these people expect of others in society? It is not too difficult for parents to change the scenario for their better existence- they have just to take to some practices in the west like re-marriage or spending all their earnings on themselves. Why should parents spend the last penny only on the well-being of children who not only can have the cruel heart to ignore them but also to abuse them physically or verbally? Norms of civilized and cultured behavior are taught and cultivated in the family as a valued member of a decent society. Unfortunately, the family itself has suffered fracture today: it slipped from a joint family institution to a nuclear family unit and that too has suffered divorce, replacing family ties by one sided master servant hurtling relations, where also complaints are the plot of novels and theme of news stories or documentaries. The example set up by the prime minister and his colleagues in the NDA government is expected to stall this slide.

Today's biggest affliction is this insincerity of emotions, this disruption of the emotions, this fouling of the norms of valued patterns of individual and family and social behavior. The overflow of commiseration for L.K.Advani or the maid servant is evidence of such feigned love, respect, concern. Today's generation has to re-learn the lessons it has deliberately chosen to forget. Apologies to the parents if you have hurt them. Do whatever you can do within your means to love them or care for them. The BJP needs and shall continue to need the L.K.Advanis as also each son, daughter and daughter-in-law will need the parents.

# India Elects & Delivers Stable Government

India has truly arrived in this election 2014. It is India that has voted this time. It is India that has delivered to itself a strong leadership and a stable government. It is the India that divisive and fissiparous forces in politics never allowed to unify and integrate the nation. They sold a divided view of India—divided into communities (majority or minority) or caste. They are known to have perfected the British policy of "Divide & Rule". India across castes, communities, gender, region, language or any other such consideration has elected after decades its national government. And this is a very big achievement. This is a crushing defeat delivered to the anti-national, anti-people forces. It is India's victory. It is India. It is the India of the knowledge society. It is the unified and integrated country. It is the people's freedom from the strangulating grip of ugly vote bank politics that has kept them subservient to political contractors & traders, who used them as fodder for civil tensions in the country all these years. Their trust has to be maintained and made an example for a great nation like India.

A great responsibility has descended on the shoulders of Narendra Modi. He has only 60 months, but he has to show results in a few weeks to start with. It is possible if he can restore public trust in the Rule of Law, which has suffered terribly at the hands of the corrupt UPA-I & II in the last ten years. Once the administration starts running as per the law and is seen to be so working, other things will soon fall in line. The rich pool of honest public servants should be given the responsibility. The Manmohan Singh government had handed over administration to known corrupt fellows who were loyal to extra constitutional authorities rather than lawful authorities.

The senior leaders of the BJP ought to realize that India has conducted a unique direct election of the Prime Minister of India, like the US President, this time and show grace in making a success of this victory of the people of India. Any attempts to harm the leader or his government will invite furious public wrath. People are watching them because of their utterances today. Any faint praise of Narendra Modi will amount to faint praise of the people of India, civil leer and sneer as also teaching others to do the same. In this moment of great hope they have dejected the nation.

The nation looks to Prime Minister Narendra Modi for deliverance from oppression and misery perpetrated on them in the last 10 years by the wicked politicians. It is a standing humiliation of this great nation that corruption of the UPA government has made even the most ordinary staple diet of the poor a luxury by raising the prices of common edible salt to Rs 24 a kg. You know it first-hand how the poor survive on dry roti and salt. Salt is India's most powerful symbol of national movement. You have to change this blood sucking of the common man. Prove your commitment to the promises made and you will find the people following you.

# Narendra Modi Sworn In Prime Minister of India

It is a turning point in democratic India's long life. It is a historic moment. More than anything else, it is the beginning of an era of hope. Unless one suffers first hand daily oppression by corruption and the misery of the masses due to it, one would never know what it was like for the more than 95% population of this economically poor but culturally rich country. The fact of it being rich culturally has made its people suffer the atrocities of the crooked masquerading as people's representative so far. India has been reduced by such forces to a mere semblance of democracy. Even monarchy would turn pale at the kind of oppression inflicted on the trusting cultured people of India. But even the nastiest of dictatorships would feel insignificant in comparison to the model of democracy developed by the forces of evil in India. They had introduced and strengthened a system of rule of political masters from the national to the village level, outside the constitutional scheme of things. Consequently we have ministers in charge of different districts, members of legislative assemblies (MLA) in charge of the territorial geography of their constituency and party office bearers at village panchayat, municipality, district, state and national level. What does it mean?

It means that no administrative function as mandated by law can be performed without the unofficial approval of these levels. Example this: a young girl is abducted and gang raped. The victim approaches the police. The police refuse to register the first information report (FIR), which can start proceedings to bring the perpetrators to justice. People don't get supply of municipal drinking water because it is diverted for illegal sale to other localities but the office concerned refuses to take the complaint or action as required under the law. In a hospital, a driver gives stitches because the doctor is running his/her private clinic at another place, but the authorities treat it lightly. Schools are run not by the government appointed teachers but those engaged for a pittance of wages by the teacher concerned, but it is okay with the authorities. Food for the poor is distributed to them on paper but generally sold in the market and tens of thousands of millions of rupees are pocked by those authorities who are under oath of office to be fair, just and honest. For such large scale operations, engagement of service providers and handlers of huge amounts of money are needed. There are highly skilled (?), effective, clever, intelligent and bold people fulfilling these requirements. They are the agents of corruption. They facilitate these operations. They are organized, networked and globally mobile. What the foreign policy of many advanced countries does to the governments of developing countries, these people can do much better. They are capable of disturbing government formation, disruption of government policies and dislocating critical functionaries of the government. People of India were sick of them. People of India were desperate to throw them out. They have done that. They have entrusted the responsibility of the government of India to Narendra Modi in the hope to see better days.

Narendra Modi has so far given ample proof of his commitment, capability and capacity. This time he has promised to prove his potential to serve the whole country (contrasted to his limited service to the Indian State of Gujarat). We trust him. The nation has reposed faith in him. He will get solid support of the people for an honest people friendly government. It is possible to achieve these targets, which will look like small goals in 2019. It can happen at less than 30% of the cost of the budgets of the past ten years, because it is sincerely hoped that the government will be determined to function honestly. It is hoped that it will have zero tolerance for corruption. There is no dearth of talent or honest knowledge workers in the government to deliver good governance to the people.

May26, 2014 has been engraved in the history of India as the Golden Day when Narendra Modi was sworn in as the Prime Minister of India. Change in the direction of the wind became obvious.

# Part II

## Election and After

# Prime Minister Narendra Modi's Responsibilities

The entire political establishment in India is nonplussed at the outcome of India Election 2014. The Congress Party is trying to find the reasons for its rout, but the BJP is no less confounded. Others like the SP, BSP, JD (U), CPM, CPI, TMC, BJD are simply benumbed. But it is so because the politicians erred in thinking themselves wiser than the people. The politician is the elite, English speaking and financially rich class and the masses are poor. Tradition has drilled into their heads a silly idea of superiority. The Constitution came into force on 26 January 1950. Sixty four years is no small time. The Constitution introduced the ideal of "equality" which politicians have not accepted in practice so far. They thought they have the divine right to rule the people of India by issuing manifestos at election time, making tempting promises during elections, launching some so called welfare scheme, distributing freebies during campaigning and garnering votes to rule in oppression over these fools for another term. Successes in elections had made them so arrogant that they started boldly terming the Comptroller & Auditor General of India reports of loooo to the exchequer to the tune of 176,000 crores or 186,000 crores and 76,000 crores as "zero loss". They had no sense of regret in allowing illegal transfer of capital from the country to foreign banks. They refused to proceed against the culprits even when their details were made available by the foreign governments like Germany. They increased their commission in defense deals which ran into billions of US

Dollars. They refused to govern and sub-contracted governance to an unconstitutional apparatus called the NAC (National Advisory Council). They tormented the masses with spiraling prices, corruption and economic stagnation indicative of the dangers to the very survival of the country. The masses expressed their strong resentment, which the ruling class ignored with the contempt it never deserved. No better allegory of such a state of affairs can be provided other than the gang rape, murder and hanging of two poor minor girls in Uttar Pradesh (UP) and the statement of the Chief of the ruling Samajwadi Party (Socialist Party or SP) during the recent elections to the Lok Sabha that boys do make such mistakes but we can't hang them for such crimes and if elected to power we will change the recent amendments to the rape law enacted post Nirbhaya gang rape and murder case of Delhi. His son and the incumbent Chief Minister of UP, displayed greater insensitivity when a journalist asked him a question about it by saying "Aren't you safe?" The political class forgot that the masses have a limit to tolerance of such lawlessness and drift, even though Mahatma Gandhi had inspired them to show maximum tolerance. The masses had long concluded that it was time to end this notorious and oppressive system.

The people were only looking for a man who could convince them of being worthy of their trust. We must rewind the chronicle. The strongest expression of people's anger came when Anna Hazare received enormous support for his agitation against corruption. Anna, however, presented no political alternative.

The masses were desperate to change the government. They were looking for the right kind of a clean and strong leader to provide the country a strong and stable government. Narendra Modi entered the arena at that crucial juncture. He had the right credentials: a successful Chief Minister who won public trust on the plank of development and growth for all, independent mind, clear headed but strong leader, a leader unafraid of the seniors in the party, devoted and dedicated and above all honest to the marrow. People decided to vote for Narendra Modi and other candidates put up by him. The results were before everyone: the BJP won 282 seats and the NDA 336. These figures drew OOHs and OUCHs from all political parties including the BJP, whose leaders publicly admitted several times that they had not even dreamt of such a wonderful majority. It was the result of the hard work put in by the BJP party workers, but more than that the image of Narendra Modi and his track record as Chief Minister of Gujarat.

However, there is a section of the BJP leaders who think otherwise. They are still under the illusion that it was their ideology which yielded the party such an astounding victory. They go solo with their views on issues that have been kept on the back burner by wiser leaders like Atal Bihari Vajpayee and create problems by their statements. The media looks for such opportunities to create controversies. It goes to the credit of Narendra Modi that he has been successful in keeping such elements under check. There are all kinds of issues before the government, many of them sensitive and complex.

A very responsible person started the application of Article 370 of the Constitution of India to Kashmir within a few days of Modi being sworn in as PM. Was it necessary to do so? Complex or sensitive issues are never resolved in such an unsavory hurry. Nobody should jump the gun in such matters and leave it to the persons handling such subjects. There are many issues before the government on which even strategic plans have not been prepared. Such impetuosity, born of a misconception of the victory being that of the BJP workers alone, affects the smooth functioning of the government. Prime Minister Narendra Modi will need to keep such elements under a tight leash lest they become an unbearable burden.

He was right in disallowing inclusion of his biography in school curriculum in Gujarat and Madhya Pradesh. It was a sign of the surreptitious attempts to play with education in the country. There is no need to imitate the Congress Party in playing with history, sociology, literature and other academic subjects. We are living in the age of the internet. People are watching the administration of the ministry of Human Resources Development. Careful supervision and superintendence of the prime minister himself will be needed because even one mistake due to unwanted zeal could prove costly. The Prime Minister is on trial by fire (Agni Pariksha). He is more than aware of it. But he has to remember that he is in Delhi, not in Gandhi Nagar. People like me have to constantly remind him of that fact. All complex issues must be handled with the aid, advice and approval of Narendra Modi, the man entrusted by the people of India the responsibilities of the Prime Minister after the success of the Second Freedom Movement of India.

China has to be seen through the lens of strategic interests. Sentimentality is to be avoided. This mistake had been made by the then Prime Minister Nehru, who displayed sentiments more than strategy in exchange with the Chinese Prime Minister Zhou Enlai in Delhi. Such visits are not meant to allow your children or grandchildren to frolic around, but for hard negotiations in our national interests. Unprepared, the government launched the forward policy but the nation paid the price. Diplomacy is never reduced to insignificant words or expressions in such strategic matters. Do we have a strategic paper on China ready even now? Even Pakistan has stolen a march over us in "tackling" China. We are still referring to the visit of Hsuan Tsang and Fa Hsien more than 1,300 years ago. Are we suggesting to the Chinese that once upon a time India was greater than China? Should we not be asking ourselves: have we reciprocated the visit by such a wonderful Chinese scholar and chronicler? Why is it that we never returned such visits in similar manner? Or did we also send our scholars who did not write their memoirs of China? We are proud of Buddhist monks spreading the message of peace and non-violence in the region, which we have long forgotten to practice in Bodh Gaya in Bihar or other places in the country. Are we really proud of having reduced Buddhism to the religion of only the depressed classes? Why is it that our academic studies do not include anything about what exactly Hsuan Tsang had written about India or what Confucius had written? What are we being taught in school or college about China? Is it limited to our anger at the Chinese aggression of 1962 or misconceptions about Maoism? Are the reasons not the same even today? Isn't India the host to the Tibetan government in Exile? Can such gaps in understanding our neighbors be considered as pardonable? The very unfortunate reality is that we have never attached much importance as a nation to understanding our own people residing in the north eastern part of the country. We have compounded this mistake by remaining ignorant about countries like Myanmar, Korea, Japan (Netaji Subhas Chandra Bose's association and Maruti Udyog excluded). Is this in India's geo-political interests? Do we guard our sovereignty without knowing our neighborhood under the influence of powers like China, USA, UK, France, Germany, Japan, Iran, Saudi Arabia, Iraq, Libya and others? Is it enough for India that we remain Mandarin challenged or other languages of the region challenged? Can we afford to continue to go slow like we have done so far?

The second freedom movement is a mandate to Narendra Modi to move away from the dynasty and create a new India that can respond to each and every issue highlighted in the foregoing. It should be the end to any reference to the scions of the dynasty: their forefathers had made valuable contributions at historic moments. Now Narendra Modi has to seize the historic moment that has propelled him to the top. A new India has to be created: an India of the dreams of the people, not of the political parties. The people have given their verdict. It is no time for sentiments.

A good leader is one who learns from everybody, including his rivals and enemies. Silence is such a virtue that all good leaders must practice. Their inexperience should not be betrayed in their zealous statements on Art 370 or China. The responsibility to ensure that rests squarely on Prime Minister Narendra Modi.

# Modi Need Not Be Thatcher, Reagan, Deng Xiaoping

A change is no change unless it compels thinkers from all walks of life to review it and comment. It is the same with a good poem, painting, novel or film. It must make people spare a moment to think about it and give their opinion. The Indian election 2014 is one such event that has caused a change of great historic value by voting Narendra Modi to the position of the Prime Minister. It has happened in spite of all efforts made to "stop" Modi. The domestic as well as foreign forces were at it round the clock to see that Modi did not succeed in his bid to become the Prime Minister. The results are before all of us. When nothing succeeds like success the cleverest are quick to change sides. Before Modi is sworn as the next PM, many of his opponents have offered their wise counsel on formation of the cabinet, portfolios to individuals and agenda priorities. Everybody has spoken excepting Modi. As his plank is development and growth, he is being compared with Ms. Thatcher of UK, Ronald Reagan of USA and Deng Xiaoping of China and many more. Let me put it straight- Modi is his own model. Modi draws from the rich Indian economic (basically socio-economic) tradition.

On face of it India looks a difficult to rule complex country with so much of diversity ranging from weather to culture. But there is one thing in which one would find India strongly united: it is economic activity. In fact, the so called caste system of India is a superb example of this well-knit economic activity. If a giant corporation can operate on the

Japanese model of a "family", Indian model offers the whole country as a single giant corporation integrated on the basis of allocation of all economic activity from production, services, marketing, research, development and newer growth avenues. Largely in this model monopolies are discouraged and opportunities are created for as many hands to work as possibly can. With a very well developed industrial infrastructure and a large managerial pool, Modi will find it comfortable to chart his own course of development largely because of this integration of all segments of society on issues concerning economic or business activity or development. Whosoever has the skills and is willing to work, gets work and not denied it because of any tag of diversity or complexity. This only those in business know. The highly skilled worker is called "kaarigar" and is better paid and treated respectfully. It is only politicians who pick up foul words from the global political sewage who try to disturb and disrupt production facilities or businesses. More than Modi, his team will be on test. They have to prove that real socialism is economic well-being rather than doling out subsidies. If people have opportunities for work or upgrading skills, they will grab them. The Indian masses are fast to adapt useful and sustainable change of any kind- economic, technological, political, social or cultural. Isn't the growing number of mobile phone users any indication? Yes, it is. But for these mobiles, India would have not changed so much so fast in the last 15 years; but for the change and empowerment of the masses on such a large scale it would not have been possible for a Modi to cross all the hurdles and break all barriers to his ascension to the throne.

Modi has promised the people "less government & more governance". It will not be a very smooth course, for systems and institutions have suffered serious injuries which will take time to heal if treated by experts. I would consider this change significant if it helps achieve these goals:

- If ethics of governance is inspired by the Father of the Nation treating the Cabinet as Trustees of the Power of the People;
- Revenue collection goes up and tax rates go down;
- Citizens don't have to pay public servants for services remunerated by the state;
- Citizens are protected from daylight robberies by land sharks, real estate builders, stock markets, financial frauds, supplies of goods & services manipulators;
- Access to education and employment is not denied to anybody for any reason, even if intake capacity has to be increased.

# Achievements of Modi's Government

An irrational debate is going on about the achievements of the Narendra Modi led government in the one month that it has been in office. Such impatience on the part of the political parties and the media owes it to the past governments who were feeding their achievements in one month or 100 days etc. through full page advertisements in most newspapers. But then those achievements were merely on paper. The time to scrutinize, evaluate and judge the new government will come very soon if they are allowed a few months' time to work. But for those who want to know the achievements without waiting, here are some important achievements from the point of view of an ordinary citizen of India:-

1. Narendra Modi has severely dented the solid structure of corruption in India, which had assumed the status of an institution. The operators, fixers, wheeler-dealers are hiding for the present;

2. The extra constitutional center of power stands demolished. There is no remote controlling the Prime Minister or proxies for ministers;

3. The game of capturing the new members of parliament by crooks' syndicates at the railway station or even before they leave their constituencies for Delhi by volunteering their services as private secretary or personal assistant has suddenly ended. The newcomers to the national capital Delhi can find themselves in utter wilderness without somebody organizing their reception and lodging etc., which is

officially arranged by the parliament office. The crooks' syndicate had perfected the art and craft of finding chinks in this arrangement to cover, capture or kidnap (metaphorically) the innocent members of parliament yet to be formally administered the oath of office. These activities helped promote the business of corruption and influenced even voting pattern in the parliament on critical matters like the vote of confidence. The dent in the corruption architecture has impacted these operations too.

4. A strong link in the chain of organized corruption in the country has been the role of the PS (Private Secretary) to the minister. These guys are officers from the public services (mostly from the IAS or the Indian Administrative Service). They were exceeding their official brief and acting as the real minister in most cases. Since the ministers were openly practicing corruption and favoritism, the Private Secretaries took advantage of a decadent system by doing all illegal things the minister wanted and also helped themselves to the extent possible. Several ambitious PS had become members of parliament and even ministers. As a career officer they would have risen to the rank of a Secretary to the Government of India, who reports to the minister. Prime Minister Narendra Modi has injected discipline in this critical link. The ministers can't appoint their relatives as PS- in fact, they can't appoint their PS these days since it is the PMO (Prime Minister's Office) that clears appointments of PS to ministers. So one really strong

and functional link in the corruption chain has been neutralized. The contribution of the PS to corruption has been greater than that of the minister as any honest civil servant would admit without fear. No mean achievement: if the foundation laid down is solid and sturdy, the structure over it is bound to be sturdy too.

5. The fear haunting the civil servants has been removed by PM Narendra Modi, who has directed them to contribute without fear towards healthy and fair decision making in public interest. They have also been directed to do their duty and not act as merely signing machines. When officers are allowed to function as per the law, there is no policy paralysis or procrastination in decision making or execution. That is how a government functions. The last 10 years of dysfunctional government bring out the contrast in the functioning of the government in the last one month. What is important is the smooth functioning of the government, a strong system and healthy democratic institutions. This perceptible change in the administrative climate is of immense value as it has already set the tone for the coming days. It can reasonably be expected that there is not going to be repeat of the last 10 years anymore.

6. Emphasis on the observance of the rules of financial propriety is going to seal the leaks of public money.

7. As the party (BJP or the Bhartiya Janata Party) was not sure of even getting a majority in the election, it was not prepared to form a government on its own. It

had, therefore, no agenda ready to govern. Its last experiment was based on a common minimum program, which in practice is a silly way to govern a democratic republic like India. Had the BJP failed to secure a clear mandate in the election, it would have again resulted in a coalition government and suffered all the ill consequences of earlier governments. Another coalition government even under Narendra Modi would have been paralyzed by a Common Minimum Program. However, the unexpected rise of Narendra Modi led BJP and NDA (National Democratic Alliance) has thrown the party in a new kind of situation it was not really prepared for. So it has one minister for Finance and Defense, only a minister of state for Commerce and Industry or Petroleum and many other ministries. It is genuinely short of qualified hands, who could be entrusted the responsibility of crucial ministries without landing up in any difficult situation like the 2G or CWG scams of the previous government. It has to fill this gap soon as the opposition is desperate to shoot at it. The media is suffering the famine of negative news for a month now and is devoting hours to non-news items like celebrity couples throwing tantrums in public and going to the police.

8. One reason for this lack of talent is the absence of tested economic, industrial, trade, foreign, defense, science, technology, farming etc. policies of the party. It has lived on negative ideas of criticizing others for their policies, programs and schemes. It has left the

party changing its course too fast, be it Gandhi, Pakistan, Bangladesh, America, China or inflation, price rise etc. It has been misled into announcing rail fare hike before the budget session. It forgot that the mass anger against the Congress Party was largely due to uncontrolled price rise for which the voter punished the Congress so severely that today it is not qualified to be even given the official position of the LoP (Leader of Opposition). By announcing such an unwelcome decision of the UPA-II government, the government unnecessarily took all the flak for the damage done to the economy by the previous government. It learnt its lessons rather fast and deferred another such unwelcome hike of petrol and cooking gas. People expect this government to check the leak of the revenue first before even thinking of any price rise of any commodity whose prices are administered or controlled by the government. The system stands so badly damaged by corruption that more than 60% revenues are eaten away by the corrupt.

9. The neo-liberals have inflicted great damage to the economy and all infrastructure. Most public services, built with heavy investment in infrastructure, have been "retired" to vacate the space for commercialization by private entities, both domestic and foreign. Health, education, energy etc. are just illustrations. Had the country suffered the misfortune of returning the UPA back to power, India would have been thrown into the conditions prevailing till

1984. Prime Minister Narendra Modi has to understand this profound truth if he dreams of making the country prosperous and strong once again. His cadres need intense training to appreciate the complexities of policies and governance so that they act more mature in matters like Art 370 of the Constitution etc.

10. The previous dispensation had outsourced governance in day to day matters also. So far, the new government has not followed them. Is it some mean achievement?

Let them work before we assess their achievements. It is great that they have not failed as their opponents have been taunting them while saying that electioneering is one thing and governing another.

# Prime Minister Narendra Modi's Security Must Be Foolproof

I am no security expert. So what I am writing is as a public affairs commentator who has been keenly watching important world developments. The trigger for my analysis comes from my internal promptings which tell me to write what I consider relevant. Red Alert is frequently sounded for Delhi and Mumbai, prompted by developments in Iraq. It would be a serious security lapse to think that Delhi or Mumbai, the two big cities, are out of the terrorists' target. The terrorists have successfully targeted the highest executive authorities globally. They attacked unabated President Bush, contributed to Obama victory in the process, began gunning for Obama after he ordered assassination of Osama Bin Laden living as a protected guest of the Pakistan's ISI in the Cantonment in Pakistan. They targeted Tony Blair. Their Indian target is Narendra Modi, the Prime Minister, whose victory in the recently held elections has dejected international terror outfits and their Indian partners. Modi does not represent Narendra Damodarbhai Modi alone. It is much more for them and it is that which is on their radar. The known terrorists are just one group that is determined to harm all prominent leaders in India but also obliterate India itself so as to establish a kind of religious fundamentalist state as some of them are trying to do in Iraq these days, but there are many hidden operatives too.

Threat to Narendra Modi comes equally from elements in India. All humane qualities are considered weaknesses by extremist elements, which generally operate on extremely low intellectual assets but unbelievable cruelty. They are barbaric in treatment of whosoever suffers their dominance. More than 1,700 people have been butchered in Iraq, more than 200 school girls kidnapped in Nigeria, hundreds of children, elderly and women massacred in strife torn conflict zones, human bombs exploded just at will anywhere in the world - their achievements (?) are a ghastly list. They have given a call for jihad in Kashmir. Pakistan has been trying to push terrorists in Kashmir across the LOC (Line of Control) for months. 40 Indian workers are in captivity with ISIS operatives in Iraq, whose release the government of India is trying. America has learnt its bitter lessons in the war on terror. It has lost the will to confront them militarily. The NATO is more than diffident. They don't know what to do and how to go about it. As open societies both European countries as well as the USA are under threat of the terrorists, who are determined to obliterate them. There is no doubt about the economic costs imposed on both of them by the terrorists. Neither America nor Europe can afford to continue any longer bearing such costs. However, there is one redeeming feature in their case: they are united in religion (largely) and foreign economic policy goals against all kinds of threats from any enemy country or terrorist group. They are militarily superior and their short term defeats at the hands of the terrorists should not be mistaken as their weakness in comparison to the terrorists. They will take their own time but will have to use all military might to finish the terrorists. That advantage is not available to India. It is in this kind of a scenario that the need to make the security of the Prime Minister, Narendra Modi, absolutely foolproof emanates. Narendra Modi represents resurgent India, even resurgent Hindutva for some, and the biggest hurdle before the ISI of Pakistan in realizing its dream of capturing Kashmir first and rest of India later in collusion with the terrorist of the ISIS type.

The network of these organizations is very strong the world over and their Fidayeen or human bombs or Rajakaars (volunteers) are present in all places in the world. These people are well versed in the local language and topography and government organization and hence possess superior capabilities to execute their designs with comparative ease. Narendra Modi's foreign visits will expose him to threats from these elements.

Prime Minister Narendra Modi should promote "Namaste" or "Namaskar" in place of handshaking, as is usual in international arena as use of chemical weapons is also in use in international arena. Anthrax had created worldwide scare only a decade ago. Only the governments possessing chemical and biological weapons know what is dangerous and what the potency of the weapon is. The Namaste is a diplomatic device, which has to be popularized internationally. India had suffered the silent murder of Lal Bahadur Shastri, one of its most loved and respected Prime Minister, in Tashkent, because he subdued Pakistan in a fiercely fought war in 1965. Terrorists from that region are leading the ISIS campaign. Narendra Modi is a victor of the same kind. The dangers should better be anticipated, assessed and evaluated by the security agencies rather than in any book. World leaders have been eliminated from remote places by sharp shooters. Today's weapons are highly sophisticated and can be precise to a point in hitting the target successfully. Security agencies have to have a detailed list of all such weapons. Mere small weapons or trained hands alone will not be able to meet the requirements in moments of critical need. Indira Gandhi's shooters could not be neutralized before they had pumped 26 bullets in her frail frame! Can the country rely upon such security for the safety of its beloved Prime Minister? Do they have any answer to laser attack? They have to think of the most unthinkable, as barbarity is no Indian DNA. History is proof that the barbaric had succeeded in enslavement of India and ruled for thousands of years. The ISIS is a grim reminder of the past and the challenge demands superior response.

Prime Minister Narendra Modi has to be his own security planner and manager. He has to acknowledge the fact that now he is 125 crore Indians. He has to understand that his safety is synonymous with the safety, security and sovereignty of India. He has not yet started what he is chosen to do. Therefore, he has to ensure that he serves India not only for the next five years but much more than that. For this, his security is the first consideration. He has also to acknowledge that he is the target of all political rivals and hate groups, religious fundamentalists busy in subversive socio-religious activities, cultural and business agents of foreign interest groups, terrorist outfits, his friends-turned-foes and several others. As he achieves success in delivering good governance to the people of India, he will go on antagonizing the elements who had reaped benefits from bad governments for so many decades. For change to stabilize, this government has to function successfully for the remaining period of its term.

# Modi's Pakistan Policy: Pakistan's Low Intensity War & Modi's Non-Violent Victory

We have already discussed the need for fool-proof security for Prime Minister Narendra Modi. He has deadly enemies in India and abroad, his own political organization being no exception. Narendra Modi is on the radar of many foreign countries, which would prefer a weak government in position rather than a strong government, decisively voted by the majority of the Indian people and headed by a genuinely strong leader.

But first the shock delivered to Pakistan, especially the ISI of Pakistan army. It is no secret that Pakistan is not a full democracy. It is a partial democracy, with full democratic exterior but under tight control of the military. The history of Pakistan post-independence is the history of martial law, not democracy. In order to justify martial law, the army needed a bogey and what could be a better bogey than Kashmir? Unethically aided by super powers for their own geo political interests, and the misplaced trust of an inexperienced political leader, Jawahar Lal Nehru, following the motto "Truth Wins", Pakistan has raised an imaginary dispute about merger of Kashmir with the Union of India. For the sake of those who have no intimate knowledge of the historical facts of the period, under the transfer of powers arrangement it was the sole discretion of the Princely Ruler of the state concerned who was given the full freedom to exercise the right to merge or not merge with the country. Some Rulers, called Maharaja or Nawab, had delusions of remaining independent - the Nizam of Hyderabad and the Maharaja of Kashmir being two such Rulers. Nothing more could vouch for their narrow thinking because of which they failed to comprehend the political change in the country. For those old rulers, freedom was an alien word for themselves and their people, whom they called praja or raiyat. But then, the high moral standards of the freedom movement leaders didn't want to thrust their decisions on those unwilling. Instead they were given the liberty to think freely, even as they resented freedom for their own people. It was this phase of indecisiveness of the Maharaja of Kashmir that prompted Pakistan to invade Kashmir in breach of all standards of international ethics between neighbors. Besides, India and Pakistan were a single nation till August 15, 1947. Had the British not played dangerous politics of divide to rule, India would have been one nation, with no separate Pakistan. But the British thought it expedient to play the communal tensions created by the Muslim League. It was such shortsightedness which is responsible for contemporary cult of terrorism in the world. The Maharaja of Kashmir came to his senses somewhat late, but realized the value of signing the instrument of accession to India. It was not difficult for India to punish Pakistan for its misadventure in Kashmir militarily, but Nehru, the Indian Prime Minister, trusted ethics more than real politics. Incidentally he was a Kashmir origin person himself and in his desire to sound absolutely objective, agreed for the matter to be referred to the UNO. Has the UNO solved any such territorial dispute in its entire life? Taking advantage of the weakness of the UN System, Pakistan has indulged in military misadventures in Kashmir more than once and has been punished for it. The last time it was broken into two in 1971 when Bangladesh was born. Thereafter it has mounted a low intensity war against India with tremendous success.

The demographic advantage that Pakistan enjoys in India is unparalleled. India is a secular country. More than 170 million Muslims constitute a section of its population. They are in all levels of positions of political power, administration and business. In comparison, the condition of non-muslims in Pakistan is miserable. Pakistan is the self-appointed jihadi state, speaking for all the Muslims of the world. Its military rulers have succeeded in befriending America, China and Russia with equal ease. It has succeeded in carving closer relations with these countries than India. It was able to exploit Khalistan movement by supplying arms, ammunitions, training and funding the movement in Punjab. The Indian authorities, especially the intelligence agencies failed to comprehend its designs on India. Due to negligence on their part the situation in Punjab went out of hand leading to the operation blue star. While Pakistani designs were smothered in Punjab, it gave a tremendous boost to the Pakistani war on India at a very low cost. The success of its operation in Punjab encouraged it to employ Indians against India at almost no cost to continue the war against India. In the process it has created hundreds of "sleeper cells" in almost all important cities of India. They carry out at its behest bomb blasts. It keeps Kashmir boiling. It has been bleeding India on a daily basis. Hafiz Saeed is just one manifestation of the widespread Pakistani terror cells network in India. It has successfully trapped intellectuals, progressive forces, secular minded civil society members, lawyers, journalists, doctors, engineers, defense personnel, airport employees, politicians and businessmen. There is just one category that it seems to have spared, that is women, excepting one or two young college girls its cadres kept for their personal pleasure against the diktats of their

64

handlers. There is no doubt that in bleeding India on a daily basis the ISI of Pakistan has excelled. It had almost finished all kinds of political ventures excepting the Congress. It supported Congress as it has been able to handle the party to its advantage operating through its agents under the garb of secularism. Taking sentimental Indians for granted and divided forever, the Pakistani Establishment indulged in daydreaming of taking over the country at any time of its choosing. It showed an attitude of superiority in governing with a heavy hand in comparison to soft India. It was here that it made another grave mistake. After the forty years of relentless efforts of the low intensity war on India, Pakistan licked defeat at the hands of a man called Narendra Modi, who scored the victory in just 40 months against Pakistan' forty years!

Narendra Modi's astounding victory stunned not only his own party stalwarts but the Congress and Pakistan. It was the biggest defeat the Pakistan ISI ever suffered at a cost lower than its own low cost war on India. It traumatized it so awfully that it took several weeks to recover from it. The visit of Prime Minister Nawaz Sharif caused added gloom for the army. India and Pakistan seemed to be coming closer, to the strong dislike of the Pak military. The Pakistani people are desperate to break the chains to their freedom that are overtly and covertly round their necks all the time. Like Narendra Modi, Nawaz Sharif poses a threat to the military rule. If democracy comes to Pakistan, can the army officers maintain their feudal life style any longer? Poverty can't be removed by simply ushering in democracy, they seem to argue. So what is the harm in continuing the martial law, moderated by occasional flashes of democracy? But they can't forget their enemy number one- India. So the ISI reactivated its agents in India. The old rhetoric of peace dialogue or Track-II diplomacy was initiated. Cadres were chastised. They pulled up their moles in the earlier ruling establishment, some of whom lambasted poor Rahul Gandhi for the defeat & loss of power. He was exclusively blamed for the defeat and charged with incompetence and incapability to rule and demand for change of leadership in the Congress party became louder. The party had to appoint the Antony Committee to examine the demand, but it recommended no change exactly as was expected under the dynastic rule of the Nehru-Gandhi family of the Congress Party. So the other plans were put into operation. The visit of an Indian delegation to Pakistan, and someone calling on Hafiz Saeed was only to send the coded messages to the cadres to come out of their melancholia, stupor and inertia as Hafiz Saeed and the ISI were desperate for action. In India it was time for festivals. The JuD, LeT and various outfits had successfully carried out acts of terror and bomb blasts during Diwali (the festival of Lights) and other festivals. The much publicized meeting of a non-active journalist's meeting with Hafiz Saeed in Pakistan where nobody is allowed to go and on whom the USA has announced a bounty of US$10 million was meant to convey the message to the cadres. Pakistan played successfully once again on the weakness of the Indian Intelligence Agencies and the media to get the message disseminated for free for days without a break. Since all its operators are not educated people who can read newspapers, the visual media played what it had sought to play for them. The absurd debates about secularism and communalism have been revived, with the media actively participating.

The target this time is Modi, Narendra Modi and only Modi alone and not the people of India. Prime Minister Narendra Modi will remain on the ISI radar 24×7 and it will strike at the first opportunity available. The Security Establishment hardly inspires confidence about the security of the Prime Minister, what with its complete ignorance of a journalist being handled by the ISI so well and making Hafiz Saeed and his operations the center-point of news and views in India and abroad and making Kashmir an issue of political debate in the world once again. Similarly our mission in Pakistan has proved ineffective. Compare the demographic advantage that Pakistan enjoys in India and our own disadvantage our mission is proud of. We have not yet been able to develop tools of better intelligence gathering. We waste our time and energy in talking silly about Hamas-Israel conflict, without learning a single lesson from Israel crossing the obstacles of demographic disadvantage worse than us in the territory. Same illogical sentimentality, same superficiality in developing global geo-political scenario, same tendency of making light of very serious issues, which has been the bane of India for centuries. All the political elements disrupting parliament on the issue were absent when Kashmiri Pundits were driven away from Kashmir. Kashmir was, is and shall always remain an integral part of India. Let Pakistan understand that its old game is now over. Narendra Modi is different. Leadership to emerge in the decades ahead will be different. They should not dream of Congress rule in India forever or a Jawaharlal Nehru being in position or an Atal Bihari Vajpayee extending courtesies to them forever to accommodate them happily. If they refuse to change now, India will not hesitate to invite a Narendra Modi to deal with them. It is in Pakistan's own interest to end this absurd war.

Instead it should acknowledge the value of peace and peaceful co-existence. War between us benefits only the weapon industry of the developed countries. Our people want peace and prosperity. We are capable of providing that to them. Let us forget war. Let us opt for peace.

The Pakistani serials on TV these days poke fun in a guarded manner at the military brass. The Fauzi (military) must take the polite nudge in the understatement of the dialogue writer and delivering actors. They are all sick of martial law democracy and its fauzi culture. They have great potential. This class of playwrights is far superior to the outdated journalists, quick to ridicule themselves to prove that ignorance is bliss. Mass media has exposed the weaknesses of the regular media, and therefore, nobody bothers for such journalists these days.

# India Budget 2014-15: Roadmap of Modi Government

Narendra Modi had established his political leadership on 16 May 2014 when he led his party to the most unexpected and stunning victory in the elections to the Indian parliament. His economic leadership was awaited for the budget 2014-15 to unveil. The budget presented by Finance Minister Arun Jaitley had nothing stunning or unprecedented about it. His speech of more than 20,000 words was nothing less than a torture of more than 2 hours! As the Finance Ministers in the past over a decade have been lawyers of the highest court of the country, their treatises were nothing less than paper books of a SLP (Special Leave Petition) before the Supreme Court. Why should our Finance Ministers speak so much, for so long, in chaste English, interspersed with King's/Queen's idioms or Harvard Business School phraseology or poetic pieces from English/Hindi/Urdu/Tamil/Bengali etc.? Can't they be brief- as brief as a 20 minute speech? In any case everybody doesn't understand everything he says inside the parliament. That is why the Finance Minister devotes several hours explaining the salient features of his budget proposal to the press and the media. Even that does not satisfy everybody, so the Prime Minister does some post-surgery care, ably supplemented by prominent members of the council of ministers, party leaders, Finance Secretary, Economic Advisers, business and industry captains, academics and common men on the street. All this elaborate exercise for nothing more than a net benefit, if there can ever be any real benefit from any Finance Minister worth his salt, never exceeding a few thousand rupees equivalent to US$ 700.

Rest of the insipid, boring budget exercise is nothing more than mathematical jugglery in the name of reduction of tax under one description only to be increased under another description. As arithmetic is hardly interesting for many of us, we don't mind getting budgeted for cheating in a clean and open official way in comparison to several other ways like full page newspaper advertisements promising 60% discount Sale (which really is discount not of 60% on all items but "up to" 60% on a few because they might have been sold by the time you arrive). In any case, the annual budget proposals open huge business opportunities for chartered accountants and taxation lawyers (the community from which some of our prominent Finance Ministers come), because nobody is able to clearly explain what exactly they mean. Interpreting such obtuse English diction then becomes the extremely pleasant responsibility of the accountant, lawyer and retired judges engaged on "chamber practice'. Consultation with retired judges or seeking their opinion on complex tax issues lends weight to the case when it is filed before the appropriate competent authority including the court. If that makes the budget speech look like a case book of an SLP, it is only appropriate.

But the question needs to be answered as to how such a practice came in to existence. India is not known to have a tradition for budget the way we witness it in democratic India today. Not even the Kautilya Arthashashtra prescribes any such drill. It is a practice of the Imperial rule in India. The British had this practice, which they imposed on their colonies. Since they were a foreign power, extracting taxes from the natives from every single economic activity, they needed to justify their tax proposals. They knew they had no moral justification for the taxes they proposed to impose on the poor natives, they resorted to coining new words and indulged in liberal use of jargon. The natives resented any such tax imposition most justifiably, but the imperial power would consistently refuse to lend any ear to public outrage. That imperial tradition continues even today, what with token cuts (of just one rupee) being rejected. The House of the Elders (the Rajya Sabha) has no power to drive any saner advice as it is only the Lower House- the House of the People or the Lok Sabha that has the power to make decisions on money bills. Even the President of India has just to okay it once the Lok Sabha puts its seal of approval on the budget proposals as presented by the Finance Minister. The British had their own economic logic to suppress local industry and business in order to promote their industrial products. They needed to create a market for their products. It mattered little if it meant closing or destroying existing facilities. Tax on production was an instrument to achieve that goal. It contributed to loss of livelihood to millions in due course. The limit was breached when they imposed tax on common edible salt. At a time, tax on salt fetched them more than 25% of gross revenues. Indian masses responded effectively to this measure under the leadership of Mahatma Gandhi, who launched the Salt Satyagraha and this movement proved to be the nemesis of the British Empire. In less than 50 years an empire over which the sun never set was reduced to an island country. The style and features of the budget speech of the Indian Finance Ministers carries on that tradition. It is, therefore, time for the Finance Ministers to introduce change in that anachronistic tradition of insipid budget speech enumerating item after item taxed or tax-exempted.

Children in Indian schools are taught to write an essay under the title "If I were the Prime Minister". I think it is time to teach them to write another essay titled If I Were the Finance Minister. These budget proposals impact economic activities across all segments of production and marketing. It is one single source of corruption in India. It is responsible for impeding the process of creation of additional jobs. It retains poverty. It talks of small savings, whereas an ordinary citizen needs millions for a bare subsistence level survival. Our economic philosophy drives away our brilliant students to complete their education in foreign universities; our talent to serve abroad; our experts to contribute to the development of other countries. We have no value for skills or talent. We want to maintain "small" in all respects. We hate prosperity of the common man. We dislike our wealth creators. We neither protect our markets nor production advantages. Unless we introduce radical changes in our thinking and functioning, we will waste historic opportunities like the one the last election to the Lok Sabha had sprung before us.

I feel that a golden opportunity has been lost on the occasion of presentation of the budget 2014-15. Explanations offered are not contested, excepting that a visionary leadership is not constrained by lack of time, since it has the plans ready in advance. This budget has one very important achievement: it has ended the unethical practice of highly insensitive neo-liberalists controlling the government to increase prices endlessly thinking that the common man has the capacity to go on paying forever the rising prices. This is no mean achievement of the Modi government. It needs to be stressed here that the Congress led UPA-II government was punished for that insensitivity. The caution displayed by the Modi government's budget, in spite of the Finance Ministry still working under that old discarded philosophy, deserves kudos. Still a word of caution needs to be sounded: the Modi government should not buy the arguments that will be thrown at it by the old school of mandarins of the Finance Ministry, who will justify every price increase. Price rise in India is due mostly to corruption, black marketing, hoarding etc. The operators comprise the powerful nexus of politician-bureaucrat-business. If these are controlled, prices will fall rather than rise. Since the budget makes no mention of any scheme to retrieve public money from the hands of such white collar criminals, this caution is being sounded. To give an example, PSU (Public Sector Undertakings) have been deliberately turned sick by such elements, which have made several attempts to completely retire them but they can always be rejuvenated only if the right man is given charge to lead them. The right choice would eliminate the corrupt practice of auctioning the positions of Chairmen & Managing Directors to the highest bidder, as was exposed in the case of appointment of a Member to the Railway Board where the Minister was alleged to have demanded rupees 100 Million from one candidate in the last government of Dr. Manmohan Singh.

The Modi government has got the best opportunity to serve the nation. It is the second freedom. Modi can set a record, like Jawaharlal Nehru did at the dawn of the first freedom, by changing the poor India in to the prosperous India. There is more than enough for India to serve all the needs of its people. There are countries in the ASEAN who have achieved that goal. The economic meltdown of 2008 affected the western world more largely because their model of economic development was dependent on wars and technological superiority providing ready markets globally. In the case of India it is different. Who understands it better than a person born and lived in a state like Gujarat? What is Modi talking about when he mentions the Gujarat model of development? Let me put it in a pith & substance manner: it is the Gujarati's Model of Development. They live globally and are not restricted to the Indian state of Gujarat alone. It is the real spirit to convert disadvantage to advantage, disability to ability and poverty to prosperity. It has to be made in to the Indian Model of Development. The one year's time between this budget and the next one needs to be employed to critically examine the text and mindset to tax; to introduce change from revenue generation for the imperial power to livelihood generation for the masses; to promote prosperity of the people instead of perennial poverty. It will obviate the present need for dividing the people socially or economically in to several categories to deliver services, benefits or concessions. Each category of Indians represents a highly skilled set of workers of a knowledge society of ancient lineage devastated by poverty of the centuries of foreign rule. Investment in reviving that spirit demands marked and focused attention for several years.

# Drag & Lift for Prime Minister Modi

The speeches of Prime Minister Narendra Modi and the newly elected party President Amit Shah at the BJP National Council meet in Delhi on 9th August 2014 were heard with rapt attention by political analysts and commentators. Soon after, analysis of the direction of the new government was sought to be culled out. Since the installation of the Narendra Modi Government 2 months ago, the news industry in India has been suffering a terrible drought situation. The TV channels, dictating and dominating the government earlier fell on bad days after the installation of the Modi government some 75 days ago. Now they are taking only longer commercial breaks and telecasting insignificant news ad nauseam. It was expected that Modi would at least provide something to talk today, but unfortunately he has disappointed them.

Whether by choice or otherwise, the first big opportunity was wasted, because the leaders reverted back to the pre-election jargon. The issues at that time, like the appeasement or vote bank politics, were relevant because the enlightened voter of India could discern the real face of the politicians of the country, who were treading the most dangerous policy of divide and rule, which the people had long concluded as the root cause of poverty and backwardness. Since Modi had sincerely served the people in Gujarat and contributed to prosperity of the people across the board without any discrimination as Chief Minister, he was accepted by the people of India to be worthy of their trust. The mandate of the people has stunned all political parties including the BJP, political analysts and foreign powers alike. The Congress party has not been able to analyze even after two months as to what had caused it such devastating defeat, which has rendered it ineligible for even the position of the leader of opposition in the Lok Sabha. Similarly, the BJP has not yet stopped wondering at its success, winning a complete majority on its own. It was expected today that the party would come up with a convincing analysis of the contributory factors leading to its victory. It only repeated its earlier exclamation! Had the party done that kind of analysis, it would have prepared a roadmap of greater value than falling back upon the pre-election rhetoric. I have a feeling that Prime Minister Modi is conscious of it but cannot voice it, for that is bound to upset the apple cart. He is experiencing the lift and the drag – the lift has been provided not so much by the electoral success alone but more by his personal conduct, policies and long tapasya. The drag, however, is the old party agenda and leadership at the local level, which is desperate to implement it. There is an open conflict between the national and the local perspective between the two. It is going to affect the flight of Modi on its path to meet the national requirement. He had asked the people 60 months' time to deliver on promises made during the election; he is left with 56.5 months! He will find it almost impossible to educate his local leaders across the different regions of the country and also implement his national agenda, because of the existing gap in education of the two levels. The local leaders have suffered discrimination and harassment at the hands of other ruling outfits and can hardly be expected to have the stomach to suffer anymore now when they have achieved historic success for the party. Unless the party meets their aspirations intelligently and also pursue national issues with the greatest sense of responsibility, it will land in a soup that even its opponents have not cooked for them. Surprisingly, the Modi team has given ample proof of a very mature leadership in the party if the impressive performance of its ministers in the parliament during the discussions on the budget is any indication. That is reassuring, because everybody was dismissive or contemptuous of their capability before the elections. Even half educated TV anchors used to misbehave by their harsh words, expressions, gestures and abominable interruptions. Some of these used to be so uncivil as to deliver long spiel before giving them the chance to answer and abruptly take a break even before they had spoken a single sentence.

The Opposition Parties will do their best to de-rail the Modi government. They are highly skilled at creating anarchy and disturb law & order in the country. Modi's victory was the biggest defeat that the Pakistani intelligence agency, the ISI, had suffered. The ISI is the most successful intelligence agency operating in India because it has a demographic edge over Indian police. In spite of the ISI, how could the BJP secure such a majority? The ISI was required to answer that question. It demanded answers from its "sleeper cells" and politicians operating as "secular forces" and liberally funded by the ISI. Since the effect of the shock delivered to all parties and others in the election still lingers on, they are under pressure to show results. In a hurry to show visible results, they started doing what they are skilled best for: riots in Muzaffarnagar. They do not think beyond riots!

Before the opposition succeeds in devising new programs to put vighna (obstacles), Modi should launch a new line of issues of public welfare covering all segments of the population. Such creative programs will help moderate attitudes and deliver public service in a visible fashion. The agitation in the name of the CSAT (Civil Services Aptitude Test) is only an example of what the inimical forces are capable of doing. I have no hesitation in saying that content and format of such examinations can only be decided by experts and not by parliamentarians. Under no circumstances should Modi get himself ensnared by the language controversy, which for the moment appears to be so simple, and which the opposition is stoking in a planned manner, making full use of the zealots in the BJP. Let me take the risk of warning the government that it will not be able to handle the situation once it develops into the full blown riots the country had witnessed in the past. There are any number of such controversial issues that the previous governments had chosen to play down, not for any other reason but political wisdom alone, which will be raked up by vested interests and Modi will have to deftly deflect them rather than permitting them to act as a drag on his flight to deliver on his commitments to the voters.

Imaginative programs for job creation will need to be thought out. If Information Technology has succeeded in creating millions of jobs, so can new imaginative programs. It is not manufacturing alone that the government should be focusing on, but the services sector too, which could generate quality jobs for the well trained youth. It will require between 12 to 36 months to train such youth and Modi still has 57+ months at his disposal. So before he goes to the next election he would have already provided the youth respectable, quality and well-paying jobs. Nothing impresses like the palpable results.

The government has to start thinking big. It has to dream big. It has to learn from its predecessors and also rise much above them. It is alright to invoke party icons. But it is equally necessary to weigh them against other local, national and global icons. The trends thus identified help draw future roadmaps for any visionary leadership. There is no time to clean the mess of the past- it is bound to accumulate again. The need of the hour is to draw action plans and implement them. Public sector banks are very unfriendly towards students, who might turn out to be national or international genius later, or an educated young entrepreneur. Can any bank, including the Small Industry Development Bank, sanction loans or overdraft to an MBA/IIT product who wants to start his own e-commerce venture? No, because the rules don't permit it. When will the rules be modified? After the opportunity is lost forever (if Ratan Tata has shown interest in this new line, shouldn't the banks have taken the initiative much earlier?). But our thinking remains the old vintage License Raj time, which was jolted by Rajiv Gandhi in 1985 when he de-licensed more than 40% of the industries included in the schedule to the Industries (Development & Regulation) Act 1951. Forward looking leadership alone can bring about the desired change.

Modi was royally ignored by the English speaking elite. One politician went down so low as to recall his humble beginnings as a small tea vendor (chaiwallah) in the railway compartments. Another had no shame in calling him Hitler. Several others mocked his success as Chief Minister of Gujarat. During the election campaign a Congress politician, belonging to the Muslim community, spoke of mincing him and feeding the eagles and crows. The Congress President betrayed lack of even barest sense of decency when she called him the merchant of death. A fellow Chief Minister ridiculed him for his lack of knowledge of history. The list is endless. But Modi ignored all of them. He showed enviable magnanimity, depth, profundity and maturity. He pursued his agenda in the party and came for attack from within. He succeeded and was declared the PM nominee by the BJP (Bharatiya Janata Party). He entered the electoral battle. He emerged victorious stunning everyone. So people started asking questions: who is Modi? What kind of a person is he? Books don't take long to reach the stands on such occasions. Articles and debates came in large numbers. Interestingly the old English speaking elite found it difficult to change their views and continued with their obduracy crediting the victory to false promises. The new ones showed neutrality and gave their own analysis. Still the inquisitive want to know more about him.

Those with a positive mindset would observe that Modi has made great sacrifices in the typical Indian tradition of renouncing personal interests in the interests of the nation. We are taught in early childhood to sacrifice personal interests if the family interests so demand and sacrifice the family interests if the village welfare so demands and further sacrifice the village interests if the country's interests so demand and if need be , also sacrifice the country's interests if the interest of the human society so need . He was married in early childhood and could have set up home, procreate and live a life of comfort. He didn't. He has not disclosed anything about it but he could not have achieved it without the overt sanction of his wife in the typical Indian tradition where the wife agrees to the husband taking any vow for the service of the country. He has since conducted himself well without any blemish on his character, though the most characterless politicians had tried unsuccessfully to tarnish him. Truth is always stronger than untruth! Modi has lived his life like a hermit or a tapasvi, which is a great achievement. Indian people have special love for tapasvis. His opponents in the last election had the historic distinction of scams of Rupees 76,000 crores, 176,000 crores, 186,000 crores and many more revealed in the audit reports of the constitutional authority, the Comptroller & Auditor General of India. Can his opponents face such a tapasvi? Besides Modi is flexible, open minded, developmental administrator, grassroots worker, organizer of the highest caliber, result oriented person and above all a Gujarati. What is a Gujarati? It is the same as the English for the European. Now he is also the darling of the masses too.

It is time now for him to deliver. The lift he has got comes to a person only once in life when the wheel of fortune turns favorable. It is the turning point in India's democratic history. It is intervention by the providence. Had it not happened at this juncture, our very sovereign existence would have come under threat due to governance paralysis, corruption and crime. Modi may not have talented people in large numbers to implement his programs because the BJP did not offer any charm to them and the Congress enticed them easily. But there is no dearth of talent, experience and integrity. He has to devise methods of inviting them to join his team because they may be hesitant for several reasons. But he will get whole hearted support for all his people friendly programs. It is now for Modi to eliminate the drag and make the best use of the lift. He is conscious of upgrading the workers. He does not speak without purpose. He asked his party workers to prepare 200 PMs for every booth, punning calculatedly to drive the message to measure up to the requirements of the Prime Minister of the party, clarifying that PM meant primary member in this context!

# Kudos to Modi Government

Creating rumpus on college/university campuses is the most favorite game of Indian politicians. They incite students even to violence. Fear prevents academicians from instilling discipline among the students. It is only a few politically ambitious students, who choose to remain on the campus longer than required for pursuing their political objectives set for them by the political party whose sole goal is to disturb studies and peace on the campuses. The Congress Party and the Communist parties have the strongest student unions affiliated to them for several decades. It was only expected that these parties, humiliated at the election 2014, would try to create trouble soon. But they would do it so soon was beyond imagination.

They found in the agitation by the Civil Services Examination aspirants against the compulsory English Comprehension paper an opportunity to strike at the newly formed Narendra Modi Government. The government amended the scheme of exams appropriately, acting fast in the matter and nipping the evil in the bud.

It was no creation of the Modi government. The English comprehension paper was there even before Modi was sworn in as the Prime Minister. The debate around the merits and demerits of prescribing a compulsory English comprehension paper has been going on for long. However, sensing the potential of trouble behind the political parties' motives in jumping into the fray, the government withdrew it. This decision gave a handle to the media to beat at the government for compromising standards since many in India think that a government can't function without the use of the English language. The insinuation was that the BJP was pushing its agenda for replacing English with Hindi. It was a sinister design to create a language controversy, which is a very sensitive matter in multi-lingual, multi-religious, multi-cultural India.

Language controversy is only one such area. Their final destination is the repeat of the dangerous language riots of the 1963 variety. Since Modi has succeeded in making inroads even in the southern states and eastern India in the last elections, opposition parties are desperate to regain their lost territories in these states. They are getting some support from Modi's own party men who have jumped to push their Hindi agenda without even understanding the complexities involved. Only ignorant people will rake up issues like language at this juncture; the sagacious will show better understanding and patience.

Prime Minister Narendra Modi will have to personally supervise the developments, as his predecessor Jawaharlal Nehru had to do in 1963. I don't want to delve any further on the subject and leave it to the wisdom of the Prime Minister. However, there is an urgent need to rein in the rogue media debates by shouting anchors and irresponsible participants, all of whom have consistently betrayed complete lack of knowledge on the subject. They have not cared to even read the constitutional provisions regarding language and yet they are livid as if they are wiser and better informed than the framers of the Indian constitution. TV channels and newspapers are owned by the same business houses and their reporting of news and views is mendacious. They are fomenting language strife in the country by their abuse of the freedom of speech. They need not be censored, but certainly the Doordarshan can beat them at their game by arranging scholarly and fully informed debates. Sadly it has been woefully failing in these matters of great national importance because under the policy of the government so far, they have been treating soft issues contemptuously and language happens to be one such issue of tremendous value. Had the significance of the language and translation been appreciated by the previous government, the politicians would not have been displaying their lack of knowledge of "translation" by calling it Google translation. They think the UPSC (Union Public Service Commission) gets its translation done by Google. What can you do other than having a hearty laugh at such ignorance? They insult and injure a whole class of human translators and some contribution from indigenously developed software like MANTRA. Can one reason with these rulers of modern India?

Next is their attack on the other aspects - Aptitude Test. Like language or translation, here also they are ill informed and politicizing a subject beyond their comprehension. They are misleading the vulnerable sections of society who aspire to enter the civil services but have no mentors to help them prepare for the job in the contemporary knowledge society where competition is extremely tough because the job requirements are tough. The political class is trifling the most competitive examination in the country by making fake assurances of getting the aptitude test dropped. Even if the test is dropped, the requirement will be there and no civil servant will survive without acquiring the necessary skills. When I wrote my IAS etc. Exam way back in 1970, after the first two papers it used to be only the serious candidates who remained in the ring. I would consider it appropriate for the aspirants to prepare for the tests, aptitude or physical. The game of the politicians claiming to espouse the cause of "students" is exposed by the fact that education stands ruined by them in their states. The condition is so awful that hordes of students migrate to other states from UP and Bihar for education because their state does not care for them. For decades, government school and college teachers have been working without salary in these states and when they agitate for their wages, they are brutally attacked by the lathi-wielding police, which hits even women unashamedly. And these politicians watch in pride and mirth. Most institutions are owned by these politicians or by their cronies, which obtain signatures of teachers on the government prescribed salaries but pay not even 10% of it. Such is the level of corruption and condition of education in many states, whose leaders are shouting for the cause of the students. They are, in fact, punishing the students for their "independent thinking" in the last General Election, which resulted in their defeat and Modi's victory. They want their vote banks to return to them, they don't care a bit if it happens as a result of mass murders, rapes, riots or other means. Modi has to beat them at their game decisively and establish his superiority.

Bihar Secondary Examination Board has shocked everyone when three of its toppers in different subjects could not even correctly tell the subject name which they have topped when asked by TV reporters on June 4, 2016. On re-test two of them had failed and their results have been canceled. The third one is avoiding the test.

The pattern of CS Exam has been devised by scholars of repute and not by politicians. It can always be improved only if justified but not because of agitations by the political parties pushing vigorously their agenda. The English paper is one of several other papers in the CS Mains. Even then the electronic media is rabble rousing as if heavens have fallen. The politicians from Bihar and UP and other states have not modified the pattern of their state civil services conducted by the UP Public Service Commission or the Bihar Public Service Commission or other state PSCs on the lines they are demanding from the Modi government for students desirous of writing Civil Services Exam of the Union. If they are really sincere in their views and genuinely care for the poor, rural and Hindi speaking students, let them first facilitate easy entry for these people in the state Civil services. They will never do that, because they are empowering their progeny with the best education in India and abroad but want to keep the poor population to remain un-empowered so that they work on their farms for free, being educated unemployed and remain vote banks forever.

Luckily, today's aspirants are better placed than us – they have access to the internet. The politician or newspapers cannot fool them, for it is possible to understand issues in depth without restricting oneself to these sources of information, which used to be the only means in our times. It is these skills alone that will come to their rescue in the highly competitive world. They should understand one thing very clearly: these skills that aspirants misguided by politicians are opposing, will get them employment in government as well as private sector, in India or abroad. Who puts the civil services at number 1? It is only the ignorant or the greedy who dream of making easy money quickly.

This round has gone to Narendra Modi. The agitating classes better remember that the agitations can also be carried out in other parts of the country against them. Have they evaluated the consequences? If not, they better do it urgently. They alone shall be responsible for the consequences. They shall be archived if it happens.

# CNN - Frozen In Time

If the American channels ignore the visit of the Indian Prime Minister Narendra Modi, no complaint need be made. But if they demonstrate a state of mind frozen in time, it does raise questions. On the concluding day of the first visit of the Indian Prime Minister, its coverage was as poor as that of some domestic channels in India. Its anchor seemed to be as ignorant of the visitor's country or the visitor himself. Her insipid questions to a person back in Delhi rather than someone in Washington, accompanied by poor visuals of people & places in the backyard of Delhi or some other place, repeated the bias of a class which has consistently portrayed a great country like India as only a "backward" country.

Such tricks of the media act to block or filter news from its domestic viewers, whom they want to feed their cooked up reports only as a great marketing strategy. If the CNN deputes its crew for visuals of modern, prosperous and developed India, I can accompany it to many such places in Delhi and elsewhere in India. The USA is home to the UNO, where the General Assembly meets. I have never seen the CNN covering the proceedings in details or discussing the viewpoints of member countries - it devotes all its resources on covering violence, violence and violence. If it learns its lessons in international humility fast it will not be wanting in giving adequate weightage to peace and happiness in the world. After all, Buddha was not born to simply preach peace; he was a natural development in an environment of terrible violence all around. America is a very young nation of less than 300 years, India is more than

8,000 years old. But it is for the CNN to decide what treatment it chooses to accord to a nation like India.

Questions are being asked as to what has Modi gained by his visit to the USA? First, Modi had not gone to gain something. He was not visiting his relations from whom he was expecting some kind of a gift. He was also not paying a visit to a disciple who is expected to offer valuable gifts to his Guru. Even then, the visit has meant great gains for both the sides. It's for the first time that the American people have witnessed real India, unfiltered by news channels, even as there was a complete blackout of some kind. Thanks to the power of the social media, the viewer is not captive to the monopoly of the media and refuses to view only what these channels dish out.

Narendra Modi has made a distinct personal impact on the viewers. People in countries like America are very busy and can't spare so much time or attention as they have bestowed on Narendra Modi. The misinformation campaigns run by paid lobbyists against Narendra Modi in the past 10 years have been effectively demolished. His critics in India and America have been shamed.

But more than that, a friendly relationship at people to people level has been established. Now the visuals shown by CNN will not succeed in misguiding the American people about India.

Let me put a question: where do you visualize America after 500 years? A robust and stable healthy democracy of enormously prosperous people belonging to a knowledge society or else? India is more than 8,000 (eight thousand) years old. India had the good fortune of experiencing all this till its obsession with peace did it in by facilitating the barbaric aggressors to vanquish it and subjugate it.

The problem America has been facing is not "terror" but war of a new variety in which human bombs are used to commit acts of barbarity and justified in the name of religion. Whether it was knowingly or otherwise but the American "war on terror" was the correct assessment of terror as a war which needed a response in the form of a war. The only problem is that America does not know how to fight this war. Its operations in Iraq as well as Afghanistan ended up in terrible fiasco only because that is not the kind of response this variety of war demands. What is the other kind is yet to be devised. But one thing is certain- you can't talk human rights or justice when responding to inhuman or unjust acts of war called terrorism.

In this region, India as a stable democracy of more than one billion people and a rich culture of more than 8,000 years holds more promise of a stable fruitful friendship to a country like America than our undemocratic, fickle and unstable neighbors. This simple strategic idea has not been allowed to take roots in the American administration by vested interests.

America cannot survive for 500 or more years on the strength of short term benefits or narrow foreign policy guideline as is suggested by its relations with India and others in the region. The cold war having gone, the world is now afflicted by terrorism, which has come to occupy the space vacated by the cold war. The media conduct contributes disproportionately to the spread of terrorism. The media can't show mercy to one category of terrorism and cruelty to the other. It has to partner in spreading civil values for the world to live a better life.

The most valuable achievement of the visit of Prime Minister Narendra Modi is this sensitization of the masses in America. America need not fight wars as in the past. Its interference in ISIS affairs has been invited by a worried world and it is for the first time that it stands on a very high moral ground. In India, prominent Congress Party leaders have openly admonished Prime Minister Narendra Modi not to partner with America in action against the ISIS. In this context, America has to view India as a mighty nation which is a votary of world peace. It has to change its view and the policy that sustained such a view that patronizing Pakistan acts as counterweight to resurging India. Pakistan, in its present form of government, will be a great drain on American resources and a waste, without contributing even slightly to world peace. Pakistan has to move towards genuine democracy for its own survival and America ought to facilitate it.

This change of perception about India and better understanding between the two mighty nations of the world puts greater value to other spheres of economic or strategic relations. The American establishment should watch the discussions on CNN & TVs to see how domineering the participants appear and how grandstanding their views on everything they talk sounds to nations like India. India does not suffer such attitude any more. Americans should talk as equal partners and two sovereign nations having distinct strengths, which they are prepared to exchange for mutual benefits. It can't always be that one gives and the other takes- after all, this give & take comes to an end sometime, if not in the immediate future, at least in the distant future as the life of the nation's runs for several thousand years. We wish the Indo-American relations also to set an example worthy of emulation by others for thousands of years. That is also the message Prime Minister Narendra Modi has driven in words or gestures during the visit. From the son of the soil, this message contains the essence of Indianess: we love and want to spread the message of love to a world suffering the consequences of acts of hate.

# What Bonds India & America?

What provides the unique bonding between India & America? Is it trade interests as some elite members of the academia or media hazard guessing from time to time? Is it political ideology of the two countries that draws them to each other? Is it global security partnership between the two countries that acts like a strong adhesive? There can be any number of such questions without any finality about the answers as it might be both yes and no or even both. However, the single strong element that bonds these two great nations is "knowledge". America enjoys the reputation of the land of knowledge, knowledgeable and knowledge pursuers, something which India has been known for millennia until it all got eclipsed.

India has always attached the highest value to freedom of thought and expression. It is our dharma or cardinal principle. So is the case with America. Both the countries are known for their professed act of faith and practice of freedom of thought and expression. America has been able to attract the best minds from all over the globe only because there was this assurance of the freedom for the scholarly to pursue their dreams as they wished, and the state providing them whatever it could. At least the American state never stood in the way of these scholars or discouraged them in any way. India could not do so in the early days of independence due to financial constraints caused by centuries of foreign rule. But even under such trying conditions, Indians never gave up their pursuit of knowledge. How could that happen? Because of what has been stated above: India has always attached the highest value to knowledge. We have been educated about it from ancient times. We have been told that the highest goal of life is knowledge or Gyan: "Gyanam Paramam Dhyeyam". Gyan is more than knowledge; even more than what is commonly meant by knowledge- it is advanced knowledge. It is that stage of knowledge after which nothing more remains to know. So, it needs no more emphasis as to what is meant by gyan, because a life span is too short a period to know all that is worthy of knowing. This remains true even after technology has empowered us immensely. With all the power of technology we have not yet made it to the several universes our scientific discoveries have identified.

Knowledge has been so vast and varied that it has been given another all-encompassing word: Truth. What is truth? All that is knowable in the cosmos is the truth. It is pure distilled knowledge. It may not be possible to define truth in any convincing manner, but questions thrown up by the human mind so far in its existence do indicate about it. What is it that we see? Is it reality or illusion that our eyes see? Is the world a creation? Is the cosmos an evolution? How do perfect laws of science come into operation without anyone visibly managing them? If someone is managing the phenomenon visible to us, what is it called? Is God or its synonyms in all the dead or living languages of the world a simple waste of time or more valuable attempts to acquire knowledge? Pre-scientific studies might have ruled the human mind till scientific studies came to prevail. How's it that science is constrained by its own limitations in getting all the answers? Does it mean that knowledge is not only the oceans on the earth alone but the whole sky whereas our scientific tools have not been able to take us beyond the limits of the galaxies? Will the human race have all the time to explore all this knowledge and render it comprehensible in the distant future? Will it end once again only to make another start from the beginning in the all-encompassing cycle of time (with T capital)? The Indian mind had explored all such dimensions in the ancient times and it inspires and spurs them even today. That explains the journey by choice of the Indian mind to that country at the other end of the globe after independence in 1947. Aren't these Indians, settled in America, a valuable asset of that country? If the answer to that question is in the affirmative, you have validated my finding that "knowledge" is the strongest bond between India & America.

That brings me to the other aspects of Indo-American relations, which have witnessed ups & downs all through these years. These variations are due to trade interests, foreign policy, diplomatic reasons, strategic consideration and failures of the intelligence agencies. These wings of the government have been regularly briefing the press and the media, who in turn marketed the version provided to them by these agencies, without independently exploring the truth. For how many journalists the principles of non-violence have any meaning or significance? How many appreciate or even understand "vegetarian" values? The global media devotes more time on violence in the world and insignificant time on good living societies. Prime Minister Narendra Modi had visited America for five days beginning 26th September 2014. The Indian community in America warmly greeted him. However, the American media seemed to be cold to the visit. They ignored even the bare courtesy of at least reciprocating the warmth shown by the Indian media in covering the visits of President Clinton or Obama and others. It is so because the American mind thinks itself superior to other countries, more so leaders from developing countries. If such a mindset influences bilateral relations from time to time, it does not surprise me. Because the bureaucracy anywhere in the world feels hurt if it finds itself in the wrong at any time and American bureaucracy is no exception. Leaders come and go, but bureaucrats survive in person or their papers. In spite of these odds, India and America will remain friends for centuries because their bonding is unique. I can't be sure if there is another example in the world of this kind of nations and the bonds of their friendship. Together these two are strategically positioned to give the world the necessary environment for peaceful co-existence in a meaningful way.

# Launch of Make in India Campaign

The Prime Minister Mr. Narendra Modi launched the Make in India campaign on 25th September 2014 before leaving for the USA to attend the UNGA Session in New York where he was scheduled to address the gathering of the Heads of States and Heads of Governments of member countries. It sent out to the world a message that there has been a change of government in India and the new government under Prime Minister Modi meant to take significant economic measures to strengthen the economy. What is the significance?

PM Modi in his address to the gathering of prominent industrialists of India and MNCs and members of the diplomatic corps in Vigyan Bhavan in New Delhi emphasized one thing: he aims to make available an "effective" government in India and not merely a "good" government. It is extremely significant and needs to be noted. It may be recalled that the Vajpayee government 15 years ago aimed to provide sushaashan, i.e. "good governance". The Vajpayee government succeeded a long era of extremely bad governance. The people demanded a change for good governance and Vajpayee did indeed succeed in giving the country good governance. But his good governance had hit the vested interests severely. So these elements, in collusion with the English media houses, managed to denigrate the achievements of the Vajpayee government. Vajpayee lacked clear majority of his party and therefore, had to exercise extreme caution in taking his coalition partners along in a pattern of political behavior that acquired a new coinage called the "coalition dharma", which came to dominate politics in the country for the next 15 years. While his opponents succeeded in breaking the coalition under Vajpayee because he lacked the skills of real politics, Narendra Modi is too clever for his rivals in the opposition or within even his own party.

Between Vajpayee and Modi, the Congress led coalition ran the government, which unfortunately earned the bad reputation of being the most corrupt government in India since 1947. The rule of law suffered the most and the whole scheme of constitutional governance in India was upended in the 10 years of the Congress run coalition under Prime Minister Manmohan Singh. Under that dispensation "effective" meant rent seekers, commission agents, deal fixers, wheeler dealers, and unconstitutional authorities exercising the powers of the government. They were the only effective people. One phone call from such elements was enough to get the desired things done, be it appointments to government positions or licenses or spectrum allocation or allocation of coal blocks or anything else. They were so effective that nothing moved without their nod, at the center or state government level. Obviously their services came not for free as public service but at attractive prices with equally attractive discounts if support for the government during the trust vote was ensured. Discipline suffered so awfully during that period that even secret government documents were leaked to unauthorized persons and even highly sensitive defense secrets like navy war room information fell in enemy hands very easily. Such was the effectiveness of these people.

Is the assurance of "effective" governance held out by Prime Minister Modi different from that kind of effective governance? Yes. Let us recall Modi's public declaration immediately after becoming Prime Minister "Naa Khaungaa, Naa Khaane Doonga "(I will not take bribe nor let anybody else do so}. It is that Modi who has now promised not only good government but effective governance. The industry needs good and effective governance to pursue their projects. They don't want irritants at every toll plaza installed by the corrupt. The industry can't suffer delays due to irrelevant laws or multiple regulators. It can't digest humiliation at the hands of authorities who are oblivious of the entrepreneurs' contribution to economic development, growth and job creation and think of industrial or commercial projects only as ventures for personal benefit of the investor. They don't even understand the difficulties and complexities of getting technology from the owners abroad or even the significance of IPR/TRIPRs. How can anybody even think of commissioning or running smoothly industrial projects? Unless the government is able to satisfactorily demonstrate that it means business and is honest about good and effective government, Make in India remains a distant dream.

But Modi is no daydreamer. He means business if the first 100 days of his government are any indication. He is conscious of the fact that it is too early to talk of branding goods as "Made in India". For that to happen, it needs state of the art technology, which is not available off the shelf. Only outdated technology and old machines are sold to the developing countries, which transfers the entire liability of environmental pollution on their shoulders while the developed countries claim carbon credits. Developing high technology, though possible, is like re-inventing the wheel and needs too much capital and time investment.

International cooperation in this field is mutually beneficial. When Prime Minister Modi launched the "Make in India" campaign, he initiated the process of transfer of latest technology in a new way by inviting technology owners to set up units in India and produce to serve the markets and contribute for developing best production facilities in India. India is no more looking for foreign capital alone. In fact, tons of Indian wealth is stacked up in foreign banks, which if invested in India will give the people tax breaks for 10 years and contribute to annual rate of growth of 8-10%.

India has been collaborating with foreign technology giants for more than 6 decades now and is a trusted partner. However, due to several constraints, lack of good & effective government being one of them, the pace of transfer and absorption of technology has been slow. I give a few examples. Take optical fiber technology. Several years were spent in fruitless discussions whether private sector should be allowed to import the necessary technology or the public sector corporation should be given the monopolistic rights to import the technology. Who was deciding on the subject? Those at decision making level had no idea of what was an optical fiber or how different it was from the jute fiber or the nylon fiber or the manmade fiber. Another example relates to manufacturing of fax machines in India. The question for decision was if it was in public interest to license manufacture of fax machines. Till date, the same mindset is in operation. The result: mobile phone handsets, plasma TV, military equipment and a long list of products continue to be imported. Comparison with China is made as if the Indian industry is not willing to manufacture all these products. Who is blaming whom? Are the decision makers helping entrepreneurs or impeding them? Do they want to promote entrepreneurship development or keep the citizens as Kisaan/Mazdoor (farmers/laborers) infinitely to harvest votes in elections in their name or poverty removal? Do they want the poor to remain in low income professions or provide them opportunities to exit the vicious circle of forced poverty? It is fresh air after 10 years of historic corruption that a Prime Minister comes to make a public assurance that he is determined to provide an effective government. And we take him at his word. We take it as a gentleman's word of honor. We want the world to trust him for his sincerity in delivering on his promise. We had very fruitful cooperation at industry to industry level all these years as entrepreneurship accepts all challenges and surmounts them satisfactorily. The Make In India campaign will only give it a fillip.

It is doable. I write so on the basis of my personal experience of successfully implementing the scheme of setting up of District Industry Centers (DIC) in every district of the country in 1977-78 and executing the De-licensing Policy of the government in 1985 against all the resistance of the vested lobbies. The De-licensing policy of the government of India removed the requirement of first getting a license before an industry could be set up for almost 40% of the industries enumerated in the First Schedule under the Industries (D&R) Act. It was the first major economic liberalization initiative in India. It was widely welcomed by industry circles. A license in those days carried more value than the contemporary allocation of air waves or coal mines, for it commanded a hefty premium under the license regime. Actually, you need honest and devoted officers enjoying the full support of the incumbent government to deliver on such policies and programs. On the basis of his performance as Chief Minister of Gujarat for 12 long years before becoming Prime Minister of India, Narendra Modi's assurance of effective and good government can be taken to be sincere and honest.

# Media Protectees & Media Fidayeens

The media, believed to be independent and objective, has often been charged of bias. It has its own favorites and non-favorites. It is different that their prejudices and flattering coinages are masked in appropriate jargon. India has been witness to this saga for more than a year ever since Narendra Modi became a serious contender for the highest office in the country. Even the BBC has not been arraigned so much for bias or tilt in coverage of the referendum on Scotland as has been the case of NaMo or Narendra Modi.

There are awfully ferocious television anchors, who had used every adjective in the best thesaurus and dictionary in the English language to attack their targets. They had no fear of loss of reputation, as they never stopped at acting media fidayeen even after expose after expose. Like the ISIS, Al Qaeda or other such outfits boastfully taking credit for human bombs, which they elevate to the level of heroes by calling them fidayeen, these media moguls or their owner companies, use journalists and their credentials to make efforts to destroy reputations of leaders of high integrity and bureaucrats of impeccable reputation. They are uneasy with a government practicing rule of law or public servants delivering public services in accordance with the law. They team up with politicians from the opposite camp and other disgruntled elements to pursue their goals. They were crestfallen when Modi emerged as the undisputed leader of India contrary to their expectations and belief, winning absolute majority in the parliamentary election. They lost their speech, so to say. They fell silent for more than a month, when their handlers goaded them to do something.

In Modi's regime, the news industry has been going through a terrible recession, as all the news becomes public through social media before the TV channels are able to give the Breaking News or the newspapers come up with banner headlines and anchor or editorial wisdom. So the newspapers started publishing full page advertisement on the first page which has come to take five pages in less than 100 days, reducing the news portion to not even 30% of all the published words in any edition. TV channels have become so boring that the viewing time has come down to a few minutes from several hours a day. Credit for this change in the news climate goes exclusively to the Fourth Estate because somewhere on the way it forgot its responsibility and took the intelligence of the readers/viewers rather casually. The news industry is dead if it does not stop acting fidayeen for one political party or the other.

It is quite interesting to note that the media which acts fidayeen for some also acts as the media security commandos for some others. The media plays favorites for the chosen ones. Its best journalists comprise the SPG (Special Protection Group). Netas (meaning politicians) in India get SPG commandos to provide them foolproof security. They have no real danger, but it has become a status symbol to be surrounded by special protection group commandos, also called the Black Cat Commandos. Like the security personnel forming the SPG for the Netas, there are journalists who protect their charge of politicians, especially from political or ruling dynastic families. So they are interviewed on TV by the best journalists but in an avuncular manner. They are serenaded in newspapers even for their silly words on any subject. Actually, whenever these "media protectees" open their mouth, they utter something fantastically ridiculous, but the journalists write wonderful articles published in the mid-day editions and next day editions, which glorify them for every such reaction or comment and educate the reader about the real meaning (contrary to what has been "mis-reported") and also its significance. While doing so they don't forget to conclude by attacking the target of their disaffection, like Prime Minister Narendra Modi or some such dignitary.

This strange role of the media costs a country like India heavily. Take for example the Prime Minister's visit to Japan or hosting the Chinese President and his visit to the USA. The media has either criticized every single achievement of these valuable exchanges or tried to revive bad past memories. The purpose was to drown the positivity created by the new initiatives taken by a leader who has been acclaimed globally.

The media has not been able to write a single story about China or the Chinese President which could provide information not already known. They could not publish even a detailed account of visiting Chinese President for the benefit of the readers, excepting criticizing the Gujarat government for the wrong translation in Chinese on the welcome hoardings in Ahmedabad. Can't the media provide the right translation, since they are ubiquitous? But the problem lies here: the Indian media is Unilingual- it can handle only the English language with a degree of confidence. That diverts their attention from the visiting dignitaries and their country, its policy and bilateral business and global ramification to pouring scorn on India, the flaws in petty things, government functionaries and the PM. It is followed by ill-informed debates, which turn into bitter slanging matches. None of the contributors to the newspapers or experts on TV shows has been able to convincingly analyze the reasons for the Chinese actions on the border even as their President was being hosted in Ahmedabad. Was it a sign to stall India's growth under a leader as strong as Narendra Modi, as they had done with Jawaharlal Nehru? Do the Chinese fear the rising stature of India because they see in it the possibility of a challenge to their hegemony in the region? Do they think that Modi, like Nehru, nurses the ambition of becoming a world leader? As communism stands buried deep now and there is no hope of Tibet ever getting its freedom back, what is it that fuels the Chinese designs on the Indo-China LAC (Line of Actual Control)? Is some internal compulsion driving China to start a war like situation as it had done in 1962 by pushing the soldiers returning from the Korean War? None of these issues have been subjected to in depth analysis by the journalist the way American, British or French journalist do. It cannot go on serving the media protectees alone. It has to serve the nation and the people.

The media, more than the Americans, will be subjected to greater scrutiny during Modi's visit to the USA to address the UN General Assembly and bilateral talks with President Obama. He will also be addressing the Indian diaspora and holding a press conference there. The media will prove itself unworthy of its role if it displays its expertise in spreading communal venom by irresponsibly using words as in India. They will get more than their appetite on matters communal in the context of the ISIS activities which they will not be able to handle as the violence is not only between the two sects of Islam but other faiths too. And our journalists are secular people with extremely limited knowledge on subjects like religion, spirituality, social stratification and several such issues. They better adopt a positive attitude so that something useful for the country comes to notice. Suffice it to say that India and America are the only two countries that are natural allies, because both lay great value to freedom of thought, speech, expression and belief. Moreover India had lived the knowledge society long ago which America is now establishing.

# Modi's Focus on Modernizing Education

Teacher's Day 2014 was different from celebrations till 2013. It was a turning point in the history of school education in India. Like in several other spheres, Prime Minister Narendra Modi leaves his footprints in one of the most vital areas of nation building-education. Teachers have traditionally been revered in India; the country takes pride in its teacher-taught bonds, better known as the Guru-Shishya Parampara. Traditionally the Teacher's Day is celebrated as Guru Parb. Teacher's Day is its modern version. But the spirit remains the same: to value the contribution of the teacher in the life of the individual and the nation. Teachers educate, develop, train and prepare the individual to become a useful productive well chiseled person. It goes down as an eternal debt, as is the love of the mother which cannot be discharged unless similarly transferred to the next generation. The demand for education in a democracy like ours is so great that we need to adopt modern methods of teaching. Prime Minister Narendra Modi has succeeded in conveying this significant message for urgent change through his interaction with teachers and student throughout the length & breadth of India. He adopted the impressively visible symbol of modernity by going for the video conferencing mode for his interaction. Without hurting the sentiments of either the "traditionalists" or the "anti-traditionalists", the Prime Minister was successful in driving his point through the target audience viz., the teaching and students community that love for tradition was as important as for modernity. As he engaged his audience in a very fruitful dialogue, he also gave demonstration of the power of technology to the children. He also demonstrated to the teachers the need to fill their skill gaps before they missed the opportunity forever as the children of today are not like traditional ones but "Born Digital". These children already know more than their traditional counterparts at that age. This generation is inquisitive and wants to know more. They have become used to getting the desired information at the click of the mouse and unless the teachers too are capable of responding as fast as the computer, their bonds will not forge as strong as the traditional one when the students worshipped their teachers. While the teachers may not know answers to all the questions asked of them, they certainly should be able to guide the students convincingly. India has to bridge this gap in skills of teachers rather fast to convert its demographic advantage to levers of prosperity. For this to happen, the government alone will need to take decisive steps.

The PM asked the question: why it is so that teaching is not the chosen profession of the people generally. Surely he knows more about it, but a few points need highlighting. School teachers are not accorded the same respect that any civil or police officer of the same rank gets from the government and the society. The teacher might get respected for his contribution to the grooming of students but he gets nothing more than that. In fact, transfers of teachers in government schools are the biggest industry in the hands of the corrupt administrative as well as executive authorities. Compared to the other variety of teachers, who have made a commercial success of their talent, the one making "sacrifice" looks a loser in real life, because maintaining a minimum standard of living for him is very difficult. Parents show respect only so long their son/daughter is getting good coaching to make a success in the entrance examinations to professional institutions. Thereafter they may not even recognize the teacher. There is no complaint for this change in people's behavior because urbanization has induced such change. I quote another funny but significant example. As a student of Sociology it is my hobby to go through various kinds of advertisements published in the newspapers. In the matrimonial columns of these newspapers, advertisements seeking grooms for their daughter all parents seek only IAS/IPS/IIT/IIM and other such professionals but none, without a single exception in the last 5 decades, has ever sought a teacher or even a Lecturer/Professor! That is our collective respect for the Teacher, whom we celebrate on the Teacher's Day.

In this background, the best teachers have regularly been changing professions e.g. entering civil services where the career prospects are fantastic in comparison to teaching. Those committed to academic profession find jobs abroad.

It is one of the greatest losses to the country that it had exported its precious pool of talent depriving the children of good teachers. To attract and retain talent in teaching, teachers need to be paid well according to their academic excellence. The private sector in India is doing that- teachers in the "Public Schools", which means private schools, are comparatively a satisfied lot because they get paid well and respected in these schools. Admission of children in these schools is a ticket to better educated, better skilled children and an assured career in life.

Should it not be the right of every child to receive that kind of education? This is the difference between the old Gurukul system of education and modern education; the Gurukul education was accessible to only the select few but the modern education is available to everyone. But the differing standards of education in government run and private schools reinforces the old tradition of Gurukul in practice because of filters applied to block the admission of every eligible child except the select few. There is denial of quality education to all children. When that is the case, can the graduates be blamed for being "unemployable"? Who has made them unemployable? Certainly not the parents nor the children themselves but the system that denies children equal quality education and equal opportunities. End this system and watch all of them turn adequately equipped to serve the vocations of their choice.

The graded education even in the government schools presents a depressing picture for the ordinary- there are Central Schools (KVS) followed by Jawahar Navodaya Vidhyalas, Pratibha Vikas Schools for the talented, government schools, municipal schools and Panchayat Schools. The largest number of children have access only to the last three schools in this list, which are poor specimen of school education.

Even if the government had provided Kendriya Vidhyalaya (Central School) education to every child in the country, the contribution of these young people would have changed the country's economic conditions long ago. Unfortunately, school education has received the worst treatment in free India. Had the British not set up excellent schools in India, our children would have suffered much more. All politicians and bureaucrats get their children admitted to the best schools run by the private sector and thereafter send their children abroad for further education. So the country has been suffering double whammy in the form of loss of talented teachers and students. We have never reviewed such huge loss of talent by way of "brain drain", much less any plans for "brain gain". We should import good teachers from wherever we can. The American success story validates this argument.

The Prime Minister should have been briefed on this aspect. There are more than 20,000 vacancies in institutions of higher learning in India. The numbers for school education are frightening. And yet the Prime Minister asked the question: can we not export good teachers sometime in the future? No, Sir. We must not export good teachers if we can afford to retain them on their terms. We have yet to achieve our targets of full literacy. A recent report published in the newspapers stated that it will only be by the year 2080 that the primary school education of girls in India could be achieved. Does it justify our objective of being able to export teachers?

Globalization has shifted the business modules everywhere. Foreign students are taking coaching from teachers operating from India. They are helping students with their homework and project work. Virtual class rooms are becoming a reality wherever they are lagging. Massive Open Online Courses (MOOC) is going to change the whole system of imparting education. I have a feeling that the Prime Minister hinted at such programs in his Teacher's Day interaction with the students. He opted for video conferencing, revealing his mind. He emphasized the need for technology and demonstrated its use through the 90 minute interaction with the children.

He is preparing the "Born Digital" generation of Indians for the responsibilities of the decades beginning 2020: learn, play, health, intellect, values, scientific temperament etc. in the technology driven decades ahead. By the time these children graduate and join the skilled workforce, they would have attained the age of 25 years, a time to own responsibility. They have more than 7 years at their disposal to visualize their future and go full steam to achieve their goals. To that extent, Prime Minister Narendra Modi has done it again.

Without giving boring speech on the occasion, he has demonstrated to all variety of students and even those deprived of education the need for education and technology. It was for the first time in the history of India that the Prime Minister spoke directly to the students taking all their questions and answering them. It was made possible by the availability of technology. The PM knew its value. His mission is clear: to connect all the villages of the country through broadband connectivity. Then every child will get answers to all his/her questions, unlike now when they are spanked for asking questions. The revolution that I see happening sooner than the Modi haters imagine is bound to change "things" in India, The explosion of knowledge occurring due to the internet will be within the reach of all students, not the select and privileged few as of now. It will cost the exchequer less than the cost of poor education, free books, uniforms and meals etc. in one year. It was the post-Independence born Narendra Modi and he was talking with the "Born Digital" generation.

Modi haters suffer from compulsive neurotic disorder and have to criticize even such a flawless, revolutionary and nationally beneficial program. Let us ignore them. It is time to achieve full broad band connectivity before the next elections. Revolutions happen due to one leader. Narendra Modi is one such leader. He should ensure program implementation.

# America Mutes All Anti-American Propagandists

American intervention in Korea or Vietnam, Afghanistan or Iraq or in other parts of the world had its critics rush to target it in the most unsavory terms. That could be justified on ideological grounds during the cold war. There was need for justification for intervention in Iraq and Afghanistan. It divided global opinion; some convinced of such action after the insane 9/11 incident, others criticizing it as a mask to indulge in unrestrained military action without lawful sanction as the United Nations had not authorized America to do that. Even the American public opinion did not entirely support the government. The count of American body bags hardly could be justified. Similarly the meltdown of the economy could not be welcomed. America had been routinely riled for behaving like the world's "policeman". But the hard reality is that America is the only policeman of the world today and is needed by the world. But for America, democracy everywhere in the world would be threatened, like it is in Pakistan or in many other countries.

America has played the leadership role in world affairs since the end of WW-II. There does not appear any other super power in the world to discharge that role. Were there another superpower matching America, the ISIS would have been wiped out long before it could carry on its barbaric acts against all humanity for so long unchecked. While the uncivilized massacres of innocent Assyrian Christians, Turkman Shias, Shabak Shias, Yazidis, Kakai and Sabaean Mandaeans, Arabs and Sunni Muslims opposed to ISIS and inhumanity that neither the Devil nor God permits or the beheading American journalists, United Nations relief workers, foreigners in Iraq continued for months, all voices thriving on anti-American rhetoric fell silent. Even the most vocal international organizations working for human rights or global peace were muted, for they dreaded the ISIS more than they followed their human conscience. Can the barbarity and savagery of organizations like the ISIS be allowed to go on unchallenged even for a day? The world has to sit up and take notice, as what is under threat is the very survival of all human values, civilization and culture. Such challenges are not for one country to face but for the entire human society as one single entity.

The world owes it to America that it has at long last accepted the role of the world leader for democracy, human rights, peace and security globally. America has been hesitant, cautious and careful before getting into limited intervention. The threat from the ISIS got somewhat reduced. It resorted to beheading journalists in the most chilling manner and video graphing the barbaric act and uploading it on social media sites. The ISIS imagines it will frighten the Americans by such nefarious acts - they are inviting solid reprisal. It will not take long for America to decimate any such barbaric organization, but before it launches into that act, others must offer to ally with it.

ISIS is not the problem of America; it is the problem of the whole world. The roots of such savagery lie in the misinterpretation of religious precepts- it is not simply fundamentalism or extremism or dogmatism even though it might sound like one of them. It is the nature of human society. Earlier it was the turn of other religions in the previous three centuries and now it is the types of the ISIS and Al Qaeda in the 21st century. It looks like the power of

Nature is silently active. There is no chance of the world being thrust into the WW-III. But can peace prevail forever? No, that is not in the nature of Nature, for change is the essence of Nature. So unless the world gets a shakeup of the kind that world wars give, there cannot be any more evolution. The human society is guilty of disturbing, disrupting and destroying the scientific balance of Nature by its excessive intrusion, interference and insensibility in polluting the environment and rupturing the outer space too. ISIS like entities are to socio-political order what pestilence is to populations. Nobody can make an ISIS or Al Qaeda sensible or reasonable. You can't reason with such elements. Nature has cast them in that neurotic mold with some purpose. The ISIS is bound to cause more serious problems for world peace and security. It will gain steam from the Saudi Arabian attempts to close down the holy shrines in Mecca and Medina or removing the remains of the Prophet to some undisclosed location according to media reports. If it ever happens, the world will see greater turmoil than the world war. The world's atomic arsenals are bound to find ready use in that kind of a situation and the consequences can well be anticipated. The human society will suffer but survive as it had done on several occasions in the past.

India had experienced such upheavals too. An aggressor by the name of Nadir Shah continued to massacre the innocent masses in Delhi for three days before the then Mughal ruler offered him his entire treasury in lieu of peace. The British rulers in India mounted no lesser atrocities on the masses. The worst has been the proxy war of the ISI (Inter-Services Intelligence) of Pakistan Army, using terrorist attacks by its religious arms like the Al Qaeda, JuD, LeT etc., which have been avuncularly ignored by America and other superpowers until the 9/11 hurt them so rudely. The world has not yet recovered from that incident and it's after-effects till date. It is worse than the nuclear bombing of Japan in WW-II by America. The economy of America and Europe has never recovered fully from the after-effects of 9/11, whereas the ISIS has proved itself the next cause of worry, rather greater worry than 9/11. It is no more "ethnic" cleansing or localized problem of one country. It is a real threat to world peace and security: whether the human society lives in an open liberal democratic form of government or a savage theocratic form of the government prescribed by the ISIS.

The ISIS does not favor "peace or peaceful co-existence". It rejects outright every single tenet of democracy or modernity. It lives to see the whole world "Islamic". So unless the root cause of this barbarity is finished, hope for world peace remains elusive. The world is going to suffer more barbarity. The ISIS cadres are trained modern war veterans, unlike their medieval predecessors, and also know the handling of nuclear, chemical and biological weapons of mass destruction. They are trying to get hold of these weapons. They might get help from the ISI of Pakistan. They could have come to possess these weapons had they succeeded in capturing the entire resources of Iraq. But for the American intervention at the right time, they were going to succeed in their demonic mission. That America has effectively checked their march is laudable. This should not be allowed to be used as a tool of American foreign policy to derive other narrow benefits excepting world peace and security, human survival, civilized society and culture. If these are assured, democracy survives; otherwise the ISIS lives.

# Financial Cleaning Now

The political capital of India, New Delhi (better known as Lutyens), stood cleaned of dirty political games played by unscrupulous politicians, middlemen, wheeler dealers, fixers, money bags, muscle power and corrupt bureaucrats in every wing of the government since May 26, 2014 when the Modi led government replaced the monolith of the Congress. Whether Prime Minister Modi leaves his mark on the political history of healthy democratic governance in India will be known only in 2019, the time till Modi has promised to present his report card. The people of India are hopeful and full of expectations of positive results at the speed of the mouse in comparison to the rope tricks we have witnessed so far. But the exercise will be complete only if the other cleansing gets completed. While political cleaning may need to be carried out unabated in order to ward off spoilers working towards pulling back the country to the old format of governance, the other cleansing yields results straightaway and stays long.

Elections to the Maharashtra assembly have brought in the new government under the leadership of the BJP. Mumbai is the financial capital of India. India has suffered more from financial misgovernance than political misgovernance. Financial scams prosper only under bad governments. Share market scandals have hit the national economy several times in the past and continue to do so. The latest is the NSEL scandal where investors have lost billions of rupees. Fly by night operators collect funds through initial offer and simply disappear overnight, without the regulatory authorities knowing their whereabouts. Banking bungles, which had led to nationalization of banks in 1969, continue unabated, although it uses advanced terminology like NPA or Non-Performing Assets now. In lay man's language it is daylight robbery of bank money. I will not get even half a million rupees for higher studies or research or starting a small business, but with right kind of connections there will be no difficulty in getting hundreds of millions for unintended projects. It is known to the banker that the intention is not to refund loans ever and still they advance loans. This is called NPA. Such borrowers are given additional funds. After sometime when even the additional funds are unproductive and defaults on payments take place, these loans are first restructured and then rescheduled and thereafter many more such exercises are resorted to, hidden from the public gaze or parliament. The airlines defunct for years now are one of the best examples of such bungling. Insurance funds are allowed to be mis-deployed and wasted and now the eyes of the vultures in the financial market are fixed on provident funds and pension funds. Black money, hawala transactions (money transactions outside the banking infrastructure), chit funds (rather they are Cheat Funds) like the Sarda Chit Fund scandal exposed in West Bengal, public deposits, units and a hundred obscure denominations have had a free run so far, skinning the ordinary investor looking for a safe investment for his meagre savings to hedge it against high inflation and meet family needs of the future. Hundreds of such cheated investors commit suicide as there is nobody to protect them or their money from such financial predators. It calls for immediate surgery to remove these financial market malignant tumors to deliver the promised good governance with achhe din or good days. The whole pricing mechanism as also the demand-supply operations of the market have been controlled and manipulated by dishonest operators who have made it thoroughly unclean.

For the realization of the Swachh Bharat it is the sine qua non that political cleansing is complimented in equal measure by the financial cleansing. Under no circumstances, the government should appear to be dithering on this score. Ultimately good financial governance is in the interests of everybody: the masses and the classes, the businesses and the bureaucracy, the political executive and the legislature, and above all the judiciary which has been repeatedly called to clean the mess created by bad financial governance of a very unholy nexus of incompetent Neta-Babu-Business. The entrepreneur in the country has been made to feel guilty by bad financial governments over the years whereas it ought to be a matter of pride to be a successful entrepreneur. The joy of producing goods or providing services that get the appreciation of the users/consumers is one of the best rewards of life. The contempt for the entrepreneur on the faces of politicians and bureaucrats and their subordinates tells it all. They are engaged on the invention of flaws in proposals requiring government clearance from the moment the paper reaches their desk. In face even in this day and age, the government postman has the cheek to open even registered letters and demand money before delivering them. You can be a whistleblower, but only if that satisfies your ego. Depending on the exposure your whistle-blowing leads to, the stakeholders might even blow you off. More than a 100 whistleblowers have lost their lives. Farmers don't get good quality seeds in season, especially in Maharashtra, where more farmer suicides have taken place than anywhere else in the country. They don't get chemical fertilizers.

Everything needs greasing of somebody's palm or purchase from the black market at higher prices. One can get as much quantity as one likes in the black market openly. Should such practices not come to end now that Narendra Modi is Prime Minister of India and his chosen party member Devendra Fadnavis Chief Minister of Maharashtra with HQ in Mumbai?

# The "Class" & Chaiwallah Narendra Modi

Delhi's elite, media barons, journalist intellectuals, news & views Moguls and remote controls of government in Lutyens' Delhi, who have been pink slipped so suddenly by Narendra Modi, are unable to come to terms with the change in the political climate in the country.

They started with mocking, ridiculing and outright vilifying Modi ever since he emerged as the serious contender for the top job in the country. Their ways are strange for the rest of India. The reasons for the sustained anti-Modi campaign lie buried deep in this entity of Delhi to the rest of India because it is only the "class/elite" of Delhi who understand it and manipulate it. They have been intolerant to new entrants, in all walks of life, whether administrative, executive, political, economic, financial, social, literary, arts, judicial, cultural or print/electronic journalism. They have shown the same contempt to everyone. They have always placed themselves high above, claiming to belong to the "class". This claim they make openly with ease in and outside India, even while speaking into the TV cameras. Wonderful class of people, who discriminate against others on the basis of Class, which is not defined by them but left to the imagination of the person or group of persons they consider beneath their class.

The Indian Constitution had outlawed discrimination on the basis of class, caste, origin, gender, language or religion; but such niceties are for others like   Narendra Modi to observe and not for our people claiming to belong to the class. It became necessary to write on this aspect because our elite of Delhi class have been desperately looking for a chink in

Narendra Modi's functioning to attack him. To add to their woes, Narendra Modi goes from success to success, at home as well as abroad. He is getting high approval ratings, which the elite of Delhi fail to understand. Hence, they think it is "oratory & Hindi" which is making Modi such a success so far. They imagine that he will fail in a few months in delivering on his words and then it will be their time to make a good meal of him and feast on it.

They are wrong, as they have always been on Narendra Modi. It is the same class that was wrong about the dark Emergency in 1975 that destroyed democracy and rule of law in India temporarily (even as the perpetrators tried their level best to continue to fool the then Prime Minister Indira Gandhi in believing that she could continue for long as PM by continuing the Emergency, she refused to bite the bait). To say that Modi owes his success to oration and Hindi is simply childish.

We have witnessed feudalism and British rule in India. While it might be a political thought that the king can do no wrong, no political ideology has ever propagated the idea that the "class" can never do any wrong. But our class has always displayed arrogance, flippancy and autocracy by never accepting their wrongs or ever apologizing for their errors of judgement or speech.

Narendra Modi emerged victorious not by oratory but character, integrity, honesty, sincerity and service as Chief Minister of Gujarat for more than a decade.

He didn't buy support of members of the Gujarat assembly to win a vote of confidence. He made no promises which he did not fulfill.

It was his career that promised to change India from a corrupted country to a respected and prosperous nation.

There has been no dearth of orators in the Congress Party and the rest of the political establishment in the country. They are all well-known orators, making millions annually by working as advocates or other honorable professions. They have been speaking nonstop for more hours than Narendra Modi. They had made success of their powerful oratory. They landed up positions of prime minister, chief minister and ministers. They threw all their weight against Narendra Modi. They failed. They failed individually and they failed their party, for they failed the people of India. Indeed, they failed mother India. In spite of their oratory skills & supremacy over Narendra Modi, their high education and Harvard or Oxford degrees, their attempts to portray him lacking even basic knowledge of history or geography, charging him of possessing knowledge of economics which can be put on a postal stamp, treating him as unworthy of joining the "class", all the competing orators were vanquished by Narendra Modi.

One highly educated member of the class as well as the party showed his concentrated derision for Narendra Modi by calling him a menial tea vendor or Chaiwallah and offered him space to sell his tea outside the Congress Party HQ at 24 Akbar Road in Lutyens Delhi after defeat in the election. The arrogance was a perfect reflection of the upper caste Hindus towards the menial workers from the lower castes before the constitution introduced the right to equality to all Indians. His body language conveyed greater sense of caste supremacy than his words. It is a different matter that Modi is the Prime Minister of India and the Class fellow is in complete disarray not knowing how to atone for his peremptory diatribe and sick mentality.

So it is not oratory skills that the despondent elite of the class are feigning to be the reason for Narendra Modi's success, suggesting thereby in their own crafty style that he continues to be only the chaiwallah (lower class than themselves) even after becoming the Prime Minister, as one of their prominent member taunted the Indian diaspora gathered in Madison Square Garden in New York to listen to the visiting Indian Prime Minister Narendra Modi that they may be rich but they don't have the class. The growing anger of the class can be gauged from outburst made publicly in the TV camera in a faraway place.

How much propaganda the class might be carrying globally through their class-network can only be imagined. They can even write books. India has been subjected to terrible exploitation by this class which is responsible for reducing the country to the status of one of the most corrupt countries. Their campaign against Modi emanates from the fear of getting exposed, investigated, brought to justice and punished for decades of corruption, which was allowed as a reward for sustaining minority or corrupt governments and dividing the country on caste and communal lines.

They have suffered defeat because they forgot to take into account the youth of India, who are able to deconstruct all their theories and return a government like that of Narendra Modi.

Much is being made of Narendra Modi speaking in Hindi. They first thought this Chaiwallah has no knowledge of the language that gives them pride, privilege and position-

English. But Modi cleared their doubts on this aspect by making a few public speeches in English. Then they started suggesting that Modi is comfortable to speak in Hindi, suggesting he is not as comfortable with English as they are and he is good in Hindi (which has been used by the class in a derogatory sense for decades due to the anti-Hindi political agitation in the South in the early 1960s). They are wrong again. Modi's mother tongue is Gujarati, but he has learnt more than one language and makes use of them according to the occasion. Why does Modi speak in Hindi? It is simply because he speaks from the heart. He does not mince his words. He is not crafty with words as a Class member can be with Winston Churchill's political language. Hindi connects Narendra Modi straight with the audience. He interacts with his audience in this language and encourages them to communicate with him in public meetings. This facility no English speaking politician in India is known to have created for the ordinary member of the audience to freely interact on the spot with the speaker.

The Class neither understands such a nuance nor wants to learn. So let them go on deriding Modi, his oratory and Hindi. We don't mind keeping the class in the archive of history as we have done with Shehanshahs, Maharajas, Rajas and Nawabs. We will add one more species to them and proceed with our mission to establish a classless society in India.

We have entrusted the responsibility to Narendra Modi presently. He is under observation. He is a very good learner, with an open mind. He has progressed a lot. His foreign visits have expanded his horizons greatly. He is not the Modi the Class has known so far. His followers have to rise to his expectations so that he succeeds in delivering a good and effective government. It would be beneficial to the Class too if it tries to understand the new Modi.

# India Lost & Found

Prime Minister Narendra Modi has been exciting unprecedented jealousy among the Congress Party top brass as also its allies. They were fuming at the crowds at his public reception in the USA earlier and Australia later. It is not only the Indian diaspora in these countries that has extended a warm welcome to the visiting prime minister, Narendra Modi, but the President and Prime Ministers of the host countries. Politicians, business & industry captains, professionals and media- everyone has been full of warmth, affection and respect for Narendra Modi. In Japan and during the visit of the Chinese President to India, the same warmth and seriousness was on display. The people back home in India have been pleased at Modi's success in building strong relations with our valued friendly countries. Only his political opponents are dejected, depressed and down.

The Congress Party's malice brigades have been mobilized to carry out demolition exercise in full steam. So, they have launched their foul mouthed attacks by calling the show as hired crowds. Actually the Congress Party has rich experience in hiring crowds and beating drums to drown their black deeds. On the morning of June 26, 1975, hired crowds were brought to express support for the imposition of the black Emergency in the country, which curtailed constitutional governance and led to suspension of fundamental rights of the citizens and the human rights of the people. The whole country was shocked at the imposition of the emergency. The notorious elements who organized such crowds in Delhi were the same who organized mass murders in 1984 in Delhi and elsewhere in the country. They have betrayed lack of basic courtesies towards presidents, prime ministers, elected representatives of the people, intellectuals, scholars and other prominent dignitaries of the country.

The informality visible during the meetings of the Prime Minister Modi with the Prime Minister of Japan, President of China, President of America, Prime Minister of Australia and other dignitaries is indicative of the charming personality of Modi. He is an unconventional politician. He has risen from the soil, unlike the earlier ruling community of leaders dropped from the deus ex machina. He ran his election campaign in the most unconventional manner; he got the kind of thumping majority mandate that qualifies to be called unconventional; he has given an unconventional governance model and earned the name and fame of the "man of action" as President Obama said during the G20 meet in Australia in 2014. More than anything else, what impresses people about Modi is his honesty, simplicity, commitment, sincerity and karmayogi personality. That is the essential India. That is the reason Modi is attracting the attention of the leaders of the super-powers and the Indian diaspora around the world.

In Modi the Indians living abroad see their dignity, honor and pride restored. The Indians abroad are no more apologetic about their country, leaders, government, values and culture. In Modi they find their moorings. Modi has suddenly proved to be the sheet anchor of the great Indian drift, a drift that was threatening to take the nation on the verge of collapse. Modi has filled their hearts with pride and hope. The world leaders have acknowledged it. They know

India much better than the brigades of the corrupt-beyond-redemption political parties and their leaders. As The Australian newspaper put it succinctly, it is after a "protracted period of weak leadership" that Modi has arrived. He has brought with him the hope of the rise and rise of India. The India that was almost lost for all Indians who love it. The past 68 years have created so many divisions at political, social, economic, security, justice and nationalism levels that the citizens cry in pain, suffer in silence and pray for salvation.

Modi has found the lost India for which the resident as well as non-resident Indians have been yearning.

Modi has fulfilled that yearning. He is a true reflection of the famed India. The world has seen the capability of the humble Indian in Modi. They have witnessed the power of political India in the last parliamentary elections. They have seen from close quarters the energy of an Indian aged more than 60 years fasting for more than a week and still going about his agenda energetically while visiting the USA. They have seen reforms taking place without unnecessary hullabaloo. They know the potential for economic development of India under a leader like Modi. They know his desire for accelerating the process of growth by harnessing technology.

Modi presents the right mix of ancient & modern values, where the longing for spiritual attainment imparts strength to the efforts to make life a happy living physical existence. The corrupt rulers had earlier destroyed the ordinary Indian both in material as well as spiritual terms.

They earned for the nation and every Indian the infamy of one of the most corrupt nations. Modi has halted this process. Modi has reversed this process. In fact, India has asserted itself: I am not a corrupt nation; I am not a corrupt person; I am as old as humanity and as modern as anybody. India had visualized the events in advance and made advance preparations. Alas! They had suffered somewhere at some point in time due to the savagery of the anti-intellectual marauding tribes, exactly the way they are performing in Iraq or Syria today. Modi is a reflection of that essence of India only. There is no need to create a halo around him or make a demigod as his opponents have done to their icons, because Indians are essentially like Modi- karmayogi. All Indians are capable of living like that provided they break the spell cast on them by the Devil, who has made them corrupt-mentally, bodily and spiritually. Life becomes rich when body, mind and soul get served equally.

India found! The young democratic republic, a member of the modern knowledge society, marches ahead under the inspiring leadership of Modi. He deserves the co-operation from all quarters. The ganging up of frustrated politicians is bound to fail, because if they win, India loses, which no Indian would allow now. They should, therefore, welcome the rejuvenated India as warmly as the Indian Prime Minister is welcome at home & abroad. Courtesy begets courtesy & respect begets respect, Truth begets truth. Satyam vadate, asatyamnaa vadate, satyamev jayate, satyam pratishtite. From Sanskrit, it means speak the truth, never speak untruth, truth wins, so respect the truth.

# Nehru's Liberal Ideas in Conservative Indian Society

Mahatma Gandhi was the first political leader in India who stood for removal of untouchability in a highly conservative Indian society. He paid the price for it by his life when one representative of that conservative society found his ideas too liberal and shot him from point blank range in full public view. The Swachh Bharat (Clean India) program of Prime Minister Narendra Modi started in 2014 broke a myth that it was the responsibility of someone else to clean his house or public spaces and he was entitled to throw garbage anywhere he liked. The Prime Minister made all VIPs to hold the broom in their hand and wield it in cleaning the surroundings in their locality.

Jawaharlal Nehru, the first prime minister of India, displayed an unwavering belief in introducing changes in the conservative society. At the dawn of Independence, even allopathic treatment for diseases was opposed by religious leaders, quacks claiming treatment by administering potions, magic or jhaad-phoonk (moving the broom up & down the sick person to drive away the evil spirit responsible for the illness). The opening of health care facilities and hospitals by the government in every district in the country was a change maker of great consequence. Irrigation facilities for agriculture, modern methods of farming, introduction of improved seeds and farming machinery, promoting the use of chemical fertilizers, schools, colleges, universities, IITs, SISIs and many other institutions introduced change at social, economic, political, judicial, cultural level in the country and led to change in attitude & perception in the masses. The old feudal system gave way to democratic institutions. Voting rights upheld the equality of all. There is no case for criticizing Nehru for any of these modernizing programs, as it emanates from ignorance. Those who criticize Mahatma Gandhi or Jawaharlal Nehru need to rise to that stature first to be able to appreciate their greatness, revolutionary work and sacrifice.

The secret of Narendra Modi's success lies in his rise to that level in spite of being in the company of those who refuse to say anything good for these national leaders. Modi has an open mind; he is receptive to ideas (his Man Ki Baat) and above all he is flexible. That trait of Modi's personality reveals the dynamism of the person which is so valuable in a leader heading a government in any big democracy. India has to play a meaningful role in world affairs; Nehru had made that statement very early through the Panchsheel doctrine & the non-aligned movement (NAM). Nehru successfully resisted the opposite pulls of the of the Cold War leaders of the two sides to join them and maintained equidistance from both sides and still developed friendly relations with all. Prime Minister Narendra Modi is likely to make equally precious contribution in this arena.

Like those criticizing Jawaharlal Nehru out of ignorance, people criticize Narendra Modi out of angst or peeve and attack him for polarization. Narendra Modi has not raised any Berlin wall; all he wants is to raise a Chinese wall to fortify the territory and integrity of the nation. His tenure is going to be as remarkable as that of Jawaharlal Nehru. Nehru had the onerous task of serving a conservative society and initiate development programs for it. Modi inherits a pool of energy of a highly talented people. This is the time to extend maximum cooperation to Narendra Modi to implement his development mission. Hate mongers doing business in the name of Jawaharlal Nehru ought to remember that none of them, without a single exception, qualifies on honesty to talk Nehru and claim legacy. Nehru had come down heavily against the corrupt elements in his party and government in 1964 itself. Claimants to his legacy have practiced corruption as never before in the history of India and earned the ill reputation for the country as one of the most corrupt nations in the world. For them, corruption is a "global phenomenon".

Nehru was one of the many freedom fighters of those days who were equal or better educated than Nehru. Nehru had not descended immediately after the end of the Mughal era. Those raising decibels need to remember that what Nehru turned out to be was as a good turn done to India by the British and not the Mughals; and what Nehru did to India was only extension of the good work done by the British. They set up colleges, universities, railways, ports, airports; organized modern Indian military, Navy, Air Force; built such a solid administrative organization in the country that it earned the reputation of Steel Frame (destroyed by the corrupt claiming legacy to Nehru). It is the British who established the Congress Party and catalyzed the Nehrus of India to think nation as against the parochial/ communal/ casteist claimants of his legacy bent upon destroying the nation. They revived the language agitation, insulted the entire territory where they lost in the last election and took the Congress further down.

Those who claim Nehru's legacy should take a vow today to practice honesty in life and serve the nation with utmost honesty.

# Policy for Development in India

India is like a tree with several varieties of fruits hanging from it. We dream. We are encouraged to dream. Our leaders after independence have nudged us to dream and partner the government in its developmental tasks. Centuries of foreign rule had robbed us of all our innate entrepreneurial capabilities. Our own production units were closed down, converting us in to a mere market for foreign goods, which used machines for mass production. We had lost our own models of economic development. Market for our own goods had shrunk. Unemployment brought poverty and backwardness. Our struggle for freedom from the foreign rule was inspired by the dream of regaining our old position of economic glory, summed up in the epithet sone ki chidiyaa or the golden bird.

At the dawn of our independence the world was divided in two models: the capitalist model & the socialist model. Capitalism was synonymous with colonization and its consequences. Who better than India knew the real face of capitalism, demonstrated by operations of the East India Company and the British rule? Socialism was a new creed. It had a magnetic appeal because of the magic of its rhetoric. The one was associated with the rich and the other with the poor. A poor country like India was naturally drawn to the latter. It was a conscious but careful choice. India wanted to draw from both models the best features for its own strategy of economic development. In lay discourse it came to be called the middle path. Credit for devising this policy was given to the first Prime Minister, Jawaharlal Nehru. It is called Nehruvian policy even today.

For all these years since 1947 the Nehruvian economic policies have been the stated development charter of the country, with amendments, modifications, liberalization and small doses of reforms from time to time. However the Nehruvian economic policy approach did not satisfy the industry, business or entrepreneurial requirements because it turned out to be slow & costly. It got regular flak from international agencies like the World Bank, IMF and developed country governments. There is no denying the fact that it was indeed slow and tilted towards socialistic pattern, but this was the only course for a country short on capital, technology, plant & machinery. None of these important elements of economic development was available easily or on easy terms. India needed a plan for the improvement of the economic conditions of its vast population. For years, we had to import food grains like wheat to feed our people.

This model, debated for decades, has become a hot issue after Narendra Modi became the Prime Minister. One view in India has been advocating adoption of swadeshi or indigenous model. There is a strong opinion within the BJP of the Prime Minister about swadeshi. A perceived conflict between the Nehruvian and indigenous models is getting more than rightful attention. The Nehruvian model neither ignored indigenous means of production nor closed down existing facilities. Rather it lent full support to village industries and small units. It only acknowledged the gap between the capabilities of the two for facing the challenge of accelerated development, for which modern industrialization was the only choice. It was the awareness of the fact that the swadeshi model lacked the potential to fulfill the total developmental requirements. This fact cannot be controverted even today and yet the advocates of swadeshi stubbornly go on with their movement without any blue print of development.

The conflict between the Nehruvian and swadeshi models, therefore, is misconceived. The remedy for the abject poverty of the masses is economic reforms on a vast scale at a faster pace than ever and a change in attitude. Nothing should hold us up; India has paid a very heavy price in the form of lost opportunities because of our hatred for capitalism inspired by the rhetoric of socialism and its success in a few countries. The left rhetoric is engrossing but hollow for sustained development for improving the living standards of the masses across all sections of society. Thus, the task cut out for the new government is nothing less than a very big challenge.

Since Prime Minister Modi has woven dreams of acche din (good days) ahead, expectations are high. The Prime Minister is sincere about his promise and his interactions with the stakeholders including the bureaucracy tend to strengthen it. But it hardly can be fixed with band aids. It demands change of gear. Success of Modi will depend on the fact whether he is ready to do that.

Criticism is always welcome. So I hold no apology for the Nehruvian policy. However, it must be noted that today nobody would have been talking of development or growth had the Nehruvian policies not been implemented. The difference of growth and development in different states within India even while the Nehruvian policies were being implemented validates the point that those who marched along had achieved vastly better results than those who failed to act in time. Nehru should not be treated as one individual alone but a collective decision of the best minds at a given point of time when nothing better was on the table.

Today it is a different India that is talking development. Modi is a product of the Nehruvian policies, whichever way you interpret them. Those who dislike the very name Nehru should place on the table their vision of development during the period 1947- 1967 that should have been acted upon. Similarly those who tend to portray Nehru as a demigod should also remember that even during the British Rule, Indians were getting educated abroad in Europe & America. Nehru himself was educated in England. So were several other freedom fighters, who knew better than Nehru what was needed for India. They chose to delegate the responsibility to Jawaharlal Nehru after due deliberation and we must respect that. Rest is matter for research in social sciences. That post mortem not being the focus of this book, I revert to the main issue: strategy now.

The new government would do better if it makes clear choices and devises a new model to achieve its goals. The choice is between economic intelligence and continuing the current project approval procedures. The present project approval methods slow down commissioning of strategic projects by decades (the coal based power projects are a case in point) whereas a decision may need to be taken in hours. That kind of fast decision making is possible only if we put value to economic intelligence rather than premium on delaying procedures where everyone only puts spokes by way of objections whenever his approval is required without even knowing the ABC of the project. Let me give an illustration. Media reports say that a new fiber optic has been developed which will change the world of internet communication.

How long should India take to get this technology? Should it not grab it? That is possible only if we are investing in economic intelligence and processing it for our use. Instead, we expect (rather ask years later), our embassies abroad for such information. Thereafter it takes years to decide whether the technology should be canalized through a public sector enterprise or allowed to be imported by the private sector. Serious discussions are held in various high powered committees comprising experts from the technical field, bureaucrats and other stakeholders for years. Such important decisions cannot be taken any faster in government, but are the staple of private businesses; in government careers are at risk if anything goes wrong, in private sector money alone is at risk. Even the evaluation techniques of the two are different: for government regional development may outweigh economic consideration or social-cost benefit considerations might influence decision making affecting the health of the project adversely later, but for the private sector business interest would be supreme and if there is the right opportunity worth investing it will finalize technical and/or financial collaborations even before the news gets broken to the market. The time difference may be of the order of several months or years and it is as valuable an input for the entrepreneur as capital or machinery, land or skilled manpower. Prime Minister Narendra Modi sounds convincing when he asserts that it is not the business of the government to be in business. Its true import can be appreciated in a case like this.

For accelerated development it is essential that the country scouts for the latest technological developments, market surveys and other critical economic information to match countries like China, Japan, USA, European countries,

Australia and every big or small country. Ideas can sprout anywhere in the world and we need to acquire the wisdom without any delay. It should be possible if we develop our own growth model. It may be called by any name such as the Modi Model. There is nothing sacrosanct about the Nehruvian model, it already stands modified to suit the requirements. Now it is time for competition. To be competitive, we need to devise new sturdy strategy fast. It calls for commitment of all stakeholders.

The absence of a committed and trustworthy leadership after Nehru had driven away committed public servants, leaving the field open for sycophants and corrupt elements to abuse the licensing strategy for personal gain or crony capitalism. The country has been exploited by such elements so much that India came to be considered a country where ease of doing business was only an economic fable. Modi has raised the hope of dismantling the anthills of such elements, but what is required is its replacement. All developed countries are investing on economic intelligence for decades. Why should India lag behind?

Whenever technological upgrade is talked, questions are raised about the perceived loss of jobs. Introduction of new technology, though disruptive, also creates new jobs. In many cases it leads to net addition to jobs. But it saves a lot in the form of reduced waste and rejects and higher consumer satisfaction. HMT (Hindustan Machine Tools), a government of India enterprise, is closing down its watch making facilities due to losses over decades. The domestic market for watches can sustain the industry for another 100 years. . The question of making losses should never have arisen. It would have been in the black all these years. But it is not a watch manufacturing country in the same way the Swiss companies are. The difference is technology. Wrist watches had remained a product reserved for development in the small scale sector for decades. Big ideas of setting up a Horology Centre have not materialized so far. The small scale industry has been importing watch movements from abroad and marking them as locally manufactured and selling. While the business has grown manifold, little progress has been made for development of skills, technology and facilities for making it into a cottage industry as in Switzerland, to create jobs for the millions to replace the harmful industry like beedi making (rolled locally made cigarettes). The market holds promise of large scale job creation besides livelihood for another million people. Wrist watches are now valued pieces of jewelry, crafted by artisans of very high skills, helping expansion of the market for their products while also retaining their traditional markets. They craft custom made pieces of great value. They are costly. They are good business. They are worth emulation. Even then the public sector HMT makes losses and decides to close down operations. This culture needs to be abandoned. It is just to illustrate the point that vested interests would not take kindly to any such idea. The entire manufacturing sector needs to be revisited and modernized. Only the new government can show the necessary boldness to step in and take healthy decisions.

Why do we complain of shortage of power in India? Are we really short or wasting energy? Our incandescent lamps, power hungry industrial pumps, heavy electricity consuming vintage machinery etc. tell a different story. We have any number of excuses to justify continuing with outdated technology. We love old, as old is more than always gold in our view. But technological advancement in the past 40 years has ushered in the 21st century with a bang. We cannot afford to be left behind. Just imagine the situation we would have been had we not embraced the computer technology in time. The result is India is today counted among the leaders in the field of software development. Today, if Prime Minister Narendra Modi takes pride in stating that India is no more the country of the rope trick performers but mouse movers, it is entirely due to Rajiv Gandhi, who took bold steps to introduce computerization in office work to make the country ready to welcome the 21st Century. When import of super computers/technology was denied, India developed its own supercomputer and supercomputing technology and showcased the PARAM computer.

My book titled *"Aarthik Sudharon Ka Sutradhar: Rajiv Gandhi (Initiator of Economic Reforms: Rajiv Gandhi)"* written in Hindi was returned by a publisher only because it brings on record the revolutionary initiative of late Rajiv Gandhi for economic liberalization without which India would have continued to suffer the ill effects of the discredited License Raj. Development was a mantra not dear to many. I learnt that the publisher was politically affiliated to the party to which Modi belonged, and which had no love for Rajiv Gandhi or his achievements. It goes to the credit of Modi that he has not only adopted development as a mantra but also raised it to the level of the magic mantra to win the elections. When prominent columnists credited PVN Rao & Man Mohan Singh for economic liberalization, they chose to ignore the stellar contribution of Late Rajiv Gandhi, who actually initiated liberalization in India and dented heavily the License Raj in India. Rajiv had introduced structural and policy changes which were impossible for his successors to upturn. They had no other option but to continue with the reforms launched by him. The Congress led UPA-I & II governments, with Man Mohan Singh as Prime Minister, rather than carrying forward the policies of Rajiv Gandhi, fell for revival of the License Raj. It meant the revival of the ills of those times and the consequences were before the whole world- scams & scams of the enormity of 2G, Coalgate, Adarsh, CWG etc. Had the Congress marched on the genuine liberalization path shown by Rajiv, it would not have been reduced to such a pathetic condition. Can anybody afford to ignore the contribution of Rajiv Gandhi for computerization in India? Innate hatred for innovators, initiators, pioneers, researchers, scholars and entrepreneurs is the weakness of the ignorant, backward, petty politicians. In contrast, Narendra Modi has displayed a better appreciation for the development brought about by the Nehruvian policies and Rajiv's contribution and converted it into his own vision, mission and First Five Year Plan of Narendra Modi, silently disowning the advocates of flawed concepts of swadeshi. What Rajiv had successfully done cannot be undone by anybody.

What Modi has done and has the potential to do, shall not be undone by his successors. The direction is clear: the Prime Minister has to lead the nation in similar or still better manner rather than leaving economic decisions to officials or chambers of commerce. If radicalism is required to be shown, it is in matters of development- economic, social, political, judicial and cultural. When Prime Minister Modi said something during the elections to the parliament, people trusted every word he uttered. We only hope he does not have to ever say: trust me.

Development & promotion of entrepreneurship is our very old model of development. Distance from modern technology had reduced our producers to bare livelihood earning artisan class. Let us take one illustration. I have witnessed several attempts to help the cobbler occupying a little space by the roadside in every small town. It is a pathetic situation to see him carry on his trade even after 60 years of planned development and scores of programs to help him. Is he a slow learner or are the government agencies tardy at service delivery? What should by now have become a high grade trade for the millions of cobblers continues to be a poor man's business for subsistence level livelihood. Only two companies had dominated the market – Bata & Flex- for decades before Flex was destroyed via public sector route. After the market was opened, Reebok and Lotto etc. have pocketed a large chunk of the market. The gap in the demand and supply of quality footwear has made them sell shoes for more than rupees 10,000 (ten thousand) a pair. Had we invested in technology, our poor cobbler would have regained his enterprise, market position and pride of business, living an improved life style and educating his children in good schools instead of keeping them with him by the roadside braving the fumes, dust, sun, wind, cold and rain. The underserved sector needs footwear in the range of more than 100 million pairs annually for school children, college students, office goers, women and men. Our half -hearted attempts at just improving the conditions and not changing them completely have yielded no better results than in the watch industry segment. This is so when we boast of being one of the largest exporters of hides & skins; a large population of cattle and wild life and finest craftsmen. What is lacking is tools, technology and material. The huge market for leather goods has been beckoning them for long. Only if they could be helped to craft the leather goods like shoes, Ladies' hand bags, purses, belts, saddles and hundreds of other items, India would have been dominating the world market. We have not even identified the prospects correctly, for that falls under the category of economic intelligence. The result: we are happy to buy fake purses and handbags of international brands at attractive price whenever we happen to go abroad and feel happy to be the proud possessor of such prized products! India simply exports the larger quantity of hides and skin instead of turning them into finished products of international quality, creating millions of jobs and improving the awful economic conditions of world class artisans.

The situation gets repeated in most areas of very high growth and employment potential. Regular advertisements from the government authority responsible for laying down "standards" warn people: Don't buy these products if they don't have ISI mark - cement, household electrical goods, steel products, packaged food & drinking water, medical equipment, electronic items like TV, microwave ovens and many more consumer products. As far as I know, there are no Indian Standards for services like the plumber, electrician, carpenter, mason, Air Conditioner/ TV servicing under Annual Maintenance Agreement for gadgets costing over Rs. 100,000. Unless the harassed consumer decides to put some sense in the head of corporates, domestic or multi-nationals like Samsung, LG, Nokia or others, the damage done to their gadget by the authorized service center mechanic is not even attended to. The government has so far not commissioned any survey on the waste of consumer wealth and life due to these products and services of poor standards. Rather their product figures are added to the contribution from the small & medium & large industry in the country. Is it industrialization or shadow industrialization? Technology upgrade and highest standards have the potential of more than 10% annual growth by themselves and equal or more exports growth. There has been capital shortage, but that logic fails in the face of 100 times more black money in the country and abroad. Actually we have not realized the value of these growth inputs and shown an attitude of 'everything goes on' or what its local equivalent is – 'sab chalta hai'.

The road transport facility of Delhi presents a very good example. The incompetent and corrupt government in Delhi and its officers had shown total callousness to the woes of the commuting public. The worst city bus service in developing countries is run under the name of DTC (Delhi Transport Corporation). Boarding the bus has always been an exercise in gymnastics, aerobics, wrestling and endurance for the commuting public. Getting the bus was possible only at starting points. Buses won't stop at the designated spot to take or drop passengers. Spotting a bus, all commuters would rush to board it. In the process injuries to many commuters are a regular feature. It could take several hours to get the bus. Meanwhile the waiting commuters had to endure the harsh Delhi summers, winters and rains. The plight of the commuters was exploited by politicians and officials by adding the ugliest private services called the blue line and red line, which were nicknamed killer-lines on the roads. Then came the change of government and the idea of the metro bloomed. The metro was working in England and elsewhere, if one were to draw on others' experience. As the intentions of the government of the time were honest, the right technical man came forward to take the responsibility of implementing the project. Today, Delhi metro is the life line for the commuters of Delhi and the NCR (National Capital Region).There are demands for the Delhi metro services in almost every town coming under the NCR. But for someone who decided to challenge the sab chalta hai attitude, Delhi residents would have been continuing with the painful experience of the DTC services. This success needs emulation by every public service provider engaged on skill development.

The new government under Modi has to change the sab chalta hai attitude in the interest of sustainable growth and better job creation. Indian car manufacturer Hindustan Motors, manufacturers of the Ambassador brand, have closed down, for having failed to scale up technology, restrictions under the licensing regime and trade unionism of a curious kind. The ease of doing business in India acquires significance in this situation. Here are entrepreneurs, trained workers, ready market, finance but not the right kind of technology. Such amount of technology in so vast a field can't be acquired from abroad easily. For this the only answer is R&D. There is no use quoting China every time growth strategy is considered, but we need to invest heavily in R&D. How can we hope to develop technology for cryogenic engines, submarines, light aircraft, consumer electronics, medical equipment, robotics etc. without investing heavily in R&D? We don't even employ the right brains for research as our payments for researchers are shabbily poor and humiliating, impelling them to go to countries like the USA where their skills are recognized, rewarded and also honored. When they get international awards for their achievements, we laud the achievements of the awardee as a Person of Indian Origin (PIO/NRI). But we don't pay for pioneers, achievers, discoverers, initiators, risk takers and change initiators.

Can we pay a few millions to a young research scholar for inventing for the country a product of great import substitution value? Our payment models, which artificially keep payments to below the highest paid bureaucrat or Member of Parliament, can hardly visualize such radical payment schemes. When we were trying to develop OCR (Optical Character Recognition) for Hindi, the bureaucrat ordered the technical team to produce it by a date falling after two months! What product development can be envisaged with such standards of supervisors?

The new mantra in India for a few years has been Skill Development. A commission was set up by the previous government, putting all existing infrastructure under one authority. The new government of Modi has taken it one step farther by creating a ministry of Skill Development. The biggest achievement of the Nehruvian model was establishment of institutions for skill development throughout the length and breadth of India. Even under Nehru's time, such institutions had reached right down to block level. These blocks had trained manpower to guide development in agriculture, industry, health, education and a few other areas. Small Industry Service Institutes, which were manned by technical officers, were set up in all state capitals. Employment Exchanges were provided at district level. Industrial Training Institutes were set up at hundreds of places to turn out skilled manpower for industry and service in large numbers. KVIC (Khadi & Village Industries Commission), concentrated on training for the rural youth short on formal education and training, providing training in activities like bee keeping, soap making, hand paper making, safety matches, candles, fragrance sticks, khadi cloth and apparel and leather sandals. It also advanced soft loans, raw material & marketing assistance, training, scarce raw material distribution, concessional finance and marketing assistance through institutions like the SIDO (Small Industry Development Organization). The network of these institutions helped contribute significantly to the growth of the small industrial units in every state and development of a valuable pool of managers and entrepreneurs. It attracted technical personnel to take up manufacturing in a big way. Before the creation of the new ministry of skill development, this infrastructure stood in place for several years.

However, that was not sufficient. Bringing latest technology to the small or even medium scale enterprises was discouragingly costly affairs, depressing margins to a level where doing business was simply not possible, unless one was prepared to cut corners. That situation impacted the skill development of both the owner-manager as also the government agency personnel. While technology was registering fast development, these two engines of growth were stagnating. The gap between the availability & requirement of the producer and the mentor rendered most public skill development infrastructure underutilized. Improving the situation needs huge investment, which is unlikely to become available in the near future. Small doses of investment are bound to yield unsatisfactory result because of growth constraints on public servants manning these organizations.

The remedy lies in skilled entrepreneurs to enter manufacturing in a big way. The government can extend them all required help like removing all impediments to setting up industries, guaranteed power & water connection, finance at negligible interest rate. It is anytime preferable to encourage quality self-employment than providing government jobs, since it contributes to overall economic development, job creation and improving living standards. The success made by entrepreneurs in the IT sector has contributed to enhancing the prestige of the nation besides inspiring thousands of young men and women. If the skill development program of the new government succeeds in delivering better services than so far, it would have turned a corner in the country's economic development as valuable as that of late Prime Minister Jawaharlal Nehru.

Gujarat in India is unlike many other states. It has many first to its credit. Its industrial growth is an example of the synergy of the political executive, bureaucracy and entrepreneur working in harmony for the general good of the people. As the new Prime Minister Narendra Modi comes from Gujarat, it is not too much of expectation that he will make the best use of his experience of the remarkable business acumen of the average Gujarati- be it a chaiwallah or a chief minister. The Ministry of Skill Development will leave a permanent mark on the industrial map of India if it achieves the legitimate goal of skill development to the extent where the product of goods and services matches the very best anywhere in the world and where the government doesn't have to warn the consumers of spurious or sub-standard products through advertisements in the newspapers.

The industry & business chambers have to come forward and take the responsibility of achieving these goals and make

India the best place to do business during the term of this government as the country can hardly afford to delay matters. The world is changing fast and we might be functioning in a new world economic order by the year 2020. Modernity is afflicted by the revival of medievalism and development is under attack from destruction. It can't be summed up in small terms like terrorism or counter terrorism- it is leading the world towards devastation of an unprecedented kind. Only economically strong nations will be able to withstand this avalanche. It is high time for them to march hand in hand with the governments of the developing nations. For us in India, it is time to create only white money; time to stop creation of black money.

Build your castles, but first build your nation. If the nation is strong, every one of us is strong. What else is Acche Din?

# Bureaucratic Mindsets

Bureaucratic minds tend to be more regulatory than promotional. They are no good to encourage entrepreneurship. Take the example of e-commerce. It is the brainchild of highly creative minds of the 21st century knowledge society, where innovation spurs change in every sphere of life. E-commerce has changed the whole concept of selling, marketing, buying, shopping and retailing. It has foxed the governments, especially their tax administration. Revenue administrators consider themselves a cut above the rest of the bureaucracy: the finance minister compared to the agriculture minister! However, the online selling guys left them so befuddled that the Sales Tax Administration didn't know how to cast their net over them for almost 5 years now. It proves a fact that they or the government didn't really contribute to promote e-commerce in India. But now that it has created a few giant e-sellers and shaken the traditional sales infrastructure, the Delhi sales tax department has decided to "act" (to be adopted by others). News reports say that the Delhi government's value added tax (VAT) department is scanning transaction records of big players "as a part of a drive to check bogus dealers". One may ask "were they sleeping all these years"? They won't answer because they love "inspection" to determine if there was any "undervaluation" so that they take "strict action ", and impose "heavy penalties". Because online shopping is a success they think it necessary to "regulate" the trade. And how do they do it? Simple: by scrutinizing all transactions of the last 3 years to start with. There lies the catch.

Scrutiny means power to harass every online seller. They issue notices under the relevant sections of the sales tax law seeking information that is enough to create a scare. The seller needs to engage lawyers or chartered accountants to comply with the requirements of the law. After preliminary scrutiny, final scrutiny will be held to decide what action, if any, can be taken for any "serious violation of the law" that might have occurred. No small scare to those facing the total affection of all categories of tax authorities.

The question is: should it be allowed? This is the mindset of the bureaucracy of the "inspector raj zamana" or the days of controls through license/permit/quota. This is the mindset when India used to pride in calling itself "socialist". In fact, an amendment to the Constitution of India added the word "socialist" to it. It brought into existence regulatory authorities in almost every sphere of governance including sales tax. Sales tax authorities in India are known to be thoroughly corrupt, because of the law which has favored regulation over growth. It was never growth oriented. It became an instrument of harassment in the hands of the incompetent, dishonest or outright corrupt officers in the entire hierarchy from the peon to the minister. It is high time the government decides to change the law to change the mindset to change the administration to become an agent of growth rather than obstructionist regulator of the last century.

E-commerce has come to stay here till such time its competitor uproots it. Till then, the government needs to look at it with a constructive mind and positive outlook. It should come forward to help new entrepreneurs to participate in this trade revolution. If the economic superpowers and their giant enterprises are investing heavily to capture the Indian retail market, why should the government of India and the states not do so? The approach of the Delhi value added tax department needs to be changed completely to achieve such a goal. Instead of scaring away the e-commerce entrepreneurs by threatening severe action for alleged/suspected/framed serious violations etc., the government ought to play the same role it has been playing to promote small scale industries. It has to extend all the assistance in the form of training, hand-holding, soft loans etc. to the e-commerce entrepreneur.

First of all, they should be treated as "entrepreneurs" and their online selling ventures as "enterprise". There goes a lot of input before an entrepreneur becomes an online seller, and there is too much risk before one becomes successful. Education, information, plan, resourcing, networking, platform, capital, work station, employees, management, finance & accounting, tax matters etc. are only some of the several areas that make the essential inputs of such an enterprise. Isn't a young MBA or any other professional deserving of the government's support in the interests of growth of the economy? It hardly needs reiteration that the online seller needs all the government's support. I recall the uneasiness in bureaucracy some 30 years ago when a proposal came up for decision to include "hotel" in the definition of "industry" so as to qualify for soft loan from banks. Ultimately it was decided to accept the demand and hotel became industry. Taking into consideration the quality employment potential of the e-commerce, these enterprises need government support and encouragement.

The government can take the following steps immediately:

1. It should free all e-commerce ventures from all laws, rules and regulations by providing a single window registration for them;
2. It should ensure loans from banks at soft rates as applicable under a score of Finance & Development Corporations i.e. under 3 to 5% rate of interest;
3. These ventures need less investment in fixed assets but more in working capital, because of the varying demand and supply of goods. Hence they should have the support of the banks in the form of availability of required funds just-in-time (JIT) without any delay at all;
4. Like the Bill Discounting facility extended to the SSI sector, e-commerce ventures should also be extended the bill discounting facility on sales executed by them on daily basis;
5. Banks demand collateral, which discourages development of entrepreneurship in the country. The e-commerce entrepreneur should be granted loans by the banks even if she is unable to furnish any collateral because she has already invested heavily for her education and start up. It is not only her self-interest alone that gets served by her self-employment venture but also a solid contribution to economic growth of the country and generation of employment besides reduction in dependence on the government for her own employment. If help comes to genuine entrepreneurs, the risk of default in loan servicing would not be even 1% of what big enterprises swallow (exceeding several lakh crore of rupees annually). It is time to treat the educated professional young people in the country as competent, capable

and trustworthy productive force. We need to respectfully acknowledge their creativity, innovation and enterprise.

6. Set up an E-commerce Development & Finance Corporation, if need be.

Prime Minister Narendra Modi might spare a thought for these ideas to bring to fruition his goal of creating million jobs?

# Sharing Indian Yoga Experience Internationally

The United Nations General Assembly has resolved to commemorate the International Day of Yoga on June 21. Yoga is total healthcare within the power of the individual. It promotes the idea that it is better to live a healthy life rather than be in the care of the health providers all the time and consuming more drugs than natural foods. Yoga leads to longer span of life. Since it is visited by scientific knowledge of good health, including healthy diet, it works highly satisfactorily. In comparison, a life dependent on medicines might not be long or as enjoyable as without medication. Modern living is fast and highly competitive. Overuse of computers and mobile phones has gifted some unwelcome medical conditions to our young professionals. Even FB & Twitter users suffer from addiction to their use and develop health problems. A few minutes devoted to Yoga at home or work place can restore them to good health in no time. In essence Yoga is an exercise in physical wellbeing. It automatically springs that a healthy body also has a healthy mind. A healthy body & mind prompts one to enter the realm of sublimity and high thinking. Prime Minister Narendra Modi offered to share the Indian experience and proposed to the UNO to celebrate Yoga internationally. The UNO member countries unanimously adopted a proposal to commemorate June 21 as the International Day of Yoga.

It can be said on the strength of personal experience and informed opinions that the practice of Yoga will reduce the prevalence of disease in the world by more than 80% in a few years and diseases like AIDS, Cancer, Heart Attacks, Hypertension, Diabetes etc. will largely be eliminated or reduced or brought under manageable control. Several ailments can be cured by proper Yoga exercises like Pranyaam. The world is now debating openly the excessive use of medicines or tests or surgeries and their futility in a majority of cases. Our health is our wealth and can't be allowed to become the wealth of the pharma companies or private hospitals.

Modern life has come to be afflicted by what has been termed as the "lifestyle diseases". Diseases like diabetes, hypertension, heart ailments, depression etc. are some of the diseases that can be attributed to modern life style. People are regularly taking medicines. To change this cycle of physical, mental or emotional ill health, one needs to practice Yoga. It gives one control over oneself as no medicine or healthcare giver can provide.

The world will benefit from commemorating the International Day of Yoga. It is India's gift to the global village family (Vasudhaiv Kutumbakam) without any restrictions about IPRs or royalties. The joy of sharing the fruits of knowledge with the world community is a source of continuing happiness.

# Paris Slaughter & Secularism

The terror attack on journalists and cartoonists in Paris was an act of extreme cowardice in the name of Islam. The idea of journalism and cartoon survives the attacks of those misguided youth. They were victims of misinterpretation of religious dogma. In fact, religion, of any brand, is incomplete in itself. How silly of man to think he is capable of defending God? Is man more powerful than God? Anybody who thinks so is a sinner and must undergo penance. Nobody is as powerful as God. Misconstruing scriptures, twisting their meaning and putting interpretation on it serving hidden agenda of individuals or groups is ill-informed way of human edification. They are no different from those who use political jargon to push their agenda or economic rhetoric to entice the innocent. In fact, every branch of knowledge from religion to politics to economics preys and thrives on the innocence of the innocents. What had these assassins achieved by butchering innocent unarmed people except playing into the hands of those who are pursuing an agenda of self-gratification? It reveals a conflict even within the Muslim community as the religious bureaucracy feels it is losing power to the state authority represented by the ruling class, including the military leaders, who enjoy all the fruits of material wellbeing of the community. In fact, many of them hold religion in great contempt if their actions are critically examined but use religion to give the impression of being devout. The question is: who is superior- the head of religion or state? The clash is between these two streams, because they often come in conflict with each other.

Why is it that the world calls them terrorists and their activities as terrorism? Is it lone wolf activity happening occasionally or a well- designed long term war? Why does the west shy away from calling it a war? New York is terror, Paris slaughter, London attack, but Bombay (Mumbai) was something else? When barbaric acts are qualified by carefully chosen adjectives, humanity is loaded with the price. Slaughter, massacre, arson, bombing, are no acts of bravery. Killing children as in Peshawar or women as in ISIS is not manly but cowardice. Destroying the seed in the womb is devilish. Using the ingenuity and rhetoric of the Devil to justify all inhuman acts is self-deception. Because the question is always: what is right and what is wrong? Who decides it? What constitutes right or wrong? The success of Muslim aggressors in the past had made them draw a wrong conclusion that their cruelty to human beings was the best instrument to establish the superiority of their religion. It is flawed. The acts of terrorism inspired and perpetrated by their descendants in modern times disprove it. New York has not been frightened, Paris will not be, nor any other place or people. Once civilized societies arrive at the conclusion that the terrorist mind is impossible to change, it can return the same fire with greater ferocity. That is what happened after 9/11; that is what is going to happen in Paris. Liberal societies will watch the members of the whole Muslim community with suspicion, just for a few hot headed terrorists!

Is war essential for human existence? Or is peace alone essential? Before the Muslims, the Christians had their full quota of violence. The Muslims carried it further. Both religions pursue actively the mission of conversion of people of other faith or without faith to their form of religion.

Inducements, threats, bullying etc. are weapons in their religious armory. But it creates conflicts. Had these two religions not indulged in conversions, the world would have been a more peaceful place to live in. Hinduism never practiced conversion. So did Buddhism. It is civilized to profess your religion and welcome those who are attracted to it. But conversion is futile. The better course is respect for all religions or Sarvadharma Sambhav (which translates to same feelings for all religions). No religion should be considered superior to others because there is only one superior- The Supreme!

Life is constantly in a flux. So, conflicts too will be there in life. It is bound to affect everyone, whether one chooses to participate actively or remain neutral. Why else would the slaughter in Paris shock the entire civilized world, including Muslims? Why would people feel disgusted by the massacre of more than 2000 people in Nigeria? Why don't people forget 9/11? The entire human society feels traumatized by acts of terrorist violence. Hence, solution needs to be found to end such violence. The only solution lies in stopping misconstruction of edicts of the scriptures e.g. "martyrdom/qurbani/jihad". For that purpose the state has to establish institutions to deliver correct annotation of words and expressions; interpretation of scriptural texts; promoting human values. Killing of innocents never was nor shall ever be the value of any God-loving society.

Advanced societies need to check their governments whenever they adopt violent means to suppress other societies they consider their opponents. The Devil should not find a safe haven in such societies in the name of democracy etc. The world has suffered many unfortunate wars and should not actively cause another. After the end of the Cold War, it was expected that peace would prevail. Did it? No. Rather everything was done to create problems for others after the disintegration of the Soviet Union. Chechnya, Kosovo, Afghanistan, Iraq…it went on accumulating and ultimately culminated in what has come about to be called terrorism. Human society has to take the same moral ground for action in similar situations. As stated earlier, conflicts are bound to be there but ethics alone should guide the participants and not their personal considerations of gain or loss. Today the ISIS presents that kind of a conflict before the whole human race: should the barbarous acts of the ISIS be ended immediately by all those forces against any form of barbarity or left to do whatever it wants to do?

In so far as God is concerned, human beings need not exercise their wits in defending Him or His Order in the cosmos. He is available to all. Those interested in meeting Him can do so, those wanting to feel Him can do so, those wishing to touch Him can do so, and those who want to hold Him can do so. It is so because He has a form even as He is formless at the same time. He is immortal- not born nor ever died because He exists. He can't be harmed by any weapon or cut into pieces or burnt by any fire or dried by any wind. He is omnipresent. He is omnipotent. He is not under human command though all creation is under His command. It is His world. We are only one of the millions of species created by Him to make His world lovely. Therefore, all those religious services providers, who claim sole selling rights of Divinity, are living in a world of mistaken belief of their own creation. People don't need their services to meet God. He is their God and they are His babies. The sky is God. Touch, feel and hold your God in your palms or arms. You can't see the whole sky for limitation of vision, so you can't see His totality (Cosmic View). But interacting with Him, communicating with Him and conversing with Him will give you the opportunity to see Him through His miniaturized images visible as His creations in the entire cosmos or the whole cosmos!

# Part III

## After completion of first year in office

# Who Got What: Modi Government's One Year?

Every Indian has some opinion on the one year of Modi government- it ranges from encomiums to brick bats, some justified, others concocted out of political compulsions. But everybody seems to agree that the Narendra Modi government has been functional all these 365 days; and that is no mean achievement, testing it on the touchstone of dysfunctional previous government allegedly comatose and policy paralyzed. Let us see who got what from the Narendra Modi led NDA (National Democratic Alliance) government in 2014-15 May to May.

## Nation:

India got back its dignity and respect. It can no more be treated as a weak nation. It is rightly recognized as a great nation by the world's super-powers. They have paid respect to the nation as a strong one and growing economy.

## Citizens:

Their faith in the constitutional scheme of governance restored. Their despair is gone. They feel safe, secure, confident, hopeful and cooperative. They trust their Prime Minister now. They stand empowered for the first time. They are bank account holders today. They can no more be cheated of their hard earned money by defrauders. You can never experience the pain of losing your money unless you keep it with somebody for you and being told that it has already been adjusted towards loan servicing against the earlier debt when you need it in emergency or for use. The usurers are eager to extend another loan. All of it is mere a jugglery of words and calculations which the lowest man in the pyramid does neither understand nor is capable of doing so. It brings the ugly practice of usury to an end by a single stroke of Narendra Modi government launching the Jan Dhan Yojana under which every citizen is empowered to open a bank account even with nil deposit. It has already crossed 100 million accounts and deposits of rupees 150,000 million. Now these citizens, labelled as poor or BPL (Below Poverty Line) families or other categories, will get all kinds of subsidies directly in their bank accounts, e.g. pension, cooking gas subsidy and all other similar social security assistance. Corruption was rampant in every social sector program as not even 10% funds reached the target groups. Even bogus beneficiaries were a common phenomenon. Corruption eradicated by one healthy program addressing all the needs of the people.

The poor have been extended insurance cover for a nominal sum. It is understood that already more than 700 million citizens have got themselves insured and everyone is going to benefit from it as awareness increases. Along with life cover, a separate scheme for accident insurance has also been launched successfully.

It needs to be noted that these programs have benefited the largest number of ordinary citizens, whose income ranges from zero to US$10 per day. That translates to approximately 65% of the population. Moreover, it serves the citizens without any segregation in terms of caste, creed, gender, region, education, economic stature or anything else. Another significant change brought about by these people oriented schemes is that they have empowered women as never before. Imagine the farmer or laborer woman operating a bank account and in control of her finances, unlike previously when all her income would be taken away by her husband who will drink her daily earnings away or family members. Imagine such a woman using her credit card! Imagine the woman receiving money sent by her husband or children working at some distant place in her own hands without the corrupt postman deducting his unlawful service charge which is common in the countryside and in metros like Delhi, where they open even registered letters and see the amount of the cheque to calculate their service charge. She would need nobody's help and records will ensure that there is no breach of trust. Until the British codified it as an offence, breach of trust was a common practice for the powerful and influential.

The initiatives of Narendra Modi have brought about Structural Changes in the economy with a far reaching positive impact which will be difficult to reverse. Ordinary Indian women are going to feel empowered in real sense for the first time because of Narendra Modi. They have been income generating members of the family so far who were not allowed to dispose it off according to their judgement. But a household runs well when the mother earns and uses the income to meet the priority needs of the family, such as nutrition and education or health over liquor.

### Economy:

The government is not hostile to entrepreneurs, but promotes industry and business. The adversarial attitude of the bureaucracy putting roadblocks in approval of proposals for setting up new industries or expansion or diversification of existing industries is gone. The Narendra Modi led NDA government has sent the right message to the bureaucracy to act facilitators for development and economic growth rather than acting stumbling blocks. Emphasis has been rightly placed on skill development and upgrading products to world class so that Make In India succeeds with an aplomb. Inflation has been checked, prices behaved sensibly in the absence of collusion of government with hoarders and black-marketers. Foreign exchange reserves are reassuring and CAD under limits. Interest rates are likely to fall soon as a result of these initiatives. FDI is coming and developed countries are keen to invest under the "Make in India" program as also government to government negotiations. The port, highways, waterways and railways development will prove as beneficial as the setting up of giant core industrial undertakings in the public sector by the visionary Jawaharlal Nehru and computerization by another visionary prime minister Late Rajiv Gandhi, who also initiated the economic liberalization process in 1985. Critics may ignore the effect of these programs of a visionary Prime Minister, Narendra Modi, as they had done in the case of Rajiv Gandhi by giving credit for economic liberalization to Late PV Narasimha Rao & his Finance Minister Man Mohan Singh. History has been written: nobody can forget Nehru or Rajiv; so none will be able to do to Narendra Modi.

## **Agriculture**:

The weather has destroyed thousands of acres of crops which were about to be harvested this year causing terrible losses to the farmers. The NDA government has reached out to the distressed farmers, compensating them for losses and giving them market support for their remaining produce. The government is working on bringing out a permanent solution to the farmers' woes to end their misery and distress ending in several suicides. India attaches the highest importance to agriculture, as it has changed the scenario here similar to what industrialization had done to Europe. Economic initiatives devised for all will benefit the farmers for the first time. Perennial indebtedness is a curse of the Indian farmer and starvation the most inhuman of all causes for death among the poor, especially women. Hopefully, they will become things of the past if the government succeeds fully in its endeavors, which it will, irrespective of the opposition blocking progress in the Rajya Sabha and some states. But the common good of the common man will force all political combinations to either support Narendra Modi or adopt his programs. There is no scope for anyone to go back or reverse the process.

## Constitution:

The biggest achievement of the people of India has been the restoration of the Constitution of India, which had been compromised to an extent where the country became a butt of ridicule not only domestically but internationally too. Chroniclers of the constitutional History of India will not be able to ignore the horrendous sabotage of the constitution whereby the office of the Prime Minister of India was reduced to a proxy! Nobody dared to challenge this patently unconstitutional arrangement. Can any outside body have the authority to decide on issues, policies or executive matters outside the Council of Ministers in the country under its constitution? Can such a body be funded from the Consolidated Fund of India or the Contingency Fund of India without being answerable to the parliament for 10 years? Can such an unconstitutional body go without being accountable to parliament or people? Can the expenditure of such a body remain beyond the reach of the Comptroller &

Auditor General of India or if examined by it, go without any questions asked for 10 long years? Such naked violation of the constitution had reduced the theory of Rule of Law to a mere fable. It was subjected to further humiliation by the amendment to the Office of Profit list: that continues without any amendment so far. It led to horrible trust deficit between the government and the people. It was aggravated by open corruption of historic proportions by ministers, officers and businessmen. What was being whispered among the better informed individuals soon became public when the C&AG of India exploded the scam in his report which said that auction of airwaves caused an estimated loss of rupees 176,000 crores to the exchequer and coal to the extent of 186,000 crores. The citizens could stomach no more; enough was enough; and Narendra Modi was entrusted the reins of power to clean the mess and restore the government as per law established and not through any unconstitutional authority's proxy. Narendra Modi is nobody's proxy. The decadent system is dead and the constitution restored to health. The law is supreme in India (1 crore= 10 Million).

## BJP:

Arraigned for being rightist, fundamentalist, communal or reactionary, the party under Narendra Modi has undergone an experience of perception and vision for the first time. Intimidated, insulted, ignored and ridiculed for long, the party has learnt its lessons to grow from an only opposition party to be a ruling party. The scale of perspective and vision of Narendra Modi, his success in winning friends from American President to the Chinese President and French President, Prime Ministers of Australia, UK and others, his charm over the PIO, NRI and generally the people of the countries he has visited, his quick response to disaster management in the country and neighboring Nepal, his people friendly economic schemes fulfilling the party's best agenda of Antyodaya or reaching the last man unserved by the system have blunted the opposition within his own party from old guards and rivals for office and won him new friends. His greatest achievement for the party has been a corruption free one year of governance. The BJP prides in nothing more than its anti-corruption agenda and Narendra Modi has proved it to the party stalwarts that he has delivered and shall continue to deliver success on this front. The people are sick of corruption and even if it means creating very powerful enemies within and outside India, Modi stands by his promise to the people that he will neither take nor allow others to take bribe (na khaunga, na khane doonga). At the same time, he has succeeded in chastising his over-zealous party workers, who have been reared on a solid diet of religion (not different from the Christian or Muslim outfits), and made them improve their horizons. The jarring notes have reduced considerably. Slowly, they will grow up. The party has showcased its talent by making the ministers speak at important public fora and TV shows. The PM has entrusted his ministers to explain the government's achievements to the people and all of them have done a fantastic job. It is a feather in the cap of the Bharatiya Janata Party and Narendra Modi. If it continues to grow like this and improve fully, it will give the governance that people have been looking for since 1967 when they first experimented with change of governments in 9 Indian states, failed and again experimented after a decade by changing the government at the center; failed again and changed the government after almost another decade; failed and again changed the government at the center after another decade! This time, they seem to have got the man they had been searching: Indian to the core, modern to compete with the best, clean as snow, devoted to serve the country, capable of taking the country to new heights, making every Indian proud of being an Indian.

The BJP ought to work hard on these achievements of a single individual, make its members understand such a vision and attitude, grow from narrow to comprehensive citizen, contribute to his efforts to build a strong India of people's dream and put no hurdles in his way. If the BJP does that, it will be remembered. For this to happen, the party has to assimilate modernity and sanitize the ills of tradition. Even Lord Vishnu took more than one Avatar. Why can't the irrelevant customs and traditions be buried forever? The lessons not learnt from the challenges posed by the birth of Buddhism or Jainism or Sikhism and the shrinkage of territory and loss of freedom for millennia should be taken seriously. Narendra Modi has brought the opportunity for that change- adopt it. Let every Indian get the best modern education so that each one gets equal opportunity to be prosperous. It is for the first time that the leadership has moved from north to west. The east and south are already contributing. Accept the change; be the change; make the change.

One year is too small a time period to judge any government. It is not my intention to be unduly adulatory. Neither would I like to be unnecessarily critical. But there are times in the history of man when an emergency operations have to be carried out. India was going down at a speed which was bound to prove fatal. The people of India chose Narendra Modi as their savior in such critical times. He has lived up to the people's trust. By his performance in the first year of his tenure, Shri Narendra Modi has justified the people of India in their judgement of the criticality of the situation and the potential of the man of their choice. He promises acche din (or good days) ahead and people trust him.

# Part IV

## Obstacles Overcome During the Second Year

# The Yoga Effect

It was a pleasant surprise to find the morning newspapers and TV coverage on the very next day of the international yoga day! Newspapers and TV channels, which must have delivered negativity a million times in the previous weeks till 0630 Hours IST on 21st June 2015 seemed to have been cured of their own negative impulses and glossary, just like any individual yoga practitioner experiences it. They must have been overwhelmed by the enthusiasm of the people across countries. As is usual with journalists, they were holding their own views dear to them, attempting desperately to undermine the commemoration, infect a perfect peaceful world environment with their own narrow perspective, making concerted attempts to reduce a scientific health regimen to dogma, rigging public opinion by shouting & screaming, quarreling into TV cameras, pursuing political agenda of their patron or mentor outfits, and ignoring the significance of the historic support of the co-sponsoring countries for the Indian resolution in the United Nations to celebrate the International Yoga Day.

The tremendous support and enthusiasm of the nearly 36,000 people from 82 countries at Rajpath in New Delhi proved to be too stunning for them to ignore anymore or criticize as usual. By the evening of 21st June reports of enthusiastic commemoration from other countries also started coming in. The journalist community was silenced unusually. The English language press did not carry any negative feature, sentence or word on the first page the next day! It was the Yoga effect. It reduces negativity, normalizes blood pressure, enhances cheerfulness, unburdens the mind and imparts peace. What undergoes in the process?

It is known that a healthy body is home to a healthy mind. Similarly, a healthy mind is an instrument of keeping a body healthy. Through Yoga, an individual strikes a harmony of the body & mind. Our thoughts are responsible for good health as much as external factors. Our mind flies in a fraction of a second from earth to sky, from good to evil ideas, from sad to happy thinking. We need to learn to train ourselves to manage our thoughts, direct them in the positivity zone and act in tune with our thoughts. Our conduct is influenced by the company of the people we keep or interact with. It is the effect of our thoughts only, which we temper on acquiring new ideas, new knowledge and new expressions. Bad influences are acquired similarly. Evil ideas mislead us. We tend to do things we would not like others to do to us. A few minutes in the morning preferably, otherwise any time convenient to the person, devoted to Yoga helps in improved physical, mental and emotional health. It brings about a harmony of mind and body, thoughts and ideas, and actions. There are eminent people in all walks of life, but everybody is not equally eminent. It is achievement, depending on opportunities available to one and not available to others. But more than that, it is due to a certain "wholeness" of a person, an integration of the self in the form of harmony of body & mind, the flow of unbounded energy experienced never before, which alone guides an individual to do things others have not yet done and perform acts which others did not do. They are called Yogi or Yogini. Talent, genius or eminence has always been recognized by the human society in various forms in areas like religion, arts, literature, science, technology. What we see today is an improved version, a sign of progress, a declaration of our growth.

Modernization has always been an ongoing exercise. There may really be nothing called ancient or modern in that sense. Is the sunshine ancient? Can we call the moonshine ancient? Is health ancient? Sadly, our health is threatened today. A recent study of 28 nations has cautioned that common drugs as well as chemicals are so harmful that they can cause cancer of the mouth or other vital organs. The so called highly competitive and commercial world of modern times has only a single aim, which is to enrich at our cost. While it might take decades to correct this practice, we are at liberty to manage our own health. If some ancient practice helps us, it is welcome.

We should not discard them for being ancient? Knowledge is neither ancient nor modern; it is forever. Our current scientific knowledge is decidedly modern, because it has reached areas which had remained unexplored so far. Human mind is inquisitive. The phenomenon we see is knowledge in all its vastness. One life span is too short to acquire complete knowledge of this phenomenon. But human race has succeeded in attempting to comprehend it through documentation. To live in such a vastness happily needs conscious attempt on the part of the people to use every moment in life to assimilate as much as possible. Such an effort needs continuous flow of energy. There are many ways to get this energy. Yoga is one of them.

If negativity levels can go down drastically for the journalist community in one day due to the yoga effect, it can do more for us. Namastay or May Our Mutual Positive Energy Benefit Us!

# Democracy Not From the Barrel of The Gun...

Democracy in India looks like the patient with multiple organ failure. Excepting for the changing pattern of voting in elections to the parliament, state assemblies or local self-government institutions like municipalities & panchayats, it is an exercise in controlled regulation of the outcome. There is hardly any institution in the country which has remained unaffected by this condition. Politicians have long been discredited as corrupt and criminal. Governments at the center as also in states have been infamous for corruption and inefficiency. Even the highly esteemed judiciary has not escaped the symptoms of this disease- a body & mind crippling disease. Bureaucrats, scientists, experts, professionals, specialists- none has been able to withstand the effects of this social, political, economic and ethical change for the worse. One word that sums up this state of affairs in the Indian democracy is popularly known as corruption. Public anger against this phenomenon is irrepressible. It is so because the Constitution of India promises a democracy practicing rule of law in word and spirit. Unfortunately it is anything but rule of law.

Officers of the state, inspired by the constitutional ideals, are routinely punished in order to compel them to fall in line. Functioning under the authority of the law is dangerous and hits the real power structure in the country, which is rule of man. It is a kind of neo-feudalism, where the demographically strong exercise authority in defiance of the law. As the political executive has the power to appoint, promote, post, transfer and punish public servants, it is used to tame them to fall in line. What is right and what is wrong is defined under such circumstances by the politician. The elite might call it bizarre, but rape and murder under these circumstances can easily be made suicide or even honor killing to harass the victim or her family. Headstrong public servants can be physically assaulted, mentally harassed, killed and thrown into the mighty river Ganga, burnt alive, stoned to death, threatened with dire consequences, deprived of their liberty or dignity and harassed routinely in hundreds of ways. Judicial remedy is costly to seek and can cost much more even after getting relief in one case. When fear of man prevails over fear of law, it only proves that democracy flows from the barrel of the gun. Terrorizing the public servants is more than enough to make this neo-feudalism succeed. And that is what Indian democracy has firmly established. If it faces any challenge from any quarter, it is India's soft power.

Indians by nature don't like corruption. They may silently suffer others indulging in corruption but do not approve of it. Similarly, Indians are basically peace loving people. Non-violence for them is not a slogan, as it is for politicians, but a norm practiced in daily life. Conflicts are there. Violent exchanges do take place. But they are temporary and issue based and resolved rather early with cooperation from social shock absorbers in place: someone known to the parties to the conflict would step in to bring peace and understanding to resolve disputes. Politics has, however, affected these invisible social structures, but they are very much living, though choking under the weight of growth and development in the same way as the trees lining big roads in the city choking to sickness of a life threatening kind due to their base being concretized for road beautification. The efficacy of this soft power is visible in change of government.

Whenever the corruption harassed citizens get an alternative leader, who promises clean & transparent government, they entrust him the reins of power. Narendra Modi won the mandate 2014 only because he promised to live by the standards set by the people for a corruption free government. He is facing stiff opposition from rivals in the opposition parties and in his own party. While a leader may be upright and honest, his team may lack the same. Presently, this is the crisis of commitment and perception afflicting him.

Due to our preoccupation with hard power all these years, what with wars with Pakistan & China, and continuing terror attacks sponsored by the Pakistan Army (ISI of Pakistan especially), we have left the entire soft power space for free lancers under government patronage of the favored over the meritorious and private individuals or groups. The result is limited public participation in showcasing, developing and exporting it. We have exported an exotic variety of India's soft power. When soft power development is not a prominent part of our foreign policy, we tend to export poor quality stuff.

We import the best from other countries, who consciously promote the best their country can offer. We are saddled with some kind of an inferiority complex, leading us to liberal self-condemnation. Take for example Indian films: we have not produced any Hollywood production so far but were quick to term our film industry as Bollywood! The industry has produced classics, but can it be taken for India's soft power? What do we project through these films? Our film industry was driven by literature, music, art and acting. Is it so even today? Or does it, like all other institutions in the country, also stand compromised? Can any improvement be brought about in the film industry or let it be business as usual? A small initiative of the government to appoint a chairman of the Film & Television Institute of India has raised the hackles of the entrenched vested interests, which have created a rumpus for almost 50 days or so. It is a curious case of students at the institute opposing the appointed chairman. Students undergo 4 years course in film and television industry. Shall they act as the Chairman of the Selection Committee? No. It is not students who would indulge in such wasteful activity unless vested interests incite them under magnetic slogans or comparisons of personalities. A change is bound to change how we project India and Indian creativity through cinema and television. It is going to lead to transparency in operations, improve quality and enable Indian films to become competitive in the world. For that to happen, cleanliness in the industry needs to be increased.

Indian film and television industry is worth a few lakh crores of rupees. It gets finance from several sources, including black money and underworld of crime. It is threatened to a large extent by the crime syndicates, which interferes with its casting and marketing rights. It fears any attempts by the government to clean up the mess. But it is time the government steps with greater resolve for the simple reason that projection of the soft power of any nation is too delicate to be left to the unregulated sector of the industry. It does not mean at all government interference. As in other industries, the Film & Television industry is bound to be one of the influential parts of the government body which will determine the course and content of the industry. Films alone are not the soft power, but they are a powerful vehicle to showcase it. The government will need to improve the health of all levers of soft power one by one. It has started well with the films. As business interests of the entrenched are bound to be affected, resistance from those quarters would flow naturally. But a transparency revolution in the whole soft power space is timely only.

Barrel of the gun cannot determine the course of the soft power of India, and films & television are important segments of it. It is in the interests of every one of us to improve and strengthen it. We have yet to open our soft power to the world. We have treasures unexposed. We have talent untapped. Our non-violence is but a manifestation of our soft power superpower role. Be it the peasant-farmer, artisan, labor, scholars, sublimity, Veda, Upanishad, Gautam Buddha, Mahavir, Mahatma Gandhi, film producers, directors, actors, writers or musicians or anything else, we have more than enough to dust, polish, modernize and share with the world.

# Assets and Resources of India's Soft Power

India's soft power assets are almost 5000 years old. Some of them were employed in contemporary crises as an alternative to hard power and proved their efficacy. In fact, the history of culture of the human race proves the greater enduring potential of soft power over hard power. It is equally true that hard power has trampled upon soft assets repeatedly in different geographies of the world and established its victory, but only temporarily. You can rule by the sword but live only by sonority. It reveals only the nature of the composition of our world. Largely it consists of certain qualities. Like individuals, societies too are composed of these qualities. These pertain to adherence to values, self-interest or simply harming others. Societies which experienced value based governments had been able to achieve high growth of culture and civilization. They shared their cultural attainments with other societies. There were some which managed their affairs well but without making any substantial contribution to spread of values, culture or other soft tools. There were still others, who first destroyed the attainments, assets and resources of highly developed civilizations in order to establish their superiority. They used hard power indiscriminately and are associated with barbarity and inhuman behavior.

India is a country which laid great emphasis on acquisition of knowledge (Gyan). It was a practicing knowledge society devoted to seek more and more knowledge in diverse fields such as health, longevity (Ayur Vigyan), mathematics, botany, chemistry, physics, statistics, environment, climate, agriculture, animal husbandry, astronomy, philosophy, literature, language and several other fields. They were known as Rishis or scholars. They had left for us a precious treasure of treatises on varied subjects. India has lost much of it when invaders destroyed libraries, burnt manuscripts and executed scholars. Some people took the risk to protect these manuscripts from the invaders and stored them securely in obscure places. A large number of these manuscripts were retrieved during the past 200 years. There are private and government efforts on way to catalog and preserve these manuscripts. When will the knowledge contained in these manuscripts become public can hardly be predicted, but it is bound to get published.

As these manuscripts are valuable, so are the languages in which they were written- Sanskrit and Pali primarily. India is a language rich country where 122 major languages are spoken or written by more than 10,000 people on all India basis, and thousands other languages with lesser number of users. There is rich tradition of written and oral literature in India. The quest for knowledge was such in earlier times that it needed no formal schooling to learn. A strong tradition of Katha or rendition filled the gap between literacy and thirst for knowledge. In simple easy to absorb language, knowledge was disseminated orally by the learned to the illiterate, who enjoyed it in their spare time like the summers when they were not engaged in farming activities and attended to all other activities of life such as marriage, Katha, pilgrimage, visits, entertainment etc. India associated the quest for knowledge with thirst because it never gets quenched, whereas hunger gets satisfied after a sumptuous meal.

It was understood by the people generally that ignorance is the reason for fear and poverty. It is akin to darkness. They wanted to walk into the sunshine of knowledge. Hence they always prayed to the Muse to lead them from darkness to sunshine (Tamaso Maa Jyotirgamaya). A country where knowledge was accorded such high priority needs to revive that passion, regain and re-establish its soft power resources, assets and tools.

Satyamev Jayate or Truth prevails has been the most inspiring objective of life in India. The history of human race establishes the value of this universal wisdom. Cultural heights were attained by societies which respected truth and established regimes where truth prevailed over cleverness, lies or intrigues. Even in this modern age, no country can sustain for long lies and live by propaganda alone. The total money spent on propaganda in the last 200 years might even surpass the expenditure on promoting values like respect for truth. Trust can't be built on weak foundations of lies and without trust neither friendships nor families nor nations can survive for long.

One of the ill effects of technological empowerment of people is the loss of trust: the buyer doesn't trust the seller, the seller doesn't trust the buyer (they need Brand and Contract); the couples don't trust each other till death does them part; friends don't trust each other as competitive empowerment introduces an element of inequality in the pure emotional world of friendship. Truth becomes the first casualty the moment a person attains added empowerment with the aid of technology than what is his natural share. The logic extends to nations. The powerful one errs in believing that its untruth can win it enduring power over others, the same lever that hard power gives them to influence policies or decisions of less powerful nations. But it is equally true that even a small country can challenge the might of a superpower and score a victory on the strength of truthfulness. That is the power of truth. Truth can't be colored. India has the treasure of the mass psyche that demands and values adherence to the principles of truth. The masses may be poor, they may be illiterate, they may look backward, but they build personal, social and political relations based on truth. Lies ruin even the closest relations in normal circumstances. The masses respect the teacher, doctors or judges only because they have trust in their truthful conduct. The misconduct, especially commercialization of these professions in recent decades has robbed them of that high and blind respect and faith in their reputation as adherents of truth. It has extremely deleterious effect which has led to charges of corruption. The worst is the politician, who is not considered truthful at all. Public conduct can't be the opposite of the edict Satyamev Jayate in India. India needs to regain its high stature of the country where truth alone prevails.

This is bound to change the complexion of the political environment globally. Industrial revolution, advancements in science and technological achievements in the modern times killed God, rigged morals and turned very fast to a world surviving on untruth. The world will be annihilated unless the doctrine that truth prevails is firmly established soon. Its alternative is Al Qaida and ISIS and similar outfits, which are born of lies, thrive on lies and survive on lies. Lies lead to barbarity and brutality. Its justification only aggravates the crimes of violence in a humane environment. India being an old practitioner of the doctrine of truth prevails, ought to modernize and renew it to serve itself and humanity at large.

India's ideology of non-violence is by now public property globally. It has inspired many peaceful movements leading to peaceful change of regimes. The adherents of hard power are still testing their weapons against non-violence. Can the world see the end of violent regimes? Yes, because non-violence survives violence. Violence is employed for short term gains, but non-violence is a sign of power, progress and prosperity of a nation. The time for sword wielding is over. In the next 50 years, robots will engage adherents of violence. They would emerge as the perfect match for the practitioners of violence of brutal murders, slitting of throats, bomb blasts, rapes, arson, poisoning, chemical and biological warfare etc. Violence might look an anachronism in that situation. The inspiration for much of the violence emanates from radical religions, but they never describe any war in heaven! Do human beings need protection of the Almighty or the Almighty needs their protection?

It is in an atmosphere of non-violence and peace alone that the mind is engaged in pursuing knowledge. There is so much to be known and our resources are yet not enough to unravel the knowledge visible in the universe to our eyes but hidden from our mind. That is the solid rationale for practicing non-violence. In the past, the practitioners of non-violence had suffered enormous harm at the hands of the violent, but that phase is going to end soon. The next phase is going to be for progress, prosperity and peaceful co-existence.

Indian literature is rich in content and embellished by Epics, two of them extremely captivating- The **Ramcharitmanas** and the **Mahabharat**. The TV serials on these two epics are master productions in which a lot of research and talent has been invested. When they were serialized, even international science congress sessions held in India were rescheduled to facilitate watching them. They are available on You Tube. The **Veda**, **Puran**, **Upanishad**, and other commentaries have been translated into several languages. The **Gita or Bhagwadgita** is a well-known treasure of world community. They are not being properly studied in the country under the mistaken belief that they are not relevant today. But that betrays the ignorance of the people about the treasure of the highest knowledge, including what is considered science and technology, even though the proportion may have changed.

A simple reading of these invaluable treatises triggers an explosion of queries, which if properly answered, can cover major aspects of modern knowledge in all branches. It is not because it is Indian that leads us to this conclusion but the fact that when knowledge was pursued single mindedly in the past, the quest was the same unlimited thirst for all comprehensive knowledge. It was not one man's imagination which produced these treatises but the scientific research to find answers to the emerging questions that yielded such wonderful results. It was only after finding answers to the questions crossing their minds that the authors or recorders of these treatises felt free or mukt. They concluded that learning leads to salvation (Sa Vidyaya Vimuktaye): learning frees one from ignorance and that is called mukti or salvation.

Another valuable asset of Indian soft power is its intrinsic entrepreneurship. Indians are entrepreneurship minded. They are innovative. If India earned a name and fame for itself in ancient times, it was due to, among other things, its entrepreneurs. If an objective study were conducted it would reveal that the social classification, under much stress now, was organized on entrepreneurship basis. Acquisition of skills can be through formal education or on the job training in family businesses. Concept of family business may sound contrary to professionally managed businesses in contemporary context, but even today this attitude produces better results. In fact, the hire and fire approach of modern enterprises is shifting beyond employer-employee relations and entering the crux of belonging as in family businesses. Companies are preparing to go an extra mile to retain talent. Technology was employed in businesses like handicrafts and handlooms too, but unlike in the production facilities in giant modern facilities. The difference is of level and scale. All production facilities needed the essential input of technology before setting up and production. If trade statistics of ancient India are any guide, Indian products had good demand in international market. This entrepreneurship got affected when mass produced industrial goods captured the Indian market and killed indigenous enterprises. Such unfavorable developments are nothing unusual in the economic history of a nation. But even this onslaught on Indian entrepreneurship could not destroy it forever; it only disrupted it.

When industrial revolution was leading to radical changes in production and supply of goods and services in the western countries, the Indian entrepreneur was not watching it from a distance - he adopted manufacturing by machines as comfortably as he was doing with production by hand. It didn't take much for the Indian entrepreneur to accelerate the growth of industrialization in the country. Today, India is counted as an economic power with great potential only because of its entrepreneurs. Had it been matched by governance of the highest quality, it would have yielded much better results. Less than the very best government has placed impediments in industrial development in the country. The nation is still struggling to free itself of the stranglehold of entrepreneur unfriendly systems, but the entrepreneur is going in full steam to realize his goals as an individual. And there lies the proof of Indian entrepreneurship. If they have succeeded in achieving something, it is said in elite circles, it is not because of the government but in spite of the government. Indian entrepreneurs are welcome to set up facilities in developing countries as well as advanced nations because of their high reputation as entrepreneurs. India has yet to realize its full potential to use this highly effective tool of soft power to further its economic foreign policy goals.

Somehow these resources and assets have been neglected post-independence under a perverse notion of socialism. In the changed global scenario, India would only benefit by using its soft power to develop friendly relations with other countries and contribute to peace and prosperity of all the peoples in the world.

# Conflict between Modernity & Medievalism

India is witnessing a conflict of medievalism and modernity. The elite class claims to belong to modernity, professes secularism, democracy, human rights, equality, justice and everything else that goes by the markings of modernity. As against it, a large number of people practice medieval way of life, rejecting everything that resembles even distantly as modern. Women's rights or their education is one area which depicts the contrast. There are many political influences that also stoke medievalism. Illiberalism marks their visage. They promote actively what should have been changed by now. Religion is used by all such activists across social groupings as a shield. Religion has ruled the minds of the people for ages. Monarchy has used religious organizations for the same purpose.

Modernity challenges the subjugation of human mind and body by religion or monarchy or its variants such as dictatorship. Science has proved most myths propagated by religion as empty. Philosophy and spirituality are on a different footing. Societies that moved early towards democracy succeeded in improving the lives of their members. Modernity has freed the human mind of the bondage of religion- people can raise questions without fear of excommunication or extermination under the ill-conceived notions of heresy or blasphemy. Man has not only landed on the moon but has set up a space center too. Man-made space crafts have travelled beyond the Jupiter and galaxy. Hasn't it hit the concepts of hell & heaven? Without these two levers, religion can hardly control the human mind. Scientific and technological developments have revolutionized human society. Man has created artificial intelligence successfully, produced off-springs out of the womb and is likely to create artificial life- something heretic even to think only a few centuries ago. The medieval mind is against these developments, which pose a challenge to all that powers it.

This conflict, which started as lone wolf attempts to eliminate the advocates of modernity has now culminated into ISIS. The western countries, led by America today, represent the face of modernity and the ISIS that of medievalism. Medievalism under the ISIS has taken to arms in an organized way. The strength of this organization of medievalism lies in adopting modernity to the limited extent of mis-deployment of the fruits of science & technology. After slitting throats of innocent civilians, children, women and raping girls or destroying prominent leaders or buildings, they are desperately looking for the opportunity to mount the atomic attack. That will lead to the third world war. It will be the last holocaust before a new beginning.

A bird's eye view of the markers of history appears essential before we proceed further. The epic, Mahabharat, describes a fatal war some 5000 years ago. It brought about untold destruction of life and property. It seems a whole river, the mighty Saraswati river, was choked by corpses to such an extent that it simply disappeared from the land it flowed on, and merged into the majestic river Ganga at Sangam at Prayag (renamed Allahabad), where also it is not visible. Hydrologists say the Sangam at Prayag is the confluence of the three rivers: Ganga, Yamuna & Saraswati. The climate of violence continued even after the Mahabharat had ended, till the Kalinga war during the reign of Emperor Ashok, The

Great. It must have been some 2400 to 2500 years ago. The Kalinga war led to rivers of blood of innocent people to such an extent that the emperor was filled with so much disgust that he vowed never to take to the arms again. His name Ashok means the one who never grieves. But the Kalinga war made Emperor Ashok grieve. He adopted Buddhism – the religion of peace! Emperor Ashok encouraged his children also to take to Buddhism, sent them to distant lands in Asia to take the message of Buddhism and peace and love. He set up more than 1200 vihars (meditation centers) and got the sermons of Buddha inscribed in stone and set them up throughout his kingdom. These are the famous Ashoka edicts. The national emblem of India has been taken from one of the Ashokan pillars. The Bamiyan Buddha statue in Afghanistan, destroyed by the Taliban, symbolizes the end of the era of peace after almost the same period of more than two millennia. Is it not surprising that Christianity and Islam both are no older than 2100 years or so. The striking similarities as also the dissimilarities are revealing. The earlier wars were about extension of territorial boundaries, wealth or women. They inspired love for peace and peaceful co-existence. May be even peace can't endure longer than that. Today, the world is afflicted by unprecedented violence everywhere. Clouds of war are gathering. This war is again for extension of territorial limits. It has a more potent incentive to fight: the Islam of the ISIS denomination & Christianity. This war, whenever it takes place, will prove to be the most devastating one. The freedom of the human mind is likely to emerge victorious thereafter. But will it? Or the process of further human bondage has already begun? Peace & war proceed at the same time as do birth & death (leaves falling because new ones are sprouting).

Our body has already become a slave. Can we live without technology even for a day? Just imagine a day without electricity, internet, mobile, television, automobiles, newspapers etc.? People in all likelihood are going to fall sick. The body, as also the mind, has become a slave of technology and its products. We can't lift heavy objects, construct buildings or even cook in the same way human society was doing some 500 years ago. We are addicts of technology; our body is addict of technology; our mind is addict of technology. What little has been spared will be covered by AI or artificial intelligence. All that human beings do, can be done by robots. Robots can fight wars, perform every function be it police, administration or management, fly planes, steer cars, guard homes, patrol borders. They may even write books. Once artificial life is created, organ harvesting becomes routine, hunger is controlled bio-medically and procreation ends – the cycle gets completed. The hovering dark clouds may hasten our journey. The era of peace ends soon as the era of war advances. Emperor Ashok signaled the end of the era of war. Medievalism of the Al Qaida & ISIS brand signals the end of the era of peace. It is worth noting that India has seen all of them: Mahabharat, Emperor Ashok, Gautam Buddha, Mahavir and Mahatma Gandhi. It needs emphasis that peace in India had been disturbed in the past ending in the subjugation of the country. Citizens see in sham secularism of the most unholy kind serious threats of repeat of the past. There is need to take a holistic view of the national and international scenario and fix objectively security policies on a war footing. There is hardly any time left for us as the forces of medievalism have advanced from all sides in the country. Today they ridicule expressions of nationalism as communalism, calling them divisive or communal forces even while practicing the worst kind of communalism themselves. They don't say how will they react to the arrival of ISIS in India, but seem to be ready to welcome them as forces of secularism. They are instigating medievalism among sections of society which have not experienced the freedom of the mind so far, in spite of 68 years of Independence.

Fears of high tech, artificial intelligence, artificial life and robotics have already begun to exercise the human mind. The thinkers of the world have come to the platform to oppose the growth of robotics. They have read the dangers that the robot army is going to pose soon. They fear the destruction of the human race itself. The war caused by the ISIS is going to provide the necessary fillip to the growth of the robot armies, as the WW-II provided the impetus for the atom bomb. Already the weaponry in the hands of the armed forces is devastating as has been proved by the ISIS and others in dozens of conflict zones around the globe. There is every need to be alert and avert the ultimate world war.

While the privileged Indian liberal elite keep on touting their flawed doctrine of secularism to the "majority" community in India only to push their agenda to "protect" minorities, they do great disservice to the minority by promoting and also strengthening status quo rather than modernization only to play dirty vote bank politics by widening the communal divide in India. They have so far failed to define secularism. They also limit their definition of minority to one community. They fail to profess atheism. They give the impression of being just a liberal Hindu, whichever way it might be interpreted. It gives them the right to shout down Narendra Modi and his party in TV studios without ever displaying the courage to criticize criminal threats to the majority community from the minority community loudmouths of their special affection. They are in political alliance with the outfits responsible for partition of India and loss of huge territory to communal forces out to inflict further damage to the country by using terrorism as state policy. They are doing it in collusion with local support from the minority community members playing into the hands of narrow religious fundamentalists who have always misinterpreted the majority community's liberal attitudes as signs of cowardice. They underplay the serious nature of the conflict of secularism and Muslim Personal Law activists. They betray so much vanity when they claim to "protect" the minority that one can only pity them. Their minority sympathies never touch any other community except the Muslims. On pure human consideration a minority anywhere in the world is a minority deserving same treatment. Has any secularist of India ever raised his or her voice for the Hindu minority in Kashmir driven away? Did they say a single word against the ISIS which tortured the Yazidis? What do they think of the plight of the Buddhists in China? Will they ever demand protection of the minority Hindus in Bangladesh or Pakistan? A person can never claim to be a true secularist unless he is a determined atheist. All Indian secularists practice some religion openly or silently. Funnily, a majority of them are Muslims who never oppose the outdated practices in the Muslim community. Several vocal secularists of the Congress Party are active evangelists. Many of them are communists or at least left leaning. The Congress, socialist, communist and other varieties of secular party members proudly announce their religious credentials through their surnames. Their secularism is restricted to be used as a staff to beat the Bhartiya Janata Party.

Talking of protection, it sounds so absurd coming from the mouths of the people whose ancestors were slaves to the Mughals not very long ago enjoying their protection. They will protect the Nawabs? They are so myopic that they either don't know that Nawabs exist in modern India even after the constitutional amendment had abolished the institution of the Maharajas, Rajas, His Exalted Highness, Zamindars and Jagirdars or they have chosen to feign ignorance out of political compulsion. Can such people protect anybody else? Are they not under the protection of these Nawabs for political power at the cost of the welfare of all sections of the Indian society without discrimination on any ground? Can one take their commitment to secularism at face value? In this background, their secularism is another political trick to assail the perceived face of the majority in the BJP and Prime Minister Narendra Modi.

They have done their utmost in sowing the fear of the majority in the minds of the minority in the past three years since Narendra Modi won party nomination for PM in September 2013. They fear Narendra Modi. They hate him only out of fear. Their fear was not unjustified as Narendra Modi reduced the Congress Party to such a pitiable condition that it failed to formally get the position of the Leader of Opposition in the House of Representatives (Lok Sabha). The fact is, all those sections of the Indian society which the Congress and other political parties had successfully exploited till election 2014 got disenchanted and disillusioned with them and their rhetoric. They don't trust any of them. They have made it clear that they want development, economic empowerment and developmental administration. No more doles or favors but implementation of the schemes of development and growth sanctioned by the parliament is their sole demand. As the human mind is free, any attempt to keep it in bondage of religion is not going to succeed for long. It would be in the interest of all kinds of political formulations to rise above the majority-minority syndrome. They should extend whole hearted support and cooperation to Prime Minister Narendra Modi for larger good of the largest number of people.

# Speechless Press, Orator Narendra Modi & Salad Lunch

The Indian media has failed to keep pace with Prime Minister Narendra Modi even after 16 months. They have not been able to present objectively the far reaching impact of the innovative policy initiatives and programs of the Modi government. The reason is that they have lived on negative campaign against Narendra Modi personally, treating him disrespectfully, as they do to the ordinary citizen, civil society members or anybody using descriptive words like patriot, Hindu, culture or any such thing. They have been treading on a monorail all these years of the Congress rule in India post 1947 that they got indoctrinated into ideas of Jawaharlal Nehru, socialism, communism etc. and turned into being camp followers. They had a few pet topics like corruption, backwardness, communalism, poverty, farmers etc. to the exclusion of development goals. These topics provided them enough content to publish newspapers, magazines and run their television industry.  It doesn't help them cover Narendra Modi as independent press or the Fourth Pillar of Democracy. For this they need to change pen and penning both. They don't know what to do or how to go about- they are in a fix of the kind very aptly conveyed in this Sanskrit aphorism- "kim kartyavya vimudhate" (to do or not to do?). To their utter disbelief, Narendra Modi became the Prime Minister of India winning a decisive mandate from the people. They couldn't believe their eyes or ears and waited for him to commit his first grave error before they struck hard, as they had done for decades. But Modi proved to be a man of different mettle. His foreign policy, economic policies, governance success and growing public trust graph has saddened them. The Opposition frustration is understandable but that of the media is baffling, only because it is supposed to inform, analyze and educate its readers/viewers. Take the example of brain drain-brain gain debate.

We have yet to come across a single authentic critique on the subject, though it has been a hot topic of public debate since the 1970s. Indian talent had two types of people: one migrated to foreign countries in search of better emoluments and working conditions; the other stayed back home to serve the people & the nation. It was no different story than in any other under-developed / Least Developed/ Developing country. But what needs examination is the push from the government for the educated, professional and talented people to leave the country by making life difficult for them. Lack of right infrastructure, attitude of political establishment and bureaucracy, poor emoluments and difficulty of keeping pace with latest developments in their field in other countries caused the brain drain or migration of talent from India. Instead of improvements, things further deteriorated in subsequent years. The contributions made by Indians abroad, could have been used for nation building. It is not the question of supply of surplus brain power, but the right to first use of it by the nation. It is here that the nation lost out and fell behind other countries by at least 50 years. It is in this context that the nation needs "brain gain" now. Prime Minister Narendra Modi has spoken of "brain deposit" from the American soil in his recent visit. He is of the view that the nation will get it back with interest as one gets the principal amount with interest on a bank deposit.

Unfortunately, that is not going to be the case. If these brains are of no use when the country needs them the most, they are as well of no use in the future. For the same logic expounded by PM Modi that India produces brains every day, there will be no need for the country when it becomes a fully developed self-reliant super-power. The cost of procrastination is enormous. We can't delay brain gain even by a year. We have to work out policies to welcome brains, not only the NRI (Non Resident Indians) & PIO (Person of Indian Origin) brains, but from all over the global village. We need to acknowledge that Indian brain is no trade mark. Brain from anywhere can grow immensely in right environment. We in India have to create that environment: freedom to think differently, innovative ideas, initiative, research, development, experiment, modernity, enterprise, rewards and recognition constitute that environment. We have no other option than to take the quantum jump. In the modern knowledge society, we can ill afford to wait forever: to wait for our enriched brains abroad to come and contribute for nation building or buying outdated technology & machinery from abroad to ensure India remains in the previous century longer than necessary. We have competitors, who are not obliged to help us grow because we want friendly relations with them. I wonder if our national goal of Sabkaa Saath Sabkaa Vikaas serves their interests equally. We have to necessarily develop our brain at the same level by upgrading our infrastructure and improving the environment for harvesting the potential brains and enriching the pool by encouraging emigration of the best brains from abroad to India. These foreign brains must find it more attractive to work in India than anywhere else in the world. What Prime Minister Narendra Modi is attempting to do is to make better use of the Indian brains. He needs to take it further as stated in the foregoing. The India media is expected to critique these issues, rather than getting tied to the jargon of indoctrinated communal riots columnists with copy of their printable article available off the shelf.

During the PM's visit, the UN Secretary General offered his guests salad for lunch and emphasized the problem of shortage of food in the world. There is need for better Food Management in the world. The UN celebrates special occasions such as the World Heart Day. Such celebrations cause waste of food globally. The UN ought to encourage saving of food instead of its wastage. The world population is put at more than 6 billion. Half of them may be adults. If the UN were to recognize the value of fasting, it should promote a fortnightly fast by asking people to forgo their one time meal. This will create the necessary food surplus to feed the needy. Besides, it might also help reduce heart failures worldwide by the same numbers. We get bombarded by private hospitals and other health care providers with discount coupons daily! Discount coupons for heart checkup or diabetes or cancer? It is not merely use of commercial terminology in a noble profession but crass commercialism. Here is the sample invitation for heart check up from a prominent private hospital in Delhi: 'angiography@ Rs. 6000/CT angiography @ Rs. 7500; complimentary cardiac consultation (with prior appointment); 25% off on advised diagnostics'. Reputed Indian doctors from All India Institute of Medical Science etc. have exposed unnecessary operations of normal patients by the private healthcare enterprises to meet their corporate targets once they approach them with any problem caused by food not to the liking of their stomach.

The current situation has placed the Indian media at the end of the queue behind Prime Minister Narendra Modi followed only by the Congress Party, the Shiv Sena, JD (U), SP, BSP and RJD. The distance between Narendra Modi and them measures the thinking of India 1950 and 2015. Prime Minister Narendra Modi shall continue his march with complete devotion and dedication without thinking of self-interest even for a split second or pal.

# Indian Media Terrorism against the Viewers

The press, especially the television medium, has been extremely unfair to the viewers and unjust to the targets it chooses to attack. It sells only stories, hardly disseminating news in any objective manner. It treats itself not as the independent Fourth Estate of the Indian democracy but superior chamber of the State, superintending and supervising, directing and regulating, ordering and reviewing in the avatar of the highest authority of the state. In any democracy, governments can always be pilloried on soft subjects like human rights, women's rights, gay rights, terrorists' rights, divorce, capital punishment, religious matters, freedom of speech & expression, property rights and corruption above all. However, the worst is the media trial, especially motivated participants and ignorant hosts, who possess simply one quality i.e. shouting/ screaming/ lecturing/ arguing/ interrogating/ accusing/deciding in advance. They are prejudiced against the voices of reason, state organs or even the law. They are often too demanding to place the construction they want on words, expressions, laws. In a way, they deem themselves autonomous, not answerable to any authority, person or even their viewers. They take offence at the gentlest nudge from the state to mind their words or priorities. That is obnoxious. They exceeded all limits of proportion, good sense and propriety in running highly provocative and mean but endless debates on the hanging of the convict of the 1993 Bombay blasts. Their audacity went to the extent of running commentary on the judgement of the Supreme Court of India insinuating that it was flawed in their own judgement. Thankfully they escaped getting lynched by the irate masses and families of the dead or seriously injured & disabled because they were operating from their secure studios. The media forgets that knowledge is no more the monopoly of the few when journalists and editors used to occupy a higher position in society. Today, they sound vainglorious by running such stories: the people may not hit them physically but hit the remote button to switch them off!

The other debate relates to government ban on porn sites on public demand and gentle nudge from the Supreme Court. In less than 48 hours, the press and television channels raised such a hue and cry as if heavens have fallen and the very right to life has been forfeited. Vociferous demands were made from the so called liberal sections of the intelligentsia, which included the media, to lift the ban. Is pornography such an essential part of their daily diet? No, I am not supposed to raise such questions; it is only their right to question others. In any case, the newspapers have been thrusting soft porn on the readers in the form of entertainment stories and ads flashing female body from every possible angle and films and television dishing out live everything right into the living room. What is left out? Why there is such a hullabaloo about pornography? Do they fear they will be asked to curtail such coverage to limits of decency? The issue is who decides what is decency? The media feels offended under the mistaken belief of some kind of a moral policing. It tries to make it sound convincing as the present government is led by the BJP (Bharatiya Janata Party), which is perceived to be rightist and Hindu party. They attach little value to the fact that all sections of society - Hindu, Muslim, Christian, Sikhs, Buddhists, Jains & Parsis view these sites if they like them. There is no moral or immoral prescription about these sites; it is purely scientific.

India has, perhaps, been one of the very few countries in the world which had never restrained anybody from pursuing his or her interests, including what is called porn today and erotica or sex earlier. A scientific approach to any subject is different from its commercialization. Students of medical science are taught in every detail all aspects of human anatomy and man-woman relations. Has anybody ever called it porn? No. Same is the answer in art- nudity in paintings or carvings in stone or wood have never been termed porn. But the fare being dished out by these commercial websites is decidedly pornographic. But nobody is bothered so long as they don't pop up on screens of viewers without being accessed. That is criminal, that un-accessed display is indecent and vulgar and objectionable.

For the votaries of freedom of expression, I would seek for them special TV channels airing XXX films 24×7, which they can watch in the company of their parents, siblings and children. They can even invite their friends and neighbors. Neither the government nor the judiciary should come in the way of such freedom of the initiated, who are better placed to handle such content even in the company of their near and dear ones. Public protests are directed against unhindered marketing of porn to protect the innocent and impressionable minds. They are the target market for these sites. The opposition to these sites is purely scientific; it has nothing to do with morals. The science concerns human health in society. We would not like India to become afflicted by AIDS or HIV at the same scale at which it has harmed developed countries in the west and developing countries in Asia and Africa. We don't want Ebola type diseases to destroy public health. The big multi-national pharma companies seek to expand their markets and addictive practices like pornography help them achieve their goal. Is it healthy to watch porn all the time or go through the whole experience of life through lawful marriage of man & woman? American scientists have even counted the number of times one can perform the act (36,000?). Is such valuable prowess to be wasted by indulging in porn watching and its unhealthy consequences? Is it about morals or morality? Or is it pure science? Besides health concerns, porn is law & order problem. It instigates and triggers responses that are unable to control ending up in serious crimes like rape or attempt to rape or rape & murder. Science says that the male-female ratio is skewed in nature, only some 867 females against 1000 males. The potential for damage by porn sites can be acknowledged in the background of science, without seeking license to do anything in the name of free speech and calling perceived adversaries as mere moral police.

The media that has been charging the government of assault on free speech is blissfully ignorant of the extreme and very dangerous assault it mounts on its viewers round the clock. Is it the fundamental right of the media to torture the hundreds of families who lost their men, women and children in the barbaric bomb blast on civilians in a city like Bombay (Mumbai)? When the same terrorists killed a dozen journalists in France, they were condemned by everyone and the Indian journalists never rose to support the terrorists. Do they think that attacks on Indians are justified but not on Europeans? What better example can be given of crass commercialism in the Indian media? It is not journalism, the famed Fourth Estate, but a dirty media industry, which has thrived on open corruption of blackmailing the corrupt in the past 68 years in India? In fact, the Late Nirad Choudhary had referred to corruption in the Calcutta (now Kolkata) Municipal Corporation in 1925 and the Military Department in 1945, even before Independence. Journalism in India was born to follow such acts of omission & commission of the corrupt in India post- independence but soon became a part of it. The corrupt face of the Indian journalists was exposed by what is now known as the Raadia Tapes. Many fervent advocates of the free speech today were shamed and named in those tapes as the middle persons to fix political and bureaucratic appointments and exchange of illegal money called bribe in public parlance. Do they have the right to cry of perceived assault on free speech (we are not talking moral right but only legal right)?

Is this not atrocious for the media to run for days all kinds of stories about the rape and murder of two sisters in a distant village in UP? They are just not concerned with the hurt they cause by their lust for TRPs by running lurid stories on a poor man's tragedy? The family in mourning is oppressed by all kinds of questions from the TV crews, who display lack of any sensitivity while firing their questions. There are a number of examples of media atrocities on the viewers. Ads are run for hours by giving a one line news in between to meet the legal requirements and same films are run throughout the year on a few days interval. If the state tries to bring some discipline to this anarchist breed, it can't be objected in the name of free speech.

Nobody, the media being no exception, can indulge in defamation. The credibility of the media in India has suffered so much that the newspaper industry is on the verge of closure and TV channels are getting poor ratings from the viewers, even though they might manipulate the figures to claim to be at the top. Even the corrupt politicians occupy the top positions, but they are rated very low by the people unless they establish their integrity. The media has lost all credibility in the recent times. Their noise about the hanging of the bomb blast accused or advocacy of the free porn has further eroded this credibility. Social media will prove the final nail, unless they regain their credibility sooner than later. People dislike suckers and confidence tricksters. The media should not take the viewers for granted. They are internet empowered knowledge society members.

Why are they so agitated about porn sites? The answer is: it is big business; windfall profits at minimal investment. In the past 4 years, they have condemned, criticized and castigated MPs & MLAs watching porn on their mobile phones inside the official premises of meetings venues. If they think it is the right of everybody to watch porn, why such noisy debates for days on TV channels, defaming people's representatives as if they have committed an offence? As sin, like morals, has no place in the modern secular glossary of the liberal civil society champions of porn sites, it can be called only an offence, but it is no offence under any existing law as far as I know to watch porn sites for these MPs/MLAs. Why, then, is the journalist community so outraged at them? Is it only because they are politicians and thus soft targets for blackmailers of the media? But it is business so long as the porn sector is restricted to only Indian TV channels, films and newspapers. Were the government to open the sector and allow porn magazines from the west to sell their wares in India, open sex shops as in the west and run open markets like the SOHO, our free speech champions will go all out to tear the government to pieces on moral grounds which they are averse to now as it does not serve their commercial interests. Let it be clear that nobody is afraid of porn business in India. It will be viewed as a part of the oldest profession and given the same treatment. Indian psyche is superior in that it raises such complex scientific subjects as romance and sex to a very high level, if the Kamasutra, Khajuraho or the custom of Nagar Badhu (City Bride) are any indications. In fact, there are some Religious Orders whose saints or guides have discarded robes and walk freely without any inhibition even while giving discourse to their followers.

But there is absolutely no freedom for porn sites to indulge in hard sell by popping up uninvited. There is no difference between adult or child porn – it has the same effect on impressionable mind. The government is duty bound to preserve and protect the rights of the citizens who do not want the media to act funny in serious matters like porn, hanging of blast accused or terrorists and other criminals. If there are reasonable restrictions on the citizens' right to free speech, how can the media be not subjected to the same restrictions?

They are not super Executive or Super Judiciary. They have no right to stoke disaffection among sections of people by tendentious and motivated reporting and debates or stoke communal violence or provoke citizens raising their blood pressure by vulgar debates or outright disinformation or campaign against the state from morning till night. The media is equally answerable to all the charges it is levelling against the government, including assault on free speech. Unless the citizen gets the full opportunity to rebut the media's colored views, detoxify it of the venomous language, disabuse it of the prejudiced mind, make it see reason and take a holistic and objective view of issues, it will be one way fare for it to harass, oppress and hit hard the viewers daily, and get paid for it too.

There is an urgent need to stop this dominance of the media on citizens, governments and the judiciary. In fact, the government should restrict telecast hours to 4 hours from 5-9 in the evening with immediate effect to reduce psychological pollution and disturbance. Nobody has the stomach for 24 hour news and entertainment. It is as harmful to the mind as is smoking or drugs to health of the body. One leads to psychiatric disorders while the other causes other health disorders. Unless regulated by law, the Indian media is likely to land the country into a psychological endemic. Our day should not start with breakfast made of negative news and language. Like fresh air, we must first take in good measure positive thoughts and good words to maintain a high energy level throughout the day. For that we must abhor newspapers and TV until after lunch time.

# Verbal & Visual Violence

Verbal & visual violence poses a threat greater than that of the terrorists. Those who use words for stoking hatred, disaffection, disharmony in society, only show disrespect to the gift of words they possess. Knowledge evokes respect, but if misemployed to cause devastation, it invites scrutiny. Historians have no other choice but to be honest with facts. History can't be made to order. If India has suffered subjugation under the Muslim Rule followed by the British Rule, it stands out as an undisputable fact. Neither of them had come to India to serve the people of India or their welfare. They came, terrorized, subdued, massacred, frightened, enslaved and dictated the ordinary people. Seeing them as great as Emperor Ashok or Maharana Pratap or Shivaji is not history but a mere hypothesis. If someone has twisted facts to manufacture some kind of an imaginary history, people are bound to question it and correct it. How can someone cry foul of new breed of historians sieving facts again and looking for evidence ignored by earlier scholars? The objections to such scholarly pursuits remind one of the court historians of yore, who would sing paeans in praise of their masters to earn their livelihood even at the cost of truth and facts.

Scientists have come to occupy a place of pride in the modern society. They claim exclusive rights to rationality and knowledge. But knowledge is prevalent in the cosmos. Scientists are only unraveling it. Gravity , magnetism, mass, energy, space, time, life, galaxies, stars, planets, light, darkness and everything else already exists in reality. Can scientists create any one of them to replace the existing ones? If not, then it is rational to believe that there are limits even to scientific knowledge and that even scientists should not cross their limit by indulging in politics or propaganda. They would do themselves justice to devote themselves wholeheartedly to the pursuit of scientific knowledge. Misuse of knowledge is a recipe for disaster and needs to be restrained.

Science & technology has given mankind huge power. Power tends to spur the desire to get more power and get monopoly over it. It breeds a generation that tends to control all information and deploy it for propaganda to perpetuate the rule of a coterie of persons. Such clubs block dispersal of knowledge, which is contested by those deprived of it. It generates conflicts between those controlling all levers of information and others demanding free access to all information. In such a conflict, which of these two blocks should be tolerant? Which block can be called "intolerant"? Obviously, those fearing to lose control would call the other group intolerant. In that case, the allegation of intolerance against the newcomers becomes untenable.

Intolerance is a seemingly harmless word but aims hard at anybody resisting the devious designs of religious fanatics out to capture new territories or clients. The violence inflicted on innocent men, women, children in the last 15 years in the conflict zones of religious fundamentalism highlight the stakes they have in pursuing violent course to establish their control. Human history is full of wars fought in the name of religion. The 20th Century saw two world wars, instigated by religious fundamentalists.

The hate mongering by these religionists has continued even after the wars. The intensity of hate, the hard hitting language of the hate mongers, the designs of these elements are all beautifully summed up by William Shakespeare in his play 'The Merchant of Venice' in the court scene.

These religionists are intolerant of other faiths but seek complete freedom for themselves from other faiths. They incite hatred against the natives, their religion, values, customs, beliefs, Gods & Goddesses, rituals and tradition. They challenge their intellectual attainments, scriptures, thought at the cost of all reason only to establish their non-existent superiority. They put to brazen misuse money, material and machine power to shake, shatter and subdue others. They move about stealthily to achieve their goals throwing all morals and values to the winds.

If resisted, they charge people with intolerance. If there is any community in the world which is the most tolerant, it is the Hindu community of India. This community has an open mind, gives due respect to all views, seeks no converts to its faith by treachery or guile or inducement or weapons on the head of someone. Those dreaming of taking over India once again through such devious means should forget about it and learn the value of peaceful co-existence. They should either pursue their own religion peacefully or the Hindu religion. They don't have to convert to Hinduism to pursue the religion and are free to leave it any time. They will feel happy at the freedom they enjoy here- the genuine freedom of thought and expression. What more is there to tolerance in the world?

It is not as if the world is witnessing knowledge explosion or science & technology for the first time. There may be no written records available of such growth and achievements in society, but great literature and treatises throw up enough evidence of their earlier existence. The legendry Ravan, misnamed the Demon King, is a superb example of a man of outstanding scholarship, scientific knowledge, technological prowess and a great poet in one. Unfortunately for him, so much of power in his hand made him so proud that instead of employing it for society's good he started abusing it all for his personal gratification. The result was his destruction and heavy loss of life and property of the masses.

In this age of instant communication, journalists have become tabloid journalists and worse, and television anchors street fighters of their employers or their political parties. India, a country of many languages is being maligned by the English language print and television media as intolerant. The media is hyping "intolerance" for illegal money from foreign masters, political parties and religious fundamentalists out to spread their religion through violent or unethical means in India. India saw one party rule for a long period under Prime Minister Jawaharlal Nehru. He became Prime Minister of India in the fervor of the Freedom Movement. He was surrounded by highly educated, modern, liberal, visionary leaders and bureaucrats, who devoted themselves to the service of the people wholeheartedly.

How the sense of service changed to self-service is a sad commentary on the evolution of democracy in India. It didn't take much time for the undeserving to slip into the good books of the establishment to capture positions of power as the country needed skilled and trained manpower. In less than 10 years of the coming in to force of the constitution of India, dishonesty and corruption in public life started replacing honesty and clean governance. Nehru had to resort to cleansing operations under the Kamraj Plan in 1964 itself. Immediately thereafter, events in quick succession led to the growth of a culture of feudalism, since they were familiar with feudal environment more than democracy. Nehru died that year, India faced a war with Pakistan in 1965, Prime Minister Lal Bahadur Shastri died in Tashkent next year in suspicious circumstances and Nehru's daughter Indira Gandhi became Prime Minister, who split the Congress Party to control it for her political interests. That was the beginning of a culture of feudalism, which was nothing more than brazen subservience.

The voice of merit was muted and sycophancy of the lowest kind encouraged. The journalist community joined all other seekers of government bounty and largesse. It was the time when newsprint was imported and black market in newsprint made millionaires overnight; wages of journalists were raised by the government; license-permit-quota Raj spurred journalists to seek "out of turn" allotments of scooters/cars/plots of land/houses built by government agencies as they fetched huge premium on black market; foreign trips as official entourage of the PM or President and many more favors.

The media had no qualms of conscience in doing the bidding of the government, dish out stories favorable to the Congress Party and Indira Gandhi. Its job turned out to be image makers or image spoilers. The silence of the press on issues of public importance for favors gained, tended to ignore the complete collapse of law and order in the country, leading to imposition of Emergency, whereby Indira Gandhi suspended all Fundamental Rights of the people guaranteed by the Constitution and press censorship was imposed. Only

Ramnath Goenka of the Indian Express at that time stood against loss of freedom of the press; others were toeing the congress Party line as they were doing till April 2014. The kind of stability the country had seen earlier was lost for long. Indira Gandhi was assassinated. Her son Rajiv Gandhi too was assassinated. A period of minority governments led to complete decline in democratic values, climaxing in the horrendous corruption of the Man Mohan Singh led UPA government, which was struck by policy paralysis and ended up completely dysfunctional. Dual center of authority created a situation where Sonia Gandhi (widow of Rajiv Gandhi) came to exercise real power, pulverizing Man Mohan Singh in to just a signing machine. The Indian press & electronic media exploited fully such decline in governance and approved of everything it did.

The journalists were not alone to get disproportionate benefits out of these developments. Poets, writers, novelists, film producers, academics, scientists and everybody who could take advantage, made a success of triviality, mediocrity, faked qualifications, sycophancy, servitude, feudalism, arrogance, vindictiveness, conflict with law and loyalty to the party chief over values. Unfortunately for such people and fortunately for the people in general, the invisible power of correction of the ills in society came to the rescue of the poor people of India. Narendra Modi, from nowhere, suddenly descended on the scene, most unwelcome by the Congress Party, English press, television channels, contractors, middlemen, fixers, wheeler dealers, black marketers, black money, parallel government, extra constitutional authority of Sonia led NAC (National Advisory Council), beneficiaries of the largesse of the government, undeserving occupants of various autonomous institutions of national importance (Sahitya Akademi, Lalit Kala Academy, Sangeet Natak Academy, National School of Drama, Film & Television Institute of India, Indian Institute of Mass Communication, Indian Council for Social Science Research, Indian Council for Historical Research, Indian Council for Philosophical Research, Centre for Molecular Research and hundreds of such other organizations), national awardees of civil or literary honors like Padmashri, Padma Vibhushan etc. They found themselves in a highly uncomfortable position. Suddenly they lost their comfort zone, fixing appointments, transfers, postings of officers or defense deals, machinery purchase, highways, ports, airports, medicines etc.

They don't trust Prime Minister Narendra Modi. How can they? Unlike the culture of corruption in the Man Mohan Singh led UPA government, Prime Minister Narendra Modi, has already threatened them by declaring publicly that he would neither indulge in corruption himself nor tolerate others to do so. It is this "intolerance" of the Prime Minister Narendra Modi, which some journalists, writers, poets, historians, film makers and scientists are opposed to and protesting vehemently and loudly before the global community. Their foreign partners in guilt are busy giving it added spin. They need to correct their blurred perception of India, Indians and Indianness. Carrying the vilification campaign any further will lead to complete collapse of reliable resistance to the really intolerant segments of human society called terrorists. Its alternative can only be the Third World War. Who can stop the intolerance of the ISIS, Al Qaeda, Boko Haram and scores of similar outfits which practice naked intolerance against the minorities, weak, old, girls, youth, elderly & women?

The country of the Buddha needs no lessons in tolerance from the practitioners of wretched violence and Inquisition elsewhere in the world. India is the only country in the world whose Emperor, Ashoka The Great, vowed never to start a war, prohibited killing of animals, promoted non-violence, peace and love more than 2500 years ago. India came under Muslim rule only because of such a high level of tolerance. Who can claim greater tolerance than India? Can those who started two world wars or those creating conditions of the third world war claim to be more tolerant than India?

What do they want? Do they want India to lose her freedom once again so that they can prosper? If peace in India is disturbed, peace everywhere in the world will be disturbed. When India was trying to draw the attention of the global community to Pakistan sponsored terrorist attacks in India since long, the world chose to turn a deaf ear. Who paid the price? America on 9/11, Europe later, Middle East now. If the global community repeats its response of the past, and fails to rein its hyper intolerant vilification troops, they should be ready to pay a greater price.

The chorus of the Indian slave dynasty-II about intolerance is perverse, mischievous and motivated. The government must enlarge the field of choice to promptly replace all the dated heads of all autonomous institutions. There is no dearth of experts of high integrity to render the necessary services. They were marginalized during the reign of corruption because they refused to partner in sins against the public. They should not be expected to approach influential levers of the current establishment to influence the government for their induction. This is the country of the saints, sanyasis, rishis and yogis. Modern day public servants are their modern version, if the government values them. India has a rich pool of talent.

If there is anything most difficult in life, it is "service". The breed of such public servants started getting marginalized as explained herein before. Their numbers dwindled because their services were not availed of. But that doesn't mean their supply has dried up totally. The government will have to go strictly by merit alone and see plenty of public servants of this quality. The tamasha or charade of protests in the garb of intolerant atmosphere will disappear in no time if the government is able to replace all such elements forthwith. Their departure is already delayed.

# Literary Writers No Politicians

Writers are not politicians. By nature a writer is "intolerant'- intolerant to injustice, violence, discrimination, backwardness, poverty, prejudice, bias, irrationality, taboo, cliché, distortions, exploitation, abuse, torture and several other similar issues. A writer is no writer if s/he is tolerant to a chosen one and intolerant to another. There is no subject under the Sun which is outside the coverage of literature. It is this universality of literature and the objectivity of the writer which places literature above everything else, though it may or may not be a commercial success. But writers are neither in commerce nor in politics, though there is no subject outside the jurisdiction of literature. For writers, judges, judiciary and the justice dispensation system are as good subjects to write about as political ideologies, economic theories, social critiques or scientific knowledge. They are not afraid to write about God or theology. It is this fearlessness, independence, objectivity, neutrality of a writer that makes his endeavor great and immortal. We don't know who wrote the Vedas, but we read the Veda even today and admire the quality of their content. Milton may be dead but Milton lives forever. Can someone kill Shakespeare or Kalidas? Yes, their works may be burnt by someone for some reason, but they will continue to occupy the mental space of the society and memory of the learned.

The drama played in India in 2015 by some Sahitya Akademi awardees for literature in the past in the name of growing intolerance in society is facetious and hence laughable, because they have been "tolerant" to all the wrongs listed in the opening sentence above for no less than 60 years!

224

There is no bar on poets, dramatists, playwrights, novelist, short story writers, essayists or critics. They have always enjoyed complete freedom, excepting the Black Emergency for 21 months, and could have used the power of their pen to hit out at whatever they consider "intolerance" today. But they have converted it into an ugly political saga only after the rise of Narendra Modi. Do they feel that they are unlikely to enjoy the political patronage enjoyed so far by them under the previous dispensation? They also seem to have lost the ground, with the new dispensation publicly professing zero tolerance to corruption and development of all and togetherness of all. The average writer thrives on material fit for political propaganda and breaking news in the most superficial manner, selecting his target according to the nuisance value, indulging in overflow of emotions of hatred against whoever or whatever s/he considers in conflict with her/his personal view or perception. Such literature has a short life. A writer is a visionary, who is farsighted and capable of evaluating issues most dispassionately beyond the compulsions of here and now only.

Once the divisive and fissiparous forces lose the battle and the masses see through the game being played in the name of literature or journalism, it is the end of a decadent literary culture and the beginning of a new era. In India, the advent of this new era has been considerably delayed by putting a premium on mediocrity at the cost of precious literature. As the year 1947 was a turning point in the history of India, so is the year 2014, which changed many things. Literature can't remain chained to the past. It has to break free of the culture of political patronage and establish its power to influence society and provide it intellectual leadership. This demands a new mindset and work culture. The change brought about by the people of India in 2014 promises to change attitudes, perceptions and resolutions of the masses as also the classes. India has changed. It is a promise to honestly translate the vision encapsuled in the Constitution of India. When all in the society rise together, walk together, put in their best efforts together, the result is all round development, prosperity, peace, harmony and happiness. Perhaps our award-returning (derisively termed Award Wapasi) writers find it awful to handle themes in such an environment. They need the illogical viewpoints, self-created conflicts, divisions in the society, slogans and vitanda (mere argument for the sake of argument to prove the rival point of view unacceptable because the objective is to defeat the opponent, real or virtual). Only literature suffers in such a climate. Even the best of event management companies can't salvage literature from the Literary Festivals of the community of such writers.

It is a healthy sign that they are vacating space in the Indian literary world, occupied for long by them through political patronage, literary brotherhood and commercial interests. It will allow the new talent to bloom, which has so far been kept at a distance forcibly by erecting barriers to block the entry of new talent & fortify themselves from any inroads of fresh air of literary creativity. That explains the total famine of good literature in the country for several decades. Is it any wonder that I cannot suggest even a single literary magazine of high standard today whereas I could have suggested at least a dozen 50 years ago?

Are the writers responsible for all this? No, no, no. It is due to the lure of the electronic media, especially the television, which offered high commercial returns for their talent. But high payments don't come for free. The television channels, like the newspapers, are owned by top business houses. Slowly and slowly, writers learnt to meet the market demands and editors started taking orders from the owners The owners are wary of risks in business and don't play Ramnath Goenka anymore. Editors have tasted prosperity, power and influence for the first time and don't let go of it. The condition of the "unrecognized" writer is comparable to that of the workers in the unorganized Sector of the economy. Readers started losing interest in literary works of low quality. Consequently literature suffered so much that poetasters donned the role of poets and wangled awards from Sahitya Academy and regional academies, which they returned under orders from their political masters to malign a transparent government under the leadership of Narendra Modi.

Globalization, social media and the internet has contributed to the decline of literary creations of immortal quality due to the unprecedented explosion of information and knowledge. No writer can take the reader for a ride, as comparisons of available material, reliable information, profundity and incisiveness of writers elsewhere in the world pales poor outputs for which the market fails to find buyers. In such a scenario, only the best quality of writers can stay on course. Others must accept the reality gracefully. Technology has been disrupting businesses for years. In the new environment, the writer has to grow up. There is hardly any reserved space available for writers thriving in monopolistic environs. It is a competitive world, even in the literary arena. The ongoing upheaval has thrown up a challenge to the writers the world over. That includes Indian writers too. It has opened opportunities for the members of the global

227

knowledge society, to promote new breed of writers to take up issues of the new society, in a new expression suited to the contemporary life, in a novel genre or improved literary genres. Literature is forever.

# A World Falling Apart

What is happening to our world? Is it falling apart? Only 20 years ago we celebrated globalization. We were immersed in colorful dreams of the world as a global village. I too celebrated the development and drew attention to the Indian view of treating the world as our family (Vasudhaiv Kutumbakam). However, the world seems to be disintegrating in less than a quarter of a century. Do we hold our progress responsible for it? Distances have shrunk, communication is instant, smart living is fast replacing human effort, test tubes have substituted the womb, cloning is a reality, we have conquered hunger & disease largely, we have captured all the knowledge in a single DVD. At the beginning, religion acted as the bonding material for people to become community. It was the sole purpose of living. Wars were fought- won or lost- in the name of religion and for or against religion. As the world attained advancement, political ideology began to replace religion. Ideology could not sustain longer than religion. Economics fought to trounce it in order to reach the top. Industrialization gave early advantage to the technology owning countries, who sought newer markets for their products. As they found the new way of domination in economic colonization, conflicts among the industrialized countries assumed threatening proportions and led to World War-I, exposing the weakness of economic colonization in the form of The Great Depression. There was no peace among the powerful countries, which soon resulted in World War-II. That hardly was any solution to the real problem, which was the search for newer economic colonies or markets. As competition grew, it put pressure on trade prospects, further shrinking the markets. Another instrument called globalization was devised to solve this problem, but it turned out to be a double edged sword. Knowledge cannot remain for long the sole possession of a few. Globalization led to poor countries becoming industrialized economic super powers like China and India. The global economic development surprisingly led to the birth of terrorism as a counter to civilized modern liberal society. It surpassed the barbarity and violence of the Medieval Age by using human bombs to constantly challenge the might of the atomic powers and their atom bombs. The plight of the terrorism affected countries like India, which practiced a policy of no aggression and peaceful co-existence were ignored by the super powers until 9/11. America declared the war on terrorism only after 9/11. By that time it had already extended its operations globally, demonstrating its influence by carrying out indiscriminate "terror attacks" against select targets in Europe, American Embassies and tourist spots visited by people from the west. Security costs and falling exports affected the American economy leading to the Meltdown of 2008. The world economy has been tottering since then. It has further been jolted by the slowdown in the Chinese economy since 2015. A new threat of European migration from Syria, Afghanistan, Pakistan and other countries has put to hard test all claims to human rights. The worried Christian countries have expressed fears that soon the Muslim refugees will turn in to a majority rendering them a minority in their own country! Suddenly the market has not only disappeared but also threatens to create chaos and anarchy in Europe. This may end up as a well thought out strategy of terrorism to capture new territories through humane means without fighting any war! The question is: what does this world stand for? Surely it is neither religion nor politics nor economics. The soup of all these elements can be seen in ISIS territory. What is happening there is not religious war, even though it is sought to be justified in the name of Islam. It is not capitalism versus communism also. It is not to fight poverty in the region. It is no ancient, medieval or modern form of war or peace. Nobody knows exactly what it is and how to face the challenge it poses. Isn't it baffling?

Consider the nature of all that we see around us. How has it emerged? Modernity restrains us in calling it Creation and religion has been propagating it as an act of God. Our modern thinkers display a rare level of confidence in changing the world and to make it a happier living for all of us. Their plans somehow missed the entry of the ISIS in this 21st Century, when the world was engaged on projects like colonizing the Moon and the Mars. The world has moved from arms race to arms limitation strategy when the ISIS makes a dangerous entry like the bolt from the blue. Security becomes the prime concern of the world. Considerations of security have impacted the march of the human race. The world spends more money, time and energy on security related issues today than on research & development. The world unity to achieve the millennium development goals stands challenged by the disintegrating effect of ISIS, more for its backward looking religious fundamentalism than the violence it has let loose. Will it disintegrate the world? Will the global village fall apart and restore the old composition of nations, societies and communities based on race, religion, creed, caste, clan, language, region or gender? Is there an invisible cycle of change in this narration? Is it only a story of growth & decay? The prosperity to poverty and poverty to prosperity cycle hints at that cycle. Wealth is known to constantly move from one owner to the other. It can be a person or a nation. Empires emerged and disappeared. All those born so far died without leaving statistics of the total number of the dead. Epochs have gone by. Universes have been born and disappeared. We are witness to cycles of seasons, day & night, birth & death. We are aware of all this change occurring constantly. That gives us energy to improve living standards. Under the spell of our achievements, we tend to become oblivious of happening change. The cycle goes on and on and on. Was this the famed Indian concept of zero (Shunyabad)? Life is a point in the very large all-encompassing zero (meaning a circle); so our world, and our universes too. If the life of the universe is taken to be 100,000 years, the life of our world may be less than 10,000 years and the individual life only 100 years! The motion may be slow or fast but the movement is unstoppable. The rise and fall of our world appears to be in exact proportion to each other: slow to slow and fast to fast. As the globalization part is over, it is time back to localization. Disintegration or falling apart looks to be a natural corollary, as nothing holds our world together—neither religion nor ideology nor pure economics! But it will emerge again as a beautiful world as always. The good, better, best or bad, worse, worst cycle will go on. We are content to call it Satyug, Treta, Dwapar and Kaliyug cycle. The world is living in the middle of Kaliyug and hence experiencing all the pain of astounding progression and bewildering regression, stupendous prosperity and horrible misery, overflowing granaries and mass hunger, superb healthcare and debilitating disease, superpower status and alarming midgets. I am noticing a strange phenomenon of poverty among the highly rich in megapolises. Why are the super-rich organizing poverty camps? Has richness robbed them of all human qualities experienced liberally among the poverty afflicted people, e.g. family, marriage, children, social architecture?

Is the world in need of new leadership? Can India contribute something? If Prime Minister Narendra Modi succeeds in giving a good government to the Indian people for the next 10 years at least, it may provide a model for replication elsewhere.

# Intolerably Tolerant India

It is only in India that even genuinely intolerable persons, newspaper Editors, Columnists, television anchors, and their guests indulging in verbal fights can deliver sermons on tolerance to the society and are tolerated. No Charlie Hebdo type incident has happened here. At times one feels like invoking the heavenly Order, if they allow us to say so, with the prayer for Sadabuddhi Wapsi to them. If they regain their good sense or Sadabuddhi, they will not misuse their knowledge of words for upending logic and spread communal hatred by being lenient to the real culprits and harsh on innocents.

If they get re-endowed with Sadabuddhi, they will desist from misusing the blessing bestowed on them by the Muse. They are pleased when one refers to the Muse but are intolerant when she is called Saraswati. They read Hindutva in it and term it communal and complain of "growing intolerance in India", troll on social media, hold nonstop TV debates, organize seminars and return whatever award whichever organization might have given to them.

When this does not satisfy their hunger for revenge, they organize Lit Fest or Literary Festivals, which is a cover for carrying on sustained campaigns against society and the government. They feel the pain of losing their primacy in decision making and governance to which they had become accustomed.

When the whole world is worried about barbaric activities of the ISIS and the dangers of developing warlike situation, stray incidents are being blown out of proportion insinuating that the Prime Minister must supervise policing at the Thana (Police Station) level, knowing it too well that it is the primary executive responsibility of the Chief Minister concerned. Law & Order and policing is a state subject (List-II of the Constitution of India). Is it any wonder that neither editors nor journalists nor politicians of any shade have so far asked the Chief Ministers concerned the questions they desire to be answered by the PM? They are scared of addressing their questions to the chief minister concerned being fully aware of the intolerance of the Chief Ministers concerned to any criticism from media or writers. It exposes their concerns and commitment to tolerance.

Actually they have no desire to promote tolerance if they get their privileges back in lieu of backing off and calling off the agitation. There is a more devious agenda of reviving the dead empire. They want to silence the people in general while they pursue their nefarious designs silently. By mixing Hindutva and intolerance, aren't they giving away their devious plan? They have always served the political interests of their patrons by contributing to widening of communal divide and fanned feelings of disaffection among different segments of the society.

The long reign of a single party, rather dynasty, at the center and in some states is proof of those political gains. It stalled evolution of a healthy democracy and parliamentary conventions in the country. It is worthwhile to extract a few sentences from an article written by Harish Salve, noted Constitutional lawyer, appearing in the TOI of 27th November 2015, titled "Constitution is sublime, failings are of our own making": Ambedkar in his speech to the Constituent Assembly quoted the powerful words of

Grote[the Greek historian] "…The diffusion of constitutional morality…is the indispensable condition of government at once free and peaceable …Since even any powerful and obstinate minority may render the working of a free institution impracticable even without being strong enough to conquer ascendancy for themselves."

The violent minority is posing the biggest threat to society, which has been thrown in to caste or communal conflicts by politicians and irresponsible writings. The aim is to make these differences bitter. Seeing "growing intolerance" where none exists is a political device used by them for attacking the government, especially the Prime Minister Narendra Modi. With a view to upgrade the tirade, Lit Fest or Literary Festivals were chosen to camouflage the vilification campaign against the government.

It was known that litterateurs and book writers on specially chosen subjects would be deployed in full force to establish the so called growing intolerance in India after the Modi government took office and shall continue till 2019. And if Modi is given another 5 years term by the people thereafter, the campaign to stoke communal violence through Lit Fests will be aggravated further.

Any research scholar in mass media & communication can cull out hate words and sentences deployed by the Congress loyalist media and self-proclaimed progressive leftist journalists and self-styled secular press in the past 30 months to malign Narendra Modi and the so called majority community. They are intolerant of the very presence of Hindu or the Hindu thought in India and have been relentlessly pursuing the game of portraying them as such. Their divisive politics ensures fissures in the society are forever so they can go to any extent in attacking the Hindu intellectual and cultural assets & interests, simultaneously promoting the Non-Hindu interests, even if that is outright unconstitutional. They take a nondescript Prachi and paint her as the representative of the Hindu mind, but ignore the highly provocative speeches of the other side. Such partisan response to communal and caste matters is used as a tool to divide society by creating phobia of one another. The victory of Modi in the general elections in 2014 and decimation of the Congress has not been digested by the protesters. They are beneficiaries of the previous corrupt government. Their language has been corrupted due to it. Hence, what should have been intolerable to them has become tolerable and what should be tolerable now is intolerable to them.

There can be no justification in civilized society for the TOI editorial descending to such low level: "In which case, will the finger of suspicion soon also point towards that indefatigable globetrotter whose frequent forays abroad have earned him the tongue-in-cheek distinction of being India's first NRI PM"? Its starting sentence itself betrays the hate mongering by the media against the prime minister: "Should Antonio Costa, the Goan-origin newly elected prime minister of Portugal be charged with sedition against the Indian state?". Should a national daily have fallen to such low depths as to be irreverent to the Prime Minister of a sovereign country - Portugal?

Its game becomes clearer if one takes a closer look at the topics for discussion for the Lit Fests this newspaper organized in Delhi and the people directing, contributing or hosting the discussions. Among others, it was scheduled to discuss:

1. Critiquing Hinduism; Ideologies of Social Dominance- Kancha Ilaiah in conversation with Assa Doron. (The conclusions to be drawn and direction it is going to move into can be easily guessed)
2. Ramayan: A Retelling by Daljit Nagra- Introduction by Gill Caldicott, British council.
3. The Argumentative Hindu- Wendy Doniger in conversation with Sagarika Ghosh
4. At Home In India: The Muslim Saga- Salman Khurshid
5. Creating The Hindu Mind: Past And Present -Aakar Patel, Santosh Desai, Akshya Mukul,
6. Writing On Namo: Deification Or Demonization – Rajdeep Sardesai, Madhu Kiswar, Kingshuk Nag
7. Writers And Protest
8. Iconic Indians And The Idea Of India - Sunil Khilnani & Shobhaa De

All these people are known Modi bashers. They have been woefully myopic about everything to do with patriotism, nationalism, communalism, Hindu, Scriptures, writers, civil society members and now even bloggers. They have always sat on a higher pedestal, talking to the people, lecturing and preaching. They started their careers when India cared a bit too much for these English journalists as not even 1% of Indians had proficiency in the language like these journalists. Today more than 20% Indians use English in a superior manner than these journalists. Basically most of these journalists should have voluntarily retired as their thoughts and ideas are outdated. But they refuse to hang their boots and want to keep kicking.

Either they get back their good sense soon or more and more Indians learn English to realize the potential threats to social disintegration in cool looking words like tolerance, intolerance, secular, communal, socialist etc. These propagandists can be matched only by better education on all issues confronting the world today.

# Literary Festivals: Anti-Modi Campaigns?

Considering a sustained campaign against Narendra Modi by the media I had expressed my apprehensions about the true motives of The Times of India Lit Fest and its organizers and the political objectives behind this contrivance. It has been advertised as literary festival but its aims and objectives were to defame, deride and devastate Narendra Modi in the eyes of the English educated Indians, foreign missions in India, and writers in foreign countries by beguiling them in the name of literature. The sole purpose of this festival of scare-mongering was to terrorize the Indian society in general through continuing propaganda under the veneer of growing intolerance. Its mask was off on the very first day. The genie was out of the bottle. It found the right word to take a direct aim at Prime Minister Mr. Narendra Modi-"silence". The participants alleged silence on the part of the prime minister. The same press was insulting his predecessor for his "silence" and changed his name from Man Mohan to Maunmohan (maun in Hindi means silence). Its political, religious and commercial objective was not only to hit the majority (believed to be Hindu), but its beliefs, traditions and icons. Any pretensions to independence of the press or the Fourth Estate were unabashedly thrown to the winds. It is only India's hyper tolerance that quietly suffers such provocations, otherwise such misuse of language is enough for it to experience a Charlie Hebdo anywhere in India.

The Lit Fest was organized in sensitive zones to plaster on the Muslims their Muslim identity over Indian identity, but they have stoutly snubbed all such attempts to the chagrin of the political sutradhars (mover of the strings in a puppet

240

show). But that hardly deterred the commissioned Don Quixote to continue tilting at the windmills. By associating select foreign writers, an impression was being created that it was a real literary festival, but the topics chosen exposed its true nature. It drilled exotic topics like gay law mixing them up with literature, economic matters and other non-literary topics. It devoted all its energies to virulently attack what it calls "Hindutva".

The Times of India is guilty of uncivilized attacks on Hindus. It instigates its columnists to use filthy language of the missionaries of the past which is enough to cause violent reactions instantly. Sample these: "Intolerance has a name, and it is Hindutva, not Hindustan". If Hindus were not hyper-tolerant, such provocation could not have gone unpunished. Had this newspaper, its columnist or its political sutradhars dared to say any such thing so nonchalantly in Saudi Arabia or UK or USA about Islam or Christianity, they would have been taught good lessons for life in no time. Such audacity is possible in the Hindu society in Hindustan only and still the Times of India spreads the political chess for the Congress Party of India to sell the imaginary idea of growing intolerance to create disturbance. If there is any doubt about it, here are some more examples of hate writing from the same columnist: This intolerance debate has been wrongly framed (emphasis on framed given by me).The problem is…Hindutva. As an ideology, Hindutva is unappealing, unintellectual, and even unaesthetic. My big problem with Hindutva is that it is also dangerous". Even the Devil will think twice before saying such things when India has been put on alert for terror attacks by ISIS in collusion with LeT, Al Qaeda, JeM etc. Unless the columnist and Times of India are in cahoots with international terror organizations to harm the country, such demonstration of immaturity need to be restrained. Freedom of speech cannot pose threats to internal security or defense of the country. But the TOI and its columnist is doing exactly that with impunity. Even the Press Council of India ignores such objectionable writing, though it amounts to stoking rioting. The columnist does not stop here. He moves on with Satanic invocation for direct action: "The vagueness of the intolerance debate has allowed the Hindutvawadis to position themselves as defenders of India against the pernicious troublemakers like Muslim film stars and liberal writers". After ruing "poor show" put up by Rahul Gandhi, the columnist gives the call for writers' jihad in these words "The intolerance debate should have a clear demand: Hindutva must stop poisoning our land'. So the cat was out of the bag finally!

Why was/is the national English language daily like the Times of India indulging in such an anti-social conspiracy? It is not the TOI alone, but it is leading all those members of the press and electronic media, who were "committed" bedfellows of the Congress Party for various reasons. One was that the Party was in the vanguard of the freedom movement and had respectable national leaders on its policy formulating body. But this shine was lost in 1969 when it was split by Indira Gandhi. It divided the press into two. the free press and the committed press. If the blame for molesting the constitution of India goes to Indira Gandhi, it goes in equal measure to the committed press. Ramnath Goenka and his Indian Express newspaper then were the only voice of free press in India. Today things have woefully changed in the Indian Express for the worse. The press and the journalists bartered away their integrity and morals for official largesse in the form of out of turn allotments of scooters, cars, houses built by government for the public to get a roof over their head, accommodation from the government pool in Delhi & elsewhere in India, foreign jaunts accompanying the Prime Minister, membership of committees & commissions and all other kind of influence wielding. They became one as you see them today ganging up against the new government led by Modi and the devastated Congress reduced to the status of not being eligible for the position of the Leader of the Opposition in the Lok Sabha. If India witnessed open loot, scams of historic proportion, policy paralysis, and bad governance in the 10 year (mis) rule of the Congress Party as UPA-I & II, it was due to falling morality and competence in government as also the decline of standards in the press and media too. Had the television industry been independent and free, Man Mohan Singh would not have won the vote of confidence as it was supplied a CD of the attempts to buy votes of MPs, which was not televised. On the contrary, the complainants were subjected to ignominy by a highly questionable and controversial verdict of the then Speaker of the Lok Sabha, who belonged to the Communist Party (Marxist) of India. But that verdict could not stop the exposure of scandals of humongous proportions and the complicity of the media barons in it. Some journalists were named and shamed by these exposures. That kind of system nursed them all. It was virtually the Parallel Government. It produced a Parallel Economy-also called the black money economy.

That illegitimate structure crumbled unexpectedly when the disgusted people of India chose a clean man as their Prime Minister. The Press and TV channels are big business, owned and controlled by big business houses. It acted like an attachment of the corrupt government. They acted arbitrary, assertive and a government over the government. The architecture of that decadent system, which was in practice for decades, was destroyed by Narendra Modi, who has failed to provide the media the opportunity to blackmail him in the name of corruption so far. The imaginary intolerance is merely a device to defame him. It was tested by creating an artificial motive for returning awards by a few writers of no consequence. Their contribution to literature has been insignificant as they have not produced any epoch making book. The system of writing, publishing and giving awards is a drill of the Parallel Government and drew contempt from discerning readers. Therefore, their returning the awards (though there is no system), was to prepare the ground for attacking Modi on a larger scale by obtaining the approval of scholars and leaders in the country and abroad. A genuine Lit Fest can provide that opportunity. Modi has been making waves and receiving very warm welcome in every country he has officially visited after becoming PM. The Congress suffers gripe at his success. Moreover, the religious fundamentalists carrying out conversion quietly of the poor Hindus by inducement or threat, are afraid to continue their illegal activities abusing the freedom of faith and its propagation in India available to all its citizens. It is the foreign Fundamentalists forces who accuse India, Indians and the Hindus of "intolerance". For these elements the Congress, especially Sonia Gandhi & her son Rahul Gandhi, are more useful than any other government. They have unlimited amounts of money to spend and well-designed plans to achieve their objective. They are organized, skilled, internationally networked and most intolerant to any legal hurdles. That explains their indecent attack on Hindutva and

Hindus. They have engaged the media, especially socially disgruntled elements, to further their agenda against the Hindus.

The whole scheme of the Times Lit Fest was nothing more than a well-designed contrivance to execute that plan of the foreign religious fundamentalists, pushing the world towards the third world war. Fortunately, the migrants seeking refuge in thousands in Europe have panicked them. They don't know how to handle such mass exodus of people from the Muslim countries (Syria, Iraq, Afghanistan, and Pakistan). They are already under pressure due to their old colonies in Asia and Africa sending their subjects in hordes. The politicians in Europe have expressed their fears of becoming "minority" in their own country soon because of the immigrants! That proves their insincerity to tolerance. They demand tolerance of others, like the Hindus in India, because it serves their fundamentalist goals and other economic interests. These columnists are bound to embrace soon "intolerance" they are seeing in Hindutva or Hindus, once Europe or America slam the door on them.

Literary circles globally have to protect genuine literature from such crass commercial and political ventures. The economic condition of the newspaper industry is pitiable, as people get all the news online, which is more trustworthy than any newspaper with political strings attached to it. Magazines have largely disappeared. TV channels are experiencing economic crisis like the failing world economies. Writers, journalists, editors have lost their jobs. Worse they have lost the plot, the theme, content for their writing and have taken to rioting instead to protest imaginary intolerance as their books don't sell, the publishing industry is feeling the stress from the internet on the one hand and the lack of footfalls in Book Fairs. The Buddhijeevi (living by the intellect) tribe of writers has no remunerative jobs anymore in newspapers, magazines, television industry or writing books. They have earned their livelihood from the previous system, which is now demanding of them returns in gratitude. The poor writers gaining recognition by the benevolence of the extant system can't afford to refuse to repay their debts. They are holding protests as ordered by their political patrons. If you can't live the life of a buddhijeevi, the next best option is politics, which has insatiable hunger for workers (hangers on really).

The irony of the festival is that it has been organized by The Times of India in collaboration with Rajanigandha! Those in foreign countries who don't know what Rajanigandha is, it is clarified that it is a powder of the betel leaf and nut with other ingredients, popular among writers of insignificance and paan loving people in India, Pakistan, Bangladesh and other countries inhabited by persons from these countries. It is advertised as the choice of the people, but can cause cancer. Isn't it a good combination? One can cause cancer of the body and the other cancer of the mind. Beware Indian writers of some merit, writers & scholars in the English speaking world, civil society, people of India, political leadership, Government Of India, liberal thinkers, philosophers, political scientists, economists, sociologists, scientists, technologists, public servants, religious scholars, Hindus and every other section of society in India of this psycho terrorism unleashed against us in pieces, exploiting our diversity by Fundamentalists torturing the world community in the name of religion. There is no need to be unhappy. Soon they will be exposed. The day the Indian news industry is thrown open to foreign companies, it is certain that nobody will even look at a biased newspaper like The Times of India.

As I awaited coverage of the proceedings, it occurred to me that in all likelihood, a resolution would be adopted which would be crafted, drafted and edited by the sutradhars operating from behind the scenes. It would attack the Prime Minister, his party and Hindu community. It wasn't far from it.

# Not My Idea of India

A highly motivated campaign against India has been going on for many months. It was politically motivated as Bihar was going to elect a new assembly and Modi was likely to score a victory. All kinds of disparate elements got into an alliance. Such campaign helped them score victory, but as a sort of counter revolution to Jai Prakash Narayan's Sampoorna Kranti (total revolution).It fell silent after the Bihar elections. People started asking why have the cacophony brigade dropped silent after achieving their political objective of stopping the BJP from forming a government in Bihar. That gave the necessary impetus for restarting the campaign.

Popular cine stars, their wives and children, foreign to the very ethos of India; writers residing mostly in rich countries of Europe or America; litterateurs who wangled national awards in a corrupt regime returning them now after decades and years insinuating central government responsibility for failure of the state government executive responsibility of bringing to justice rapists, murderers and lynching suspects; blaming the government for the murders of rationalists in the past when the Congress Party was ruling in the state; politicians going to Pakistan beseeching the audience publicly to remove "Prime Minister Narendra Modi"; patronizing a criminal of an MLA who openly threatened to cut Narendra Modi to pieces during the General Election 2014; alliance of the anti-corruption crusaders from the Anna Hazare team calling a Bihar politician and Union Minister of the Man Mohan Singh government as an "epitome of corruption" till 2014 and hugging in 2015 the same person in a tight fraternal embrace and raising hands in unity in the motion of world leaders at a summit made common cause to stall parliament and all reforms. Newspapers, especially the English press and media and its journalists & editors having deep and long bonds of loyalty to the Congress party and foreign agencies, launched themselves into steady action publishing canards for news, malicious views and outright propaganda likely to seduce the reader into taking everything at face value. It is only the experienced, discerning and analytical minds which can see through their games. It is really the time to stop subscribing to newspapers and television channels. Unfortunately, they have addicted people to their daily dose of negative mental diet without which the victims experience lacking something in the mode of the drug addicts. I am pretty sure that beginning one's day with a reading of classical literature or scriptures is a better option than the morning national daily newspapers as it provides so much of good ideas full of positive energy in cultured language that both health and happiness are assured.

My idea of India has no place for spurious writers. I don't visualize my India crowded with superficial poets, novelists or other writers. There is no place in my India for business oriented writers, whose sole aim is to write in English to sell their books by painting India black. These writers belong to neither here nor there- they belong to wherever they can sell to make profits. What do I have to do with immoral, dishonest and criminal politicians or ministers? I have no use in my India for women bartering away their dignity for positions of power or pelf. I cannot tolerate dishonest teachers, doctors, engineers, bureaucrats and other professionals. My India does not need wimps for Army, Air or Navy Chief. My India can't stand a corrupt judge even for a split moment. In my India social justice does not mean benefiting the family or clan. My India will not compromise on promoting knowledge and equal access for all the citizens. I refuse to give up non-violence until the independence and sovereignty of my country dictates otherwise. I treat myself as part of the global family, which my knowledgeable forefathers bequeathed to me in these zillions of Dollars' worth words: Vasudhaiv Kutumbakam, meaning the planet Earth is my family. I refuse to give up this world view of mine for the satisfaction of  vilifying paratroopers. My India does not need sermons on religion from sect leaders from abroad, which were not even born when my India had already reached the pinnacles of glory, unless they offer me a superior choice over Sarvadharma Sambhav and Din-e-Ilahi. My eyes and ears are wide open all the time for new ideas. Unfortunately, my own writers, in all branches of knowledge without exception, have failed to raise my spirits high. While the world rightly boasts of inventions, discoveries, patents, brands, institutions, Nobel awardees and thinkers, my own fellows consider it a big achievement to return their awards given for small achievements of no consequence. They suffer delusions of grandeur only by exclusion mostly of the past achievers who stand taller than them even today. Their whole work is to assail, re-tell, malign, condemn or reverse the work of the authors of ancient India or their genius. They are incapable of even understanding the classics. They have tried their best but never succeeded in even being shortlisted for a Nobel in literature, science or technology, sociology, political science, medicine, law or any other discipline. My idea of India envisions a very large number of such talented men and women contributing to the wellbeing of every individual in the spirit of Sarve Bhavantu Sukhino, sarve sant niramaya, sarva bhadrani pashyanti, maa kashchid dukh bhag bhavet om shantih shantih shantih. Are the contemporary Indian writers able to produce works to reflect such noble ideas? They are rather crass; and that is the tragedy of resurgent India. Every effort is being made to stall progress, reforms and all round advancement of the country because the Prime Minister, Mr. Narendra Modi, is seen as a result oriented person who has delivered results fast and is going to deliver much more that the country has not witnessed but desired for long.

It has given pangs in the stomach of foreign powers and domestic forces thriving on exploitation of the country by defiling and misusing the British policy of divide & rule. The British had failed to divide India as much as the post-independence politicians and writers have done in the name of social justice, reservation, castes, tribes, gender, region, religion, socialism, Marxism, revolution, total revolution and many more such divisive ideas.

When Narendra Modi gave a call for Sabka saath sabkaa vikas, India rose in unison as one giant and entrusted the governance of India to him. That is the idea of India, not the one adopted for sales promotion of books or documentaries by many. My India welcomes ideas, thoughts and views from all scholars and right thinking people but no sermons from salesmen of motivated agenda wrapped in seductive language.

India has always promoted the concept of simple living and high thinking. If India could survive the ignominious millennium of enslavement, it was because of drawing strength from such ideas and their application in day to day living. A neutral assessment of the ideas and language used by these protesting writers organizing their literary festivals in the national capital is likely to throw up the only conclusion that it is anything but simple living and high thinking.

Simple living does not mean living in abject poverty nor does high thinking mean only the Sahitya Akademi awardees or Padmashri & Padma Vibhushan awardees. There will be no pejorative expression that will not be used in denigrating the idea of India as brought out in the foregoing paragraphs. They will fail the test of tolerance themselves by not reciting openly the Satanic Verses or organizing a seminar on Taslima Nasreen's novels defying the ban imposed by the intolerant Congress regime and the Communist Party of India (Marxist) or majestically avoid even a passing remark against phenomenon of intolerance of the ISIS, which has gripped the people of the world in depression, gloom and doom. What an irony that the leaders of the protests in the name of intolerance have always professed to be leftists or progressive or Marxist writers, artists, actors, film producers and even politicians! It is further another irony that they are attacking the incumbent government without passing any resolution against the intolerance shown by the Congress and the Communist Party governments!

These writers hardly buy the books published by their fellow writers as is evident from the number of copies sold. No publisher is prepared to risk his money on these writers who can't sell even 500 copies! Even then, if they feel like going to foreign countries, they can go to Paris, Brussels, London,

New York, Mosul or anywhere else. But they will always miss My India that is for sure!

# Breach of Tolerance

Suddenly silence has befallen the preachers of tolerance to India. Just a single instance of religious fundamentalists demonstrating their intense hatred to civil society in Paris has filled newspapers with frightening headlines, though they have been practicing these inhuman tactics on liberal societies of Asia and Africa with excessive impunity because of tolerance of these societies. European nations are already in the grip of intense fear because of the enemy lurking in the neighborhood and attack their population at low cost but high devastation yield. Civilians are terrorized. Air transport in holiday season stands disrupted. Metro train services stopped for fear of bomb blasts. Normal life across Europe and America stands disrupted as never before. These headlines speak it all: Donald Trump leads Islamophobia in US; Africa in middle of new arc of terror; Militants freed those who could recite Quran; IS threat to White House; Brussels goes into lockdown fearing a Paris-style attack and Metro Shut In Home Of EU, NATO HQs; Portraits of Black professor defaced at Harvard; Palestinian poet in Saudi gets death for apostasy. Where have all the writers, poets, rationalists, secularists, leftists, Jawaharlal Nehru University intellectuals, IIFT and other self-proclaimed "tolerance" groups disappeared? They are not raising their voice against such crass intolerance in Europe and America? They have not returned a single National Award in protest nor held a demonstration at Jantar Mantar in Delhi and other cities nor taken a procession from Parliament House to President's palace, the Rashtrapati Bhavan, nor resigned their official positions in autonomous institutions nor declared their decision to go on self-exile nor insisted on naming an international airport after any of the internationally reputed terrorist, who took to terrorism only because of the actions of Europe or America. Is it because they are no more supported by European, American and Gulf funds? Or is it because these countries have stopped all political, propaganda and tolerance support to them? They have been only sanctimonious so far about tolerance in their own countries and India or other countries. Normal life comes to a standstill as terror attack may occur unannounced anywhere any day any time. Sports events are postponed out of fear, concerts canceled, metro shut down, people warned to avoid shopping centers, airports, train stations because of serious threats. That exactly is the goal of terrorists-disrupting normal life. The tolerance of these preaching countries has simply evaporated in no time.

It needs to be mentioned that the target of their hate agenda in India, the majority community, has not punished even one person for apostasy in its history of 5000 years till date! Does Indian tolerance need more evidence? Tolerance for the majority community in India is a way of life, not a slogan. It is its DNA. But for tolerance, India would not have been home to Hinduism, Buddhism, Jainism, Sikhism and dozens of other sects. But for ingrained tolerance in Indians, there would have been no Parsi community in India. What Paris suffered on 7 January 2015 or America suffered on 9/11, India as a highly evolved cultured liberal country suffered long back as a result of excessive tolerance and non-violence when they came under barbaric attack from the invading Muslims, the ancestors of these present day terrorists going under the names of Al Qaeda, ISIS or dozens of their variants. Even before any other country suffered terrorist attacks in the last 35 years, India had suffered. It is not significant what name they take, but it is the tactics which they adopt: massacre of innocent unarmed people, killing children, raping women and selling them, looting property, destroying cultural assets, burning libraries, destroying standing crops, poisoning sweet water resources and conversions to Islam under threat of death. In a nutshell, everything inconceivable in a civilized society is done by these marauders in the visibly most barbarous manner.

The preachers to India and the Indian propagandists don't even understand and acknowledge the complexity of this widespread phenomenon, which leaves nations with one of the two options to either give it back to them in their own language or surrender to them. Taking to their barbarism is neither simple nor acceptable to most civilized people nor is meek surrender to them. Recently civilized countries in Europe and America, which promoted human rights, civil rights or women's rights after the tragic world wars, had no experience or understanding of realities. Even then, they never tried to learn from the Indian experience. Now that they have personally experienced the consequences of barbarism in the name of Islam, they are in uncontrolled panic. Their response to the challenge posed by the new variant of war, which I would call the War of Barbarity in Modern Times, by terming it simply as terrorism is ostracism of history without any parallel. Such wars are not possible to win by hard power alone. They demand novel ways to counter. Savage minds make no distinction between "we & they"- whosoever is perceived as opposed to them meets the same fate as co-religionists or others.

Promoting human values of love, cooperation, non-violence and peaceful co-existence may be one of the several answers.

Religions have to interpret their scriptures to promote these values. They should not be misconstrued to spread hatred for other religions. Nobody has any right to convert anybody else to his religion by inducement or threat. It is irreligious to even think of doing any such heinous thing. Only the Devil thinks like this. Unless religions do so, there is every possibility of mankind moving towards self-destruction sooner than later.

# The Secularist Offensive

Secularism suffers no universal definition. Such a lack of clarity allows the advocates of secularism the license to define it whichever way they like. In a multi-religious country like India, there is hardly any prominent world religion that would have no followers. India is a secular country in the sense that it is not a theological state- it has no state religion. It gives equal treatment to all religions. The state follows the age old traditional approach of equal feeling towards all religions or Sarva Dharma Sambhav. It does not mean inter-faith discrimination. Majority of the population has been practicing the Hindu religion from time immemorial. The ancient treatises of Veda and Puran are well known to the knowledgeable the world over. And yet the democratic India opted for secularism rather than a Hindu nation. This was so under the worst provocation of division of the country by the receding British Empire into India and Pakistan. Pakistan was created on religious grounds by conceding to the demand of the communal Muslim League and claims no pretence to secularism. It is an avowed Islamist country. Even though the Muslim population in India exceeds the population of Pakistan, it remains a secular country.

In the facts & circumstances of Pakistan being the greatest sponsor of terrorism, social harmony in India gets easily disturbed. I have been noting it since 1980 that every Hindu festival is celebrated under threats of terrorist strike. It raises a pertinent question: are there limits to secularism?

How can it survive for long under threats from Pakistan sponsored terrorism? Can India meet this challenge through secularism, peace and love? Is terrorism a real threat to other countries? Is there a real clash of secularism and anti-secularism? Are Hindu sections alone expected to remain secular in India while all others can pursue their anti-secularism agenda? Can an India without the Hindu population be visualized? Can Hinduism be allowed to be attacked by the anti-secular segments? Can India without Hinduism have any identity? This question has become important in the light of sustained attack on the Hindu beliefs in the last 20 months or so in the name of tolerance. More than a million words must have been spent on decrying the Hindu belief by the media and the politician. Should the Hindu section of the nation give up its belief only to establish its secular credentials? Is there no value to the living tradition of Sarva Dharma Sambhav, which is nobler than simple secularism? Sarva Dharma Sambhav is definable and defined concept than the wooly secularism. Secularism had long been "rejected" by the Muslim clergy and the Christian authorities.

Had secularism been as well defined as Sarva Dharma Sambhav, the media and politician would have spared themselves the negative spin to an incident of lynching. Neither the minority is weak in India as is deviously portrayed nor are there killers freely roaming in the streets in villages. It is a matter of public knowledge that such heinous crimes are sponsored by the politicians eager to harvest Muslim votes in India whenever an election is held and blame the political parties branded as Hindu (Hindu Fundamentalist in BBC speak) or rightists. Even before an inquiry takes place, the leftists and centrists pronounce the Hindu parties guilty. Thereafter starts the media blitz. But are these people not supposed to delve deeper and logically, if not scientifically, examine these beliefs?

If the Hindus consider it unholy to eat beef, it should be respected. How does anybody acquire the right to attack their faith? Claiming diversity as something unique to India amounts to ridiculing Nature, which itself is not for uniformity. India has always respected the sentiments of others. Even in non-vegetarian households, non-veg food is cooked in a separate kitchen in one distant corner of the house. I don't eat meat or egg and I can't stand the smell of fish being cooked in the vicinity. Is it too much to expect that due care shall be taken of my sentiments? It is more than sentiment: I shall throw up if I suffer the smell. I prefer to go out for more than an hour if I find my immediate neighbor low on civic sense. If the Hindu feels hurt at beef, where is the need to make it an issue?

Even otherwise, there are not as many cows as human beings if all of us took to eating beef. Excess of everything is bad; it is so in this case. The allusion to the happenings was necessary but the issue here is something different.

The question is: what is the purpose of war? Isn't it establishment of peace? A war lasts for days or weeks or a few years at the maximum. Thereafter begins the era of peace. How long can peace endure? Surely till disturbed by the next war. Violent societies face wars very often, but the non-violent ones witness it after considerable lapse of time. India being an ancient civilization has experienced both. The Mahabharat was a war fought for 18 days and cost millions of lives. Thereafter, Emperor Ashoka vowed not to wage war. He took to Buddhism. Both Buddhism and Jainism propagated non-violence as the best religion (Ahinsa Parmo Dharma). Mahatma Gandhi used it as a weapon during the freedom struggle. The division of India took place because of the non-violence of Mahatma Gandhi and violence of the Muslim League led by Jinnah. Jinnah threatened and instigated a civil war in the country, getting a Muslim Pakistan but Mahatma Gandhi got no Hindu India. He asked only for a secular India. So the tragedy of partition, with mass scale migration of people on both sides, could not achieve complete exchange of the population on religious grounds. So, while Pakistan is a Muslim country, India is a secular country.

After Emperor Ashoka, India had suffered loss of its freedom. The millennium of subjugation, first by the Muslim aggressors and thereafter the British & other European powers, had completely shaken the self-confidence of the Indian masses, till Mohandas Karamchand Gandhi revived it and woke up the sleeping giant out of its numbness. Independent India went for democracy, which was welcomed by the masses. However, India had no tradition of democratic rule at the national level. Democracy demanded a large number of leaders to take responsibility to deliver governance to the people. It is here that India failed miserably.

The new leaders have established the superiority of violence in daily life and governance. They have abused the power of the vote. They started with booth capturing, scientific rigging, misuse of money power to purchase votes, use of criminals to win elections, dividing society into communities, castes and even sub-castes. In a matter of just some 35 years, they have reduced civilized discourse to a nasty war of words. They have denigrated every single national icon. They have grown swollen heads on their shoulders. In their lust for power they have forgotten even Lord Krishna and the cow so dear to him. The politicians indulging in such sacrilege betray only their own intellectual bankruptcy.

Lord Krishna is reverentially remembered by people not because he was God but because he demonstrated the best qualities of a mass Leader and his capabilities to change the lives of the people. Lord Krishna was born when the infamous Kansa ruled Mathura. He had established a reign of terror after imprisoning his father. He used to kill children, get all the milk & butter from the villages depriving the children of the only source of protein. He impoverished his people to such an extent that young girls could not afford a change of clothes while taking bath in a river or pond. Kansa would regularly dispatch his oppressors to harass the masses to extract their loyalty to him. An atmosphere of gloom, fear and hopelessness pervaded all around. Krishna challenged the power of Kansa and infused confidence in a people in despair. He revived their spirits by making them feel happy. He advised the milk producers of his community to stop sending milk and butter to Mathura and feed their children first. He formed his children's volunteer group to execute his social responsibility. The earthen containers of those trying to stealthily export milk to Kansa or Mathura were stoned and broken on way by the volunteer force. The hungry group helped itself to belly full of milk, Dahi (yoghurt) and butter without fear or guilt feeling. As the children grew healthy and masses confident, Krishna advised women to keep a change of clothes handy while taking a bath at public places.

Initially the innovative revolutionary methods and tasks performed by the volunteer force of Krishna caused a flood of complaints to his mother, but seeing the public purpose behind all these activities, they started showering love on him. Seeing change coming in their lives, Krishna would play music on his flute. Under the despotic king Kansa, the people had forgotten all forms of entertainment. The flute played by Krishna mesmerized them. Even the cows and calves and birds would listen to the rapturous flute of Krishna.

It improved the local prosperity and happiness. Krishna demonstrated to the people the power of change in happiness, contrasted with the gloom & doom, which had overwhelmed them. He celebrated this change by organizing the supreme dance or the Maharas one full moon night by the river Yamuna, elevating the dead spirits of a whole people. The cow played the key role in this transformation of the life of the people. Only agricultural economists can understand the value of a cow in the economics of livelihood of a farmer. If the value of such an animal was established by Krishna and the Hindus raised it to the level of holiness, only the ignorant will view it differently.

It is a significant coincident that the lynching took place in the Brij region of UP (Uttar Pradesh), the land of Lord Krishna (His Brij, Gokul, Vrindavan, Yamuna, also pronounced as Jamuna, and Mathura) and led to verbal violence of the lowest kind when a politician in Bihar ridiculed the holy cow concept. The media has been disparagingly using the phrase "holy cow" as a metaphor for decades. The politician lost his good sense and went to the extent of stating that Hindus too eat beef! He did not elaborate whether it is a common practice among majority of Hindus or limited only to some among them. Bihar is the land of the Buddha and Mahavir.

Alas! Wars of words are more dangerous to society than real wars. There is a concept of Sur and Asur in the Indian literature. The usual translation of the words is Gods & Demons. But here is another connotation of these two words. God Almighty in the Sanskrit and Hindi languages is called Iswar. Swar in Iswar means sur or a musical note. Music in essence takes a person to God Almighty or Iswar. The Gods are consonance or sur. The demons are dissonance or Asur. What is being played out in the name of beef is this dissonance; it is the Asuras in full play. They represent the negativity, the force of evil and doom. It is not difficult to answer the Asur in his own language but it is not worth it. There is an ongoing conflict between the Sur and the Asur tendencies, mentality, attitude, speech and objectives. That is how the Life Cycle works. They provide the necessary tension to initiate motion in opposing directions, making churning a reality. The war of words seems to suggest that the time has come for violence to cease. From Buddha to ISIS it is a full cycle of time.

Non-violence, which was placed at the top of the list of virtues in civilized society, has been replaced by violence effectively. Just consider the plight of the Buddhists in Tibet. They have been forced out of their country. China calls Tibet a part of its territory. But the same China is grappling to fight a handful of violent Uyghurs. Recently 15 serial bomb blasts took place in China and one serious blast destroyed property worth billions of US Dollars and several precious human lives. The terrorists have created havoc throughout the world, attacking trade towers in New York, trains in London and other places, killing journalists in Paris, attacking American and European tourists or embassies wherever they can It is no war, even though to counter such attacks is called a war on terror. But the ISIS is a real war. It has a territory, army of trained soldiers and funds of its own to fight the war. Nobody so far knows the way to end this war. It has already drawn America and NATO in to the war theatre and Russia has marked its independent entry. The kind and level of violence and barbarity seen in the ISIS war for more than two years now tends to support the end of the virtue and value of non-violence as nobody would be able to adhere to its principles if their very survival is threatened. If violence registers success in one part of the world, it will become the creed. It seems, both peace and non-violence have reached their limits and must yield the space for violence. The Asur of Indian politics have made it public that they can adopt any violent means to capture power. For them the cow or Krishna is not secular but beef eating is secular.   The voices of dissonance pen the script of secularism in India!

Can issues concerning the poor be ever discussed dispassionately in India? Aren't 37% Indians living below the poverty line (BPL)? So, near about 460 million Indians are living below poverty line, which means they can't afford a bare meal a day; their income being less than half a US Dollar a day! Now, a cow gives some means of livelihood to such a poor person for at least a decade or so. It provides her milk, dahi (substitute for green vegetables), butter, ox for ploughing as source for cash accruals, cow for milk again. In total sum, a very good source of protein, calcium, food, fuel and cash income. I leave it to the judgement of the scientific community to state if the cow milk is superior to other milk, because India is a country where complex knowledge had been employed in the form of tradition for the benefit of the layman. Without scientific terminology like pasteurization, fat content etc., cow milk had been prescribed for babies, lactating mothers, sick persons and generally for all other people in view of easier digestibility and wellness.

Now kill the cow and you kill the source of livelihood of the BPL persons. Is it the aim of the advocates of killing the cow and eat its beef? Butchering cows by machines by the meat industry is short sighted and costly activity. It costs more rearing up animals for meat. Besides, animal slaughter houses cause pollution and noxious odor irritating many people in the society. That is why, all governments , from the central government to state governments, while promising half a million jobs during electioneering never promise opening of new slaughter houses but only free distribution of milk giving animals to the BPL families. Why? Think and then only carry on this unseemly debate about beef.

# Tolerance: Charm Bomb of Post Neo-Colonialism

What is tolerance? What is neo-colonialism? These terms need not be re-defined here as a lot of literature already exists on the subject. Interested people can use the available literature to better appreciate the emerging challenges. Direct military takeover (Imperialism), political takeover (hegemony), economic takeover (market globalization), and religious takeover (conversions by force or inducement) are part of human history by now. Almost every country has experienced one or more of these. What has not been understood, appreciated, critiqued and assessed is the new form of imperialism that has almost captured the whole world. It is cultural takeover (writers, poets, critics, dramatists, film producers, journalists and all media formats). Its potent bomb is a simple word: tolerance.

For those who have ignored the implication of the word "tolerance", it is advisable to survey the literature generated in the last 5 years on the subject. Such tolerance helps establish a new kind of imperialism. The rhetoric is liberal but the goals are hard. The new imperialism uses the soft power instead of hard power. Taking over a country culturally is cheap, profitable and sustainable. It does not require physical presence of the colonizer or pumping capital. All that needs to be done is to establish the superiority of the colonial power's writers, poets, journalists, judges, thinkers, scientists, technologists and professors, and drill inferiority in the minds of the elite in the target country. Everything from nationalism to beliefs, values, traditions, customs, and thoughts are portrayed as inferior. It is carried out in such a smooth and smart manner that the target peoples don't even become aware of it till lapse of considerable time, by which the colonial power is already securely established. It is now a test bed. It has already won the loyalty of the large numbers of the practitioners of the culture of the target country, who have become too loyal to break ranks with them. The colonial power is in a position to directly interfere in the elections, government formation and functioning now to subserve its own interests through the media, films, political supporters and market manipulators. They need not invade a country militarily. It is enough to invade them culturally.

It is being tested on a very large scale in India, because the stakes are very high in this large market for everything from hard to soft products and processes. Whatever is being orchestrated in the name of tolerance in India since the Obama visit to New Delhi in January 2015, is now a full blast campaign for tolerance. President Obama dropped the third American atom bomb in New Delhi without the government or the people being alert to its fatal consequences.

We have no moral right to question the moves other intelligent people or nations make. We too can emulate them. Cultural wars in the 21st century will not be bloody wars. These wars are left to the Jihadists by intelligent design. If the majority of the world remains engaged in armed conflicts between the terrorists and their opponents, it only serves the interests of the colonial powers additionally. The gap between the jihadi and the culture superpower is as wide as between the 9th century and the 21st century. In the contemporary times, technology will rule the roost. It has the power to capture the whole world and rule through remote control. People capable of enjoying political humor have enjoyed the unexpected events in the last 24 months in India. India the original sponsor of the NAM (Non Aligned Movement) had high aspirations as a member of the comity of nations, which was not liked by the NATO Block of nations. The last one decade (2004-2014) saw a very weak India. It was established that the Indian people are tolerant to covert invasions through sabotage of the constitutional form of government without as much as a murmur. The lawful government (de jure) was headed by Dr. Man Mohan Singh as Prime Minister, but the unlawful government (de facto) was run by an outsider (one not a member of the Council of Ministers) under a dubious mechanism of NAC (National Advisory Council). When the elections to the parliament of India were announced in 2014, the cultural colonizers had let out their full force against Narendra Modi and his party, using all print & television journalists, and others, many of whom are those who have been commanded to return the awards now in a show against "growing intolerance" even though there is none. The masses, decried as illiterate, backward and poor, saw the dirty game and defeated the Congress party decisively and mandated Narendra Modi to form the government. Those who enjoy political humor enjoyed that turn of events but others have been sulking since then.

But that is a minor point; the big thing is the atom bomb called "tolerance". It will be used to needle, bleed and stain the image of the government, especially the Prime Minister, Narendra Modi. The powers that be must have come to the conclusion that Narendra Modi needs to be dislodged before he becomes the darling of the people. He has already implemented several people oriented schemes like the Jan Dhan Yojana, Gas Subsidy and Insurance. He is out to make an immoral (corrupt) system morally strong. A cultural colonizer sees his biggest hurdle in such a leader and people. He succeeds only when the masses consider everyone corrupt or immoral as they viewed them before Narendra Modi re-established the moral values in public life. Establishing its moral superiority over the target and driving a sense of inferiority in it about its own moral standards is the sine qua non of such colonization mission. It needs a veil to hide its true colors. What can be a better tool than denigrating a society as "intolerant" and demand of it "tolerance"? That brings us to the beauty of the English language- in fact, the power of the American English.

America has already colonized the world: computers, Facebook, Google, Internet, World Wide Web, Apps, smart phones and a number of other tools have brought the users the world over under **American Technological Hegemony**. There is no doubt about it and there is no substitute for it. The world will stop the moment these power tools are down. And America knows every single detail about its users. Has the world witnessed this level of colonization earlier? What facilitates this colonization is equally interesting: it is the American English. My computer not only confuses me repeatedly but keeps on harassing me until I use the American English, not only spelling but meaning. The meaning part I accept because it is undoubtedly the better one, the spelling only partly. The British get the credit for teaching the world the English language, derided by the British themselves till Churchill imparted it some amount of self-respect and lifted its status. It has helped the Americans better than any other peoples.

So, America today is in direct communication with the users, bypassing national sovereignty and carries on business as it desires. The sheer power of its cultural assets is enough to overawe any country, short on culture or Dollars. Indians from the scientific and technology streams have long been employed on American jobs and assignments. The culture wing was embraced by the Americans slightly late because of the writers' pretensions of progressivism (communism/ leftism) and overtly anti-American writings and speeches. Television exposed the soft belly of the Indian writers soon and America just grabbed them by offering exchange visits, literary festivals, publication & sale of their books, conferences, seminars and other lollipops. Who will refuse to visit America on a fellowship? Even Narendra Modi visited America at the first available opportunity after becoming Prime Minister, as the chorus of same intellectuals had been petitioning in writing the American Establishment not to grant Modi a visa to visit America! The man has proved himself smarter than everyone in the rival camp; they are stumped, so to say. But weapons are already out. This time the shots are being fired from the shoulders of the writers, who are blissfully ignorant that tolerance is not a simple word but a charm bomb. It is a Vashikaran Mantra of immense power (captivating chant).

The situation is dangerously complex. The success or failure of the attempts at cultural colonization of India would depend on how the heirs to the Indian culture behave. As of now, they have given proof of their terrible ignorance and lack of understanding of complex issues of the contemporary Post Neo-Colonialism. They are lost in hatred, their language is soaked in hatred, their actions are ill advised, their arrogance is too offending, their egos are too inflated, their vision of the world cultural scenario is extremely limited, their capacity to absorb new ideas inhibited, their capacity for exchange of ideas very low, their skills in listening to others poor and their morals abysmally deplorable. They have proved themselves a liability to Prime Minister Narendra Modi. They refuse to grow. They could have grown had they walked with Modi. On the contrary, they want to drag Modi to their stalled walk. Is it not a matter of great concern that India has so far not appointed a stalwart to the office of the minister for culture? Only insignificant persons have so far been appointed as minister and secretary culture!

Will the Indian intelligentsia rise to the occasion? Will the elite Indians ponder over this creeping cultural colonization? Today Zuckerberg can control governments from America. He represents the power of technology. Go farther and assess the situation in a really smart world, operating from above in the sky, where all traffic is one way. Be smart or the tolerance bomb will put to hypnosis all- writers and readers forever.

# America Has Trumped Indian Intellectuals

First it was President Barack Obama who triggered the tolerance debate in January 2015 in Delhi, energizing a depressed Congress Party after the electoral defeat of 2014 to hyper activity in cahoots with a selected few Indian intellectuals portraying themselves secular and liberal. The Obama sent opportunity provided them a much needed issue to target the Prime Minister, Narendra Modi for intolerance in the country. It didn't take them much time to organize protests by some writers, instigating them to return the national awards conferred on them for their literary works by the Sahitya Akademi.

With valuable contribution from the English press, they built an atmosphere suggestive of intolerance in India after Modi became Prime Minister. They kept on harping about the riots of 2002 in Gujarat, when Modi was the chief minister, for which no judicial court has cast even an aspersion on Modi personally. But they have displayed utter lack of faith in the judiciary as it demolishes their allegations against Modi in totality. They had played up the American visa refusal also, though Modi frustrated them by not only visiting America to a rousing welcome but also making President Obama the Chief Guest at the Republic Day Parade on 26th January 2015. All this only added to their gripe. The Awards, which were returned by their writer friends, has earned the people's sarcasm as Award Wapasi. They organized a march under the leadership of Congress Party President Sonia Gandhi from the parliament house to the President's place, a small distance. That too evoked derisive laughter as the Congress was in power till May 2014 and the protesters were referring to events of that time insinuating responsibility of the Modi government. Besides, the incidents they were referring to fell in the executive responsibility of the state governments, not the Modi government at the center. But the objective was not genuine protest, only malicious propaganda. It failed because it was propaganda. People of India are aware of the growing popularity of Prime Minister Modi and the intolerance of the Congress Party for him.

Their anti-Modi campaign has not stopped since then. Even literary festivals have been used to provide a forum for anti-Modi diatribes by poets, writers and journalists. The aim & objective was to malign India in the name of intolerance before some literary audiences so that the prime minister could be put under pressure. Caught for long in the ambiguous connotations of secularism, minority and tolerance, they refuse to consider the global developments, affecting peace and civilization. They feel shy of talking about ISIS, which they consider to be the burden of the white men, especially America alone.

They view America as the country of their dreams, not because they want to contribute anything to its development or growth, but because they wish to lead a life bereft of all responsibility or restrictions or accountability. It is amusing to note this change of attitude in the Indian intellectuals, who had spread more hatred against America in the past than they are doing now to Prime Minister Modi. It was virtuous for them to criticize America for everything wrong in the world, whether it was capitalism or consumerism or world peace to claim to be progressive and liberal (euphemism for communist).They called America the world's policeman out of contempt. It was only after the disintegration of the USSR that the Indian intellectuals found themselves in complete disarray. China had split them ideologically in 1962 by invading India and activities of the Naxals/ Maoists has brought them enough discredit to permanently block their rise to power to rule India.

The internet, information revolution and other technological developments of this century have brought about revolutionary changes in the world. The new tilt towards America can be explained in this context. So the spontaneous rejection of all things American (as in the case of civil nuclear agreement) changed to warm acceptance in the Obama sermon on tolerance. They have gone hyper on tolerance and intolerance, presenting themselves as tolerant and Modi as intolerant, even without acknowledging growth of terrorism, ISIS and threats to world security & peace.

Their thinking on tolerance is narrow, motivated by vote bank considerations and Modi centric. They write editorials and interview foreign authors/ journalists invited to the Lit Fest or visiting India otherwise and ask them for their views on "growing intolerance" in India. The visiting intellectuals refuse to play to the gallery and ignore such irrelevant questions. That does not deter them and they continue with their propaganda.

Unfortunately for them, Donald Trump, the American Presidential hopeful for 2016 has dashed all their hopes. His resolve to refuse entry of Muslims to America has stunned Indian intellectual circles, who do not know how to react to his radical views. If they criticize Trump, they displease America, which they don't find attractive; but if they laud his views they prove themselves wrong for running a malicious campaign bringing bad name to India for growing intolerance. Trump has dissipated all their negative energy by a simple one liner.

Can they go on criticizing Modi in the name of intolerance, now that Obama is certain to demit office and Trump may win the American Presidency? Even if Trump fails to occupy the White House, the tremendous support he has won from the American people and which is going to grow with every barbaric act of the ISIS in the coming days, shall remain there. It is this change in the conservative view of minority, Islam, Muslim, fundamentalist, liberalism, tolerance across America and Europe and other countries in the world, which has created confusion among the Indian intellectuals.

These Indian intellectuals refuse to acknowledge the real conflict in the world between the two big religions viz., Christianity & Islam. To cover it up, they invent ludicrous excuses to underplay the issues. They advance arguments like Islam & terrorism are different or that all Muslims are not with the ISIS. When intellectuals try to be politically correct in voicing their thoughts, they do grave injustice to the people. Articles without mastery over matters like Islam or Shariyat law or Muslim mind fail to be instructive. Blaming terrorism of the Al Qaeda or ISIS kind on fringe elements and distinguishing them from the mainstream Muslim society globally is ostrich mentality. The dangers are real and need to be faced squarely. They emanate from Islam as interpreted by the authentic hierarchy prescribed in the Koran.

It is a different matter that some people try to treat such interpretations of the Koran as flawed and hope for peace against the decades of barbaric violence threatening almost every country today, irrespective whether it is America, Europe, Africa, Australia, New Zealand, Asia, whether predominantly Muslim, Christian or any other religion. This is a new format of war. This is medievalism waging a war on modernity. This is a challenge to the concept of Superpower hegemony.

The industrial revolution empowered the western world militarily so much that it came to dominate the world. It got its first serious challenge from Osama Bin Laden and his Al Qaeda. The response to the growth of Al Qaeda led to a devastating armed conflict with serious consequences of unimagined and unmanageable kind for the superpowers. Iraq and Afghanistan proved the biggest failure of superpower military might. The killing of Osama Bin Laden, who was living under the protection of the Pakistan army in their most secure cantonment area, was expected to bring an end to Islamic terrorism but it turned out to be just the opposite- it gave birth to a more deadly terror outfit in the form of the ISIS.

This outfit has created panic in the world by attacking France, UK, Australia, Russia and threatening China and all other countries. For weeks now, the ISIS is under combined attack of Russia, France, UK and America. But it is not yet subdued. Even if its leader Baghdadi is eliminated, it will not end the terrorism of the ISIS kind. On the contrary, it might create another organization. The danger is not from an Osama or a Baghdadi, it is from Islam, as interpreted or misinterpreted (depending on individual choice) by those who exercise authority over the devout under the Koran.

But this conflict is essentially between the world's two religions: Islam & Christianity. Both have fought religious wars in the past. Christianity had the advantage of science, technology and modernity, which empowered it over the remainder of the world community. Islam took time to master the same technology and science, but has used it against the Christian world. It has rejected modernity and used Islam to propagate medievalism as an alternative to establish the rule of Islam everywhere. This competitive religious fascism is responsible for the so called terrorism; terrorism for the west is a value judgement of the modern liberal western democratic world, but it is a holy war for the practitioners of Islam. That difference of perception has attracted fighters for the cause of the ISIS from almost every country of the world which has some Muslim population. The Indian intellectuals avoid writing on these extremely significant issues. It needs to be examined whether the world is fast moving to the next world war. Is there a solution to the problem created by the ISIS for the civilized world in sight?

Yes, there are solutions to every problem. The Cosmos is not regulated by the ISIS. It does not rule beyond that small territory. Diversity is the law of Nature. There is no uniformity in the Cosmos. The delusion of the ISIS of Muslim Rule is flawed in that sense. It is rather strange that Nature is neither all violence nor all non-violence! It is neither wholly war nor peace. It is struggle, conflict, competition all through right from impregnation to birth and death. Big leaves fall under attack from a micro leaf emerging side by side. This cycle is repeated. The Al Qaeda and ISIS are in the cycle of growth of the life on Earth. It will meet its end at the appropriate time. Like the leaf, its rival is already born. It will not be noticed for long- it will remain invisible like the magnetic force, but will rise to vanquish the ISIS and its ideology effectively at the appropriate time. That appropriate time will come when the ISIS reaches the pinnacle of its infamy. But to just give a hint, the woman power in the Muslim society will bring about the change Islam has not experienced so far. Islam is a comparatively young religion. It has to grow, evolve and develop beyond the narrow interpretation placed on it by the male dominated hierarchy so far. The terror attacks, mass migration of refugees fleeing conflict zones to Europe, Trump and women in election in Saudi Arabia and the coordinated attacks on ISIS are silent moves of that invisible force which will bring about changes far reaching not only for the Muslim society but civilization on the whole.

It was after almost 2500 years that Mahatma Gandhi established superiority of Non-Violence over violence in the last century. It changed the world, but the Cold War continued the arms race for fear of the enemy. The disintegration of the Soviet Union led to a drastic cut in the race. But the economic ramifications of non-violence and peace deterred the superpowers from giving up manufacturing weapons of mass destruction like bombs and missiles. Organizations like Al Qaeda and ISIS were new entrants in the weapons market. They had oil dollars in abundance. They were fired by the Islamic hegemony dream. The rest is public knowledge. ISIS will survive so long as the manufacturing superpowers sell weapons and remain cold to peace and peaceful coexistence. The day weapon manufacturers realize that there are limitations on violence and the onus of peace is more on them than small outfits like ISIS, peace will prevail in the world.

Trump has started an open discussion on a relevant subject that all liberals have been avoiding, especially in India. He has confounded them rather awfully. They don't know how to respond to Trump now, having magnified the Obama doctrine of tolerance just 11 months ago. He has put brakes on liberals marketing doctrines of intolerance by putting his views rather bluntly, bringing to public discourse the common anger ever since 9/11 against Islam and whispered only in private conversations. In India it has frustrated all attempts of maligning the Prime Minister Modi – Donald Trump has trumped Modi bashers.

Indian masses value transparency. They trust Modi is running his government in a transparent manner in spite of the Congress Party raising barriers to development on a daily basis. The political trends in Europe and America are bound to redefine democracy, religion, socialism, capitalism and humanism. A new World is about to be born. My hunch is that the world will witness a New World Order by 2050. The ISIS initiated violence will end in peace.

# A Case for Domestic CBMs

Reviewers of Narendra Modi's rise to power would certainly highlight the single most valuable factor for his success: his successful domestic confidence building measures (CBMs) with the people of India. After 24 months of his being in office, these CBMs will again be evaluated and weighed against the achievements or non-achievement in the next 24 months.

Modi has achieved great success in his foreign policy and taken the country to a level where members in the comity of nations treat India with respect. He played his master stroke in foreign CBMs, significantly among others with Bangladesh and Pakistan. His visit to Pakistan foxed many from the elite community of media moguls, journos, columnists, Captains of the so called secular forces, soft-liners & hard-liners alike, academicians, experts and foreign governments. The best part of his Pakistan visit was that it was welcomed by the people in both the countries.

How did it come through? It is because at people to people level, their emotional bonds remain sanguine. Only the terror groups and their mentors were upset, who lost no time in spoiling the atmosphere of goodwill created between the two countries and internationally too, by launching almost immediately the audacious terrorist attack on the Indian Air Force Base at Pathankot on the night of January 1 this year, that is within just 7 days of Modi's visit to Pakistan on December 25, 2015. The Pathankot incident is one among many in the past carried out by terrorists (actually Pakistan ISI trained soldiers) running their training schools for terrorism. It has again dented the CBMs between India &

Pakistan. But the success of the Modi government's foreign policy has already been stamped.

Now is the time for paying greater attention to domestic CBMs, which have suffered no less from political terrorism of the opposition, even on an important area of public interest like the GST Bill; a hostile media which has always hated him and his supporters and have refused to acknowledge the change of government in India in 2014 after almost 67 years!

Modi had written a success story for his party, the Bharatiya Janata Party (BJP) and himself that went beyond the expectations of even the top leaders of the party and the organization. The recognized leaders of the party have not accepted the supremacy of Narendra Modi. They have gone on record expressing their disgruntlement. Narendra Modi faces regular sniping from his own party men, some honorable & intelligent, others outright boorish & foolish, and yet another lone wolf journalist kind seeking to further their own career by playing one against the other between these two groups (Modi & the dissidents). They are competing with the opposition in suppressing Modi's achievements and finding faults with him or his government even where none exists.

Luckily for Modi, the people of India have not yet bought their propaganda. But there is no guarantee they would not. Modi has to attend to domestic affairs with greater commitment and care on a daily basis.

The people need the relief promised to them. They need roti, kapada, makaan, sadak, bijli, paani, school and health care facilities (bread, clothing, dwelling, road, drinking water). They are not demanding world class services; rather they are simply asking for restoration of the facilities made available to them during Jawaharlal Nehru's time but rendered dysfunctional after him by corrupt elements which ruined them to promote commercialization of education and health against the letter and spirit of the Constitution of India.

The country could never recover from that terrorism of the corrupt. In fact, the terrorist activities in India had also become a lucrative business for the corrupt politicians, bureaucrats, police, security forces and businessmen creating difficult internal security problems that continue to be worrisome even today.

The masses suffered so much that they had lost faith in democracy, government, political leaders, bureaucrats, institutions, professionals, businesses and industry until Narendra Modi succeeded in winning their trust. They entrusted the responsibility of governance of India to him. It is for him to live up to that trust and prove himself worthy of it.

As the time to show results on the ground is not more than what has already elapsed since election 2014, Modi needs to monitor critical areas like price rise, employment, transparency, black money and general well-being of the people of India.

Modi need not take unnecessary risks like in Delhi & Bihar elections, which have to be left to the local leadership. He can't reduce himself to the level of a state politician by undertaking the whole responsibility of winning these elections on his own shoulders.

The issues involved and the language employed in state elections is different from the oratorical specialization of Narendra Modi. There are more pitfalls than high grounds in politics of elections in states. Modi has all the enthusiasm of a young ebullient dynamic politician that is germane to such personalities, but he is now a statesman of a very high stature, which his party has never had. He has to live up to that image and reality. Too much state electioneering has the ill effect of reducing that stature to an ordinary politician.

It is time for actualization of promises, showing results on ground and demonstrating the capability of a new India to run a government transparently as by law mandated.

# Part V

A billion hopes to deliver in only 36 months

# Threats to Homeland Security

Sections of the media are portraying the JNU (Jawaharlal Nehru University) incidents as a fight for student rights. They are calling it an all India movement by student activists for their rights. They justify it in the name of freedom of speech. Freedom of speech does not include anti-national slogans at the behest of ISI of Pakistan or on behalf of the ISIS or religious fundamentalists desperate to expand their numbers through conversions operating under the cover of NGOs. Those who understand the meaning of freedom of speech will spontaneously respect the rights of their opponents also for their freedom of speech. Take out the respected magazines published in India during the decades of 1960 & 1970 and plagiarism of words and expressions used therein will become apparent in the politics being played up on campuses today.

The forces of destabilization were acting against Nehru, hoping his death will create a vacuum for them to "Occupy India". Indira Gandhi frustrated their aspirations for power. Now it is Narendra Modi winning people's mandate for a clean and strong government. The forces of destabilization will continue to work like this, ruin academic environment, mislead students for recruitment to their ranks (similar to silently operating drug lords and crime mafia). The decisive mandate given by the Indian voter disoriented these anti-people anti-national forces, for they had always treated the poor uneducated masses with sophisticated scorn.

They had gone into political hiding in fear for some time, waiting for Modi to commit blunders. They never considered Modi fit to be the Prime Minister. For these elements Rahul Gandhi is Prime Ministerial material. But Modi frustrated them more than Indira Gandhi. So, in complicity with their foreign investors in political upheavals in India, they started as a field trial with burning small under construction church premises, but failed to stoke communal riots and generate    anti-Modi news for foreign media. Tolerance came next and Award Wapasi gave them temporary relief for a few months before it also proved a damp squib. It ended up making writers controversial and exposing the unworthy awardees, who got them through manipulation. Then it was the incident of murder in a UP village. It was used to create disturbances on campuses. When that too failed, they tried to exploit the OROP (One Rank One Pension) issue and create disharmony in the armed forces. The Modi government settled that issue peacefully to the satisfaction of all. Then was used the JNU.

The sloganeering crowds were not "students" nor "faculty" but agents of ISI of Pakistan & ISIS recruiters. They exploited the liberal, open academic environment of the JNU and duped the unsuspecting students under the veil of a cultural evening to indulge in the most abominable act of seditious sloganeering. Students on campuses have been leftists for decades, but their leftism is different from the professional leftism of the CPI (Communist Party of India) and the CPM (Communist Party-Marxist). The split in the Communist Party after the Chinese War on India in 1962 led to the creation of the Naxal movement in1967. Naxals rejected both the CPI and the CPM and have not so far aligned with them even after a lapse of 49 years. That is leftism in India. That is why there are about 5 leftist organizations active in JNU. So it is not for student rights that the trouble on the JNU campus was fomented; it was to serve the Pakistani goals of destroying and dismembering India which is amply vulnerable because of its diversity.

India might bask in the glory of its diversity, but Pakistan seeks to exploit it to thrust the dagger. Just ponder: why did it use only Khalid to raise the slogan. It could have also employed a Kumar. But it didn't because it knew that its game will be blown off before executing if any non-Muslim were to be used for such a traitorous activity. It is, therefore, not for student rights but for ulterior motives.

There has never been any restriction in any educational institution in India on student activities or rights. But the agent provocateurs never discuss student duties. Is it not the duty of the students to successfully complete their academic studies and acquire the best skills to face the challenges in life? Should students be wasting time in pursuing useless research only because they are unemployable? Should they not be made to work hard? Nobody wastes his or her time on campuses as our students in universities like JNU. Is it not surprising that not a single research of international standard has been produced by the JNU in these 46 years of its existence? Perhaps the faculty is also answerable for such a state of affairs. It seems the faculty and students don't have adequate amount of academic work, including research projects. That is one reason of students idling their time in fake cultural evenings and useless extra-curricular activities, ruining their careers. They ought to understand that they are being sustained by the poor people by financing their studies and jobs through direct and indirect taxes and sacrificing their needs so that institutions like JNU produce excellent thinkers who could strengthen India and return the public generosity by contributing to growth and development and prosperity of the masses. They must appreciate the lurking dangers like the fires in Haryana. They are raring to create similar situations everywhere in India. For this, they will exploit student activism all over the country in the next few years.

Academic institutions are the first line of defense for internal security of India. Faculty and students are the civil society soldiers alive to any simmering threat. They are society's radar to capture all activities of the foreign intelligence agents or other vested interests operating in the country and undermining the nation, as they are engaged on learning, analyzing, debating all material developments in and outside India. Students and faculty freely debate all subjects including political, economic, social, philosophical, technological, scientific, governance and others. Since all political parties in the country try to secure student support to further their interests, they seed in their minds ideas to achieve their goals, howsoever narrow they might be. The political bosses take advantage of their maturity over the vulnerability of the students and succeed in their plans easily. It is exploitation of the idealism of the youth, who lack personal experience and knowledge about realities and unwittingly walk in to the invisible snare spread to capture them. Political jargon is full of enchanting rhetoric. It can act like hypnosis. Words like revolution can instantly cast a spell. Unless the students are careful, they can be easily misled in to indulging in unlawful activities. Resorting to unlawful activities like violence produces instant results. It attracts the media. Favorable reporting of the developments and flashing of photos in the newspapers and on television screens enthuses them. The politicians smile at their success. The students get distracted, classes are cut and studies suffer. Academic standards go down. Student scores fall. Employability of such products becomes doubtful. A kind of disability is fastened on to them. Meanwhile politics goes on merrily in the name of student activism. Ultimately society suffers.

# Propaganda Does Not Make News

Are journalists born or made? Does a journalist acquire greatness or it is thrust on her/him? Is a mere accreditation card a passport of privilege to say arbitrarily anything against a section of the society, nation or government? Should the journalists earn the trust of their readers, audiences and viewers or command it in the name of press & media? Should the journalists become spokespersons of the political party of their choice or maintain the fine distinction between the free press and committed political party?

These are some questions that arise after witnessing the continuing assault on Narendra Modi right from the days he announced his candidature for the Lok Sabha elections in 2013. In spite of all hate mongering against him, Modi emerged as a leader of the masses with a clear majority in the Indian parliament, ending the culture of corruption aggravated by the "coalition compulsions". In simple words, coalition compulsions meant "khao aur khaane do" (translating in to eat & let others eat). It was the deepest pit to which democratic governance could sink.

The harassed people of India threw out the UPA government led by the Congress Party, with Man Mohan Singh as Prime Minister. It was on the basis of a solemn assurance from Modi never to indulge in corruption or allow others to do so (Naa Khaungaa Naa Khaane Doongaa). Corruption had rusted all wings of the nation- legislature, executive, judiciary, bureaucracy, security establishment. The worst was the corrupt press and media. Names of journalists acting as agents of corruption were mentioned by investigation agencies. This meant the decline of intellectual leadership of democracy in India, following the declining political, economic, business and security leadership. The journalists lost their freedom, stood with the ruling establishment, formulated news stories as dictated by those who engaged them. The angry masses gave full vent to their frustration on the social media.

But before that, news had already become good business and a short cut to power and prosperity. It was in line with their business interests that the media persons painted Narendra Modi as a villain so that he could not win the election. Excepting for Modi, the Congress and its unholy alliance partners feared no challenge to their prospects of capturing power for another term. Had they done their duty to the society by covering the elections without bias, prejudices and predilections, they would not have come to suffer the trauma of getting proved wrong and way off the margin. By unethically attacking Narendra Modi, the media moguls lost their influence on public opinion. The journalists failed to gauge the public wrath against corruption, deceit and harm to public interest in functioning of the government because they took the people for granted under the impression that the helpless voter had no option other than the Congress, which could merrily fool the people as always in the name of secularism, communalism, minority, farmer, women, poor, schedule caste & schedule tribe. What the Lok Sabha elections revealed was the face of the resurgent India asserting its authority decisively. The journalists in employ of the political parties were crest fallen for quite some months till their political masters came up with a sturdy plan to get rid of Modi.

These journalists desperately looked for chinks in the armor of Modi and his government. They were fed on too much of anti-Modi stuff which woefully underestimated Modi's capability to run the government and believed in their heart that he will fail shortly. They ignored all the good work done by Modi in the first year as Prime Minister of India, whether in foreign policy or good governance. Journalists, who wrote their stories in the name of corruption to blackmail bureaucrats, ministers, politicians and business houses, suffered the worst economic meltdown in the news industry in the history of free India in 68 years! Modi robbed them of breaking news, because Modi himself broke it first on twitter. They goaded their masters, shared their angst against Modi and desperately sought remedial action.

Resurgent and assertive India and her face Narendra Modi caused enormous worry for the foreign anti-India forces too. Attempts were made to foment communal trouble to portray Modi and party as anti-minority. First strike came in the name of attacks on churches by carefully engineered damage to one or two under construction small structures right in Delhi. The journalists went berserk with disproportionate stories filled with choicest negative words to make a mountain of a genuine molehill. The Modi government was instantly put on the defensive because it had the potential of flaring up in to serious riots, but it understood the game behind these incidents and effectively checked them from repeat.

The ISI of Pakistan smelled an opportunity but was feeling helpless. Foreign training of Indian politicians of low intellectual caliber, who were a cause of extreme worry for the committed journalists, increased in the meantime. The mantra of "tolerance versus intolerance" was given to them in that training. Its implications didn't become clear to the masses or the elite until used by the American President, Barack Obama, before winding up his visit to India. Since then it has been intolerance all the way to create trouble for the Modi government. The Modi government was sought to be blamed for intolerance by recalling incidents which occurred long before he became Prime Minister of India. These included the murders of Dabholkar & Kalburgi. Law & Public Order, including policing, is the administrative responsibility of the state governments (Chief Ministers) under the Constitution of India (Allocation of Subjects under List-II State List) and not of the Central government (Prime Minister). If a man is lynched in UP state, the chief minister should be held accountable. But the journalists have labored hard to blame Modi for it. It is so because the journalists have not changed their attitude or regained their true freedom. They have stubbornly refused to come to terms with the reality of Narendra Modi becoming the Prime Minister of India or the Congress having lost power for several decades and reduced to less than the recognized Opposition failing to get the status of even the Leader of Opposition because of getting just 44 seats, much below the requisite minimum number in the Lok Sabha.

It has not deterred either the Congress Party or the journalists from creating trouble for the government, impacting its smooth functioning. A new weapon, a tried and trusted old one, to create unrest on the university campuses at different places in India has been released to cause disturbances by starting strikes and instigating students to commit suicide. Any political commentator would vouch for these old tricks of defaming the government before the imposition of Emergency in India. Drama on roads by carrying the dead body of a student or citizen killed in police firing or heavily bandaged heads of people who had not even been scratched superficially, getting them photographed and published in newspapers are stale tricks of the game. One can easily imagine the "power" of the journalists in spreading misinformation, disinformation and genuine information in such circumstances. First it was the advent of the television which clipped the wings of the print media, and when the television started abusing its power of the camera and the mike, the social media set it right. But the journalists refuse to budge a bit. They have now removed the thinnest veneer that distinguished them from the political party workers and spokespersons, as they have taken direct action. Today's journalists are no more than propagandists for the anti-Modi political parties, foreign vested interests  out to create communal riots in India for increasing the numbers of converts to their religion and discrediting the majority community or serve Intelligence agencies like the ISI, CIA, KGB & others.

They all have one common goal: to dislodge Narendra Modi, by hook or crook. They all have a single mission: to weaken India as a country. Their plan of action is: destabilize the government of India so as to eventually capture it with the connivance of traitors. They have started with hate campaigns.

Freedom of speech is the first in this series. It started in the Jawaharlal Nehru University (JNU) in Delhi when under the pretext of Cultural Evening, anti-India slogans were raised, threatening to destroy India and fight for independence of various states in India. The worst was the glorification of a terrorist who was behind the attack on the parliament building in the past and who was executed after exhausting all legal channels. It achieved what was sought by the agents of ISI of Pakistan and other foreign vested interests- it evoked wild reaction throughout the country. The student union president was arrested. It was virulently opposed by communist organizations and Congress leaders. They opposed any action against the seditious uttering of the students and attacked the police action and the government for it. When the accused were being taken to the court, they created rumpus in the court premises.

Journalists violated all decent behavior and had to be kept away. They clashed with the lawyers. Journalists got the excuse to criticize the government. Everything was playing to the agenda. The journalists forgot that JNU is not the only university in India, it is no Oxford or Harvard, it barely makes to the list of 100 Indian universities rated by a media house, it figures nowhere in the list of 200 top world universities, it is not known to have done a single world class research in its existence of 46 years and that there are many far superior universities in India. The journalists think that whatever is thought by the students of JNU is also the thinking of the students everywhere in India. They are grossly mistaken. Had the journalists been fair & objective, they should have moved a 100 km away from Delhi and interacted with the students and faculty in universities in UP, Rajasthan, Haryana & Punjab. But they know that their stories will fall through if they went beyond the protected garden of Delhi's JNU with its overwhelming communist dominance.

The hype created by the journalists about the JNU incident and its aftermath are in a series of well-planned destabilization campaigns starting with the return of Award given in the past to poets and writers, which is called derisively the Award Wapasi followed by a chain of Lit Fest (Literature festivals) to malign the government in the name of intolerance, vilification of the government for showing intolerance to the anti-India and pro-Pakistan slogans on the campuses of JNU & Jadhavpur universities and program for similar events throughout Indian universities. The journalists liberally contributed to fuel the fires of mayhem. Irresponsible statements, partisan news stories, motivated editorials & columns, facile TV debates, provocative language from the journalists and television anchors provoked the public immensely.

They went to the extent of justifying themselves by using the names of famous individuals like Noam Chomsky and Orhan Pamuk and newspapers like the New York Times and the Guardian.

It is so unfortunate for Chomsky to lend his name to be exploited by the highly compromised Indian journalists.

Either Chomsky is unaware of developments in India in the last 12 years or he is getting his feed from sources in India, which is second rate and colored information, unworthy of use by an eminent thinker and author like Chomsky. He would do himself a great favor to stay in India for a few years and see things for himself before issuing any fatwa on the crass anti-India sloganeering on the JNU campus by agents of Pakistan's ISI & other foreign powers.

The NYT has so far not taken a neutral view of the change of government in Delhi in 2014. It puts on a mask of leftism forgetting the damage the left has done to states like West Bengal & Kerala and its association with the Emergency rule of Congress leader Mrs. Indira Gandhi. It suffers from the same drawback of getting feed from half educated half-leftist half-socialist Indians who are prepared to give any twisted report for money.

If the NYT sincerely stands for a free press, let it send its New York based correspondents to do independent coverage in India for a year without any bias and file the stories accordingly. Carrying on with the motivated coverage as usual is poor journalism.

The Guardian has never done any news story on developments in India in the last 12 years. Had it done stories on corruption under the Congress led UPA government or the diarchy or the dynasty or the unconstitutional structure of the NAC under Ms. Sonia Gandhi, it would have earned credulity for its stories. Since it ignored all such developments and is standing with the forces opposed to the Modi government, its stories deserve no credit.

Will the NYT please answer this question: would it be siding with a mob of students and faculty on the Harvard campus raising slogans to dismember America or kill the President of America or destroy America as on 9/11 or worse on Sunday June 12, 2016 in Orlando, Florida, butchering 50 and grievously injuring 53 innocent people?

Will the Guardian be kind to students and the faculty on Oxford campus raising slogans to destroy the UK or kill her Majesty?

If not, how can these two newspapers extend support to traitors on the JNU campus? It is immoral, unethical, and unwise from every angle. These newspapers owe an apology to the Indian people immediately.

Noam Chomsky need to remember that America has invested billions on containing communism in this region and fought wars, which are still continuing in Afghanistan. Does he want communism of the JNU variety to gather strength further? Does he expect a friendly response to America from the Indian left which has always spewed venom against it and misled the people on geo political issues all these years, patronizing poverty instead of prosperity, backwardness instead of development, closed mindset instead of openness to new ideas and change?

Why should such serious matters be adjudicated in newspapers and television studios? The Indian judiciary is independent and strong enough to return the right verdict.

But when traitors and enemies of India allege "judicial killing" for awarding the death penalty to terrorists or traitors, they cross limits; when such elements poison the vulnerable student community on campuses, they invite prompt and harsh response; when they try to stop the government by media hype from taking lawful action, they seek the weak government of the past which had encouraged them to cover the distance from terrorist hideouts to university campuses. That is over now. Government has since changed in India and the people have changed in India. Terrorists must face decisive action. They saw it in Pathankot. They will see more of it. But the western countries must be prepared to face the consequences of their soft corner for them and their chief patron Pakistan. Stoking fires on university campuses is going to prove counterproductive for these countries, their press and electronic media, their thinkers and writers and others who are exploiting the host's generosity by living in comfort in those countries and surviving on foul mouthing India.

A true academic institution must promptly condemn the activities of the anti-national forces, enforce discipline among its students and impart true knowledge to them on all issues. Anything less than that is un-academic. For that the right place is the political party, not a university.

# Non-Alignment Between Cold War & Third World War

Where does India figure in the strategy of super powers? Do the superpowers give a damn to the low cost war by Pakistan against India for the last 36 years? Do newspapers, television channels, radio or other media in developed countries make even a passing reference to organized attacks on democratic India by the military dictatorship of Pakistan? Is the West safe if Pakistan succeeds in subduing India with their help? Will the minorities in India be spared by the fundamentalist forces carrying on unabated for decades the terror activities against India if India fails to checkmate them effectively forever? Who will stand by India when the fires of the Cold War & third World War impact India? At present Pakistan has three (3) superpowers backing it solidly besides some Islamic countries. America, China and Russia are Pakistan's friends. Indians have not yet forgotten the American threat to send the 7th Fleet to the Indian Ocean in 1971 to help Pakistan. China has entered into strategic partnership with Pakistan and is developing the Gwadar Port. After the end of the first Cold War in 1991, there has occurred a significant change in the Indo-Russian relations and Russia has warmed up to Pakistan. The disintegration of the former USSR has changed the geo-political power equations. The magnanimity shown by Russia in the interest of world peace has been abused by America by creating trouble for Russia and making serious efforts to weaken her. Pakistan has always been a pawn in the hands of America against the Communist Block. It has patronized the military rulers in

Pakistan in order to exercise control and influence on it. There is no Non-Aligned Country anywhere to help India if ever the need arises. The civilized mode of raising issues of terrorism in the United Nations Security Council (UNSC) have repeatedly been "blocked" by member states to extend a protective cover to Pakistan, which runs the world's most successful terror factories and exports all its produce, threatening not only international peace but also security.

Added to all these problems is the baggage of secularism, which is shared by no other country with India. In effect, the secular India has no friends to come to its rescue. This century will witness the worst conflicts of human history. The present day India is not prepared to face such a challenge because it has failed to devise any strategy so far. Every decision of the government has its opponents. Politicians speak in different voices. Even national interests are undermined for no justification. We face wars with Pakistan and China not by consensus but by majority, as the communist party had opposed openly the government when China attacked India in 1962 and the Congress is unlikely to cooperate with the government of Prime Minister Modi if Pakistan were to start a war against India now as its leaders (on a visit to Pakistan) had begged Pakistan to overthrow the Modi government.

In these circumstances the people of India have to take a decision now whether they love freedom, democracy and rule of law. There has been too much of superficial talk on almost every aspect of our life, but now is the time to take hard decisions. We need to punish traitors threatening to destroy India. We need to strengthen democracy by electing only the best persons for parliament, assemblies and all other elected offices. We must take the vow to contribute to the growth, development and power of the nation before exercising our rights- meaning we give more and take less.

Our youth must give a serious thought and decide not to give or take dowry in marriage. Our prospective mothers must give a serious thought and decide to make one of their offspring a clean person who will never fall to the lure of any kind of corrupt practices as a public servant. Our voters must take a vow to exercise their right to elect their representatives wisely, not as a once in five year task; and also to keenly maintain an oversight on the elected person with a view to seek delivery of good and transparent governance. An honest MP/MLA is worth the gold equal to her/his weight if s/he were to perform her/his duties honestly, irrespective whether on the treasury benches or in the opposition.

Irresponsible conduct of leaders in the last 20 years or so leads us to only one conclusion that the country has been thrown in to a movement of untruth as politicians, newspapers and television channels have no qualms of conscience in telling untruths and perpetuating them nonchalantly creating social disaffection, disharmony and disturbance. A single word "corruption" sums up all the malaise afflicting the country. The drama that started with award wapasi has reached the stage of Freedom of India Wapasi because the dynasty is no more in power. Presumably India can enjoy freedom only if they are accepted as the lawful ruler. India won her freedom by launching the Satyagraha Movement under the epoch making leadership of Mahatma Gandhi. Politicians are now on Asatyagraha Movement (Falsehood Movement). Mahatma Gandhi gave the call for Quit India; present day leaders seem to be giving the call "Occupy India".

# Mahatma Gandhi More relevant to India than Marx

The much talked about rural employment guarantee scheme of India, the MNREGS, is a flawed economic wellness scheme for mitigating poverty and unemployment in rural India.

Most of it is unproductive labour which creates no genuine valuable assets and also not sustainable for long, whereas the problem of poverty and unemployment in rural India not only will continue but also increase.

Urban poverty provides the painful evidence of it.

If the conclusion of the economic thinkers is that rural poor can only have the opportunity for seasonal labor intensive work in the rural area itself, then the MNREGS gets reduced to a glossy unemployment dole with many opportunities for the rent seekers to swallow a large chunk of the funds by maintaining fake muster rolls and underpayments. That has largely been the fate of the scheme.

Unfortunate though it is, this has been the fate of almost 120 other centrally sponsored schemes and hundreds other state sponsored schemes.

So what is the alternative? The Gandhian economics envisions work to each hand and food for every mouth through promotion of khadi and village industries need be pursued, instead of simply putting Gandhi's name to fancy schemes like the MNREGS.

It is incorrect to consider the products, productivity and income generating power of the K&VI sector as of inferior quality. The tag of village industries need not be misconstrued to mean non-technical rudimentary production processes. It instantly pulls them down to an inferior status in comparison to modern industries.

They are village industries because they cater to the local markets and are owned & managed by local people with local tools and raw materials. 80% India lives in villages or depends on villages. Even cities like Delhi have "urban villages". These megapolises will lockdown in no time if goods and services supplies get disrupted.

Is edible oil extraction a local product or an export one too? Wasn't cheese making a cottage industry in the West before it developed into a billion dollar export industry? Is khoya (condensed milk for making sweets) making restricted to domestic consumption or can it also be developed into a roaring export industry to meet the taste of foreign consumers? What about the downstream products made from khoya? The word burfi is now part of the glossary of most tourists who have visited India.

These Village Industries need the same technological support which cheese received in Switzerland and other countries. We can follow the Swiss in making even the wrist watch industry in to a Cottage Industry only if we seriously ponder over the strengths intrinsic to these industries and their potential for employment and growth. The village industry sector deserves a SWOT test right away. They can compete with any producer provided they get technological support and obtain Trade Mark, GI tag wherever applicable, Patent and all other kinds of IPRs.

What is made by hand is considered superior in Europe and priced higher. They add value to the craftsmanship to hand made goods, whereas we reduce the value of all goods made by hand. Swiss watches offer the best example because they claim to be handcrafted and hence a collector's choice.

As against this attitude and economic logic of the industrialized world, we have not been able to establish a brand name even for the Rajasthani Jootis/ Kolhapuri chappals, which are appropriate footwear considering the climate and cultural choice of the consumers. They are all handcrafted products. There are a number of such products.

If we applied modern technology to this sector as a competitor to industrial products, we would have reduced to a large extent all prevailing food adulteration in the country.

Sensibly worked out data will throw up amazing results such as value of products more than 200,000 Crore rupees and self-employment opportunities for more than 5 million people in one product or a basket of some products.

Industrialization creates jobs but robs natural wealth of society in the form of pollution, migration, ghettoes, crime & grime, happiness and social support systems. The jobs created by industries are not well paying for the labor class. The birth of Socialism & Marxism immediately after industrialization in Europe is testimony to it.

The remedy lies in creating livelihood opportunities for the people by creating work at their doorsteps, without fixed working hours involving commutation which disrupts normal life and adds unnecessary cost to reaching work place. As against it, the village industry worker has the flexibility to do the work according to his or her convenience, with or without help from other members of the family, and continuing with farming activities.

The residence and work place being the same place, costs of production are reduced and price advantage makes marketing competitive. Besides, the artisan adds additional value by way of individual touch to the quality or aesthetics of the product.

Such products have always been in good demand in the domestic market, and export market is also quite promising if the tourists' purchases are any indication.

A national economist, superior to the Nobel winners, can work out schemes to take an integrated view of the entire KVI, handloom & handicrafts sectors. The potential is enormous, the possibilities unlimited, the opportunities for sustainable quality livelihood assured.

India, an ancient civilization, is caught in a unique time-space warp, if I may describe it so, where we neither love wealth nor decent incomes (we treat wealth as Maya or illusion & hate it; we show contempt to labor & artisans, paying them depressingly very low wages). If we get out of this civilizational black hole, pay decent wages to the working class and improve our business model to allow wealth creation as an honorable activity, we can improve living standards of our people.

It alone is a guarantee for rural employment; others are hollow slogans.

# Schooling Up To Class VIII Meant To Be Wasted?

By the time a child completes his class 8th schooling, s/he has already attained age 14. It is a very precious time of life indeed. Raw data tends to suggest approximately 40% of these school children discontinue further education. There are many reasons for it, poverty and poor educational infrastructure being two critical reasons. A collection of data from different segments like persons below poverty line, food security, village population, urban poor, disability and underserved population throws up the only conclusion that good education in India is a "luxury" the average household can't afford. On the other hand the question "what is the use of education?" begs an answer nobody has been able to field so far. When high school (X & XII) and graduates fail to get a job, the VIII pass can't even dream of landing up a job. Is "literacy" alone a measure of our achievement?

Age 14 is no small milepost in our country where the poor as defined under all categories mentioned above, constitute about 80% of our population. The question is: What is the age at which a boy (girl) can be considered grown up enough to be given family responsibilities and prepared to face exigencies? Thinkers in the past answered these questions after collecting the requisite statistics. They had settled for 12 years. Medical fraternity will provide due justifications regarding "maturity" at age 12 purely on technical grounds. It does not mean, children aged 12 should be loaded with the family responsibilities. If they do it, there exist compelling reasons for their plight, like the starvation conditions in the family or mother/father ill or unemployed. The sheer number of such painful cases will exceed the national population of many countries. The lesson we need to draw is this: formal or informal, education must be able to turn a child in to a "skilled workman" by the time he celebrates his (her) 15th Birthday.

It means overhauling our education curriculum and system. Presently it is a horrible waste of the whole schooling of 11 years as children enter school at 3+ these days, though the right age should be 5 years if the number of children wearing reading glasses is to be reduced. Modern achievements will trash any such demand for justifiable reasons. But ponder for a moment to analyze whether it robs the child of his childhood. We are producing trained workers because once in school, they will never have time in life for themselves, running from school to college to the job market. They are an over-burnt generation. We have successfully deprived them of Children's Right to Life & Liberty and Healthy Growth of Body & Mind. Success too does not come to all children. What about the 40% not going beyond class VIII? What would they do? Are we not making them economically disabled? Is it the goal of our education policy?

We need to devise a system whereby children learn one livelihood skill in the 10 years in school on the job. It may be without any formal lectures on the theory or technical aspects of it. We learn to drive without knowing anything about the inside of the car. Photography is yet another trade to learn. Why should children in this period not learn to use the computer and the keyboard effectively? The list goes on, but the success rate is 100% in any trade selected with due care. It is somewhat puzzling to find tailoring or candle-making in the training programs of most Finance & Development Corporation of the government, which aims to serve the disadvantaged groups. They need to be supplemented with skill development in first aid, physiotherapy, pre-natal/ post-natal services and similar other non-traditional and modern trades for a satisfactory livelihood. Our education system has to change children's attitude to working with hands. We teach our children contempt for trades enumerated in the foregoing and rate a government job superior, though the well trained nurse may get more than a doctor for his services, as there has always been a shortage of qualified nursing staff and the demand is only rising. Unless we start thinking for ourselves and stop merely copying advanced countries, we will be acquiescing to the colossal waste of money and manpower that has been going on all these years.

India has to rethink her children's education up to class VIII and devise suitable policies to face the challenge before her. Let us not be too patriarchal and bossing over our children. It is our duty to ensure a healthy development of their body and mind in 14 years. They should be able to face the world on their own in their 15th year of life. Millions of the unfortunate Indians have been shouldering these responsibilities all these 69 years of Azad Bharat. Even today, children can be seen working at thousands of roadside eateries throughout India. The kind of labor they have to do should be enough to draw tears to the eyes of any good citizen. It can stop if our schools also impart OJT (on the job training).

Poverty can't be removed by slogans or subsidies. Education alone is no guarantee for gainful employment. 14 crucial years can't be allowed to be wasted so easily. Can a project be allowed to suffer non-commissioning or excessively delayed commissioning? The privileged rear their children to make it to the national cricket team, proving the potential children have. Each child is endowed with such potential, only if our school education would nurture it to deliver a finely honed young man/woman, ready to face the competition before him/her in life.

# Jihadis Challenge Democracy

ISIS has shown its fangs once again in Brussels. It can derive any pleasure in killing 31 innocent flyers and seriously injuring another 271. Even with so much barbarity it has failed to secure recognition for its heinous brutality. What has been done by them in Brussels is no stray incident. The greater tragedy is that nobody knows for certain what is happening or why is it happening.

What do they want? This question was asked by a journalist to a citizen. Obviously she had no answer. If governments don't have answer to such a question, it is because of the civilized society fumbling for an answer. But an answer has to be found immediately. Violence in New York, London, Paris, Brussels and now Orlando (Florida) can't be ignored any longer.

It is so as this is a different kind of a war- a war between medievalism of the Dark Ages and democracy of the Modern Age.

The ISIS wants the world to return to the Dark Ages. Is it acceptable? If not, an effective antidote has to be found soon.

Violence for violence, brutality for brutality, savagery for savagery is not the answer. The world has invested heavily in modernizing. It can't waste all its intellectual, moral and scientific achievements to reach this level by adopting the same means as are practiced by the ISIS or similar other terror groups. Doing so would validate their style. Besides, the modern world would find itself a weak match for the barbarity of the terrorists. Other methods would need to be devised.

The civilized societies of modern democracies have to revisit their laws. Terrorists are exploiting the laws of modern liberal democratic societies. They can't be treated to fair and equal treatment of the law. They inflict widespread casualties but suffer no consequences on arrest as they get away with the justice dispensation mechanism practiced by democracies. Inhuman elements deserve no human treatment. So, what should the world do?

One solution is that each country fights terrorism on its own. That exactly is what has been done so far. It has only emboldened the terrorist formations. They have succeeded in inflicting not only physical casualties but economic devastation too. Free societies practice openness. Nobody is expected to bomb schools, markets, airports, restaurants, metro trains, planes or hospitals. Nobody is expected to wear a suicide belt and kill oneself. But that exactly has been done by terrorists- they have been indulging in all kinds of inhuman and beastly acts. All that is considered outlawed in civilized societies is lawful for the terrorists. Their act is no simple crime or revolution. It is terror. They want to establish the Rule of Terror.

Their religion has inspired them to do so. They are guided by their religion to win the world by terror. They have come to possess the weapons of modern warfare. They aim to use chemical, biological and nuclear weapons. The world can't act like an ostrich. It has to face the reality or peaceful

315

societies everywhere suffer the misfortune of the Brussels victims till democracy surrenders to terrorist diktats everywhere in the world.

Clearly, the menace can't be faced individually by the member states of the global community. Even alliances at regional levels can't stop the ever extending boundaries of DAESH as is proved by the failure of the NATO forces after the Paris attacks.

The failure of the NATO to deal successfully with the ISIS proves the point that there is an urgent need to devise an effective global response to face the challenge posed by terrorism represented by the ISIS. It has to be a UNO devised response. It calls for a new moral code. It has to re-define all principles of civilized behavior, such as human rights, freedom, equality, justice, equity, fair play and natural justice etc.

It needs to be noted that it is a different kind of war. The enemy is unknown but attacks from him are spectacular. He has no defined geographical territory. He may operate from the mountains in Afghanistan or somewhere in Iraq & Syria or elsewhere. He dreams of capturing the entire earth. His soldiers are not stationed at one place for his enemies to bomb and eliminate in a few days. They exist in all countries. It is confident of getting recruits to its ranks regularly for centuries. He draws all his power from this confidence. He operates in the name of Islam. There lies the secret source of his power.

While modernity has promoted secularism, the ISIS has promoted the medieval form of Islam. That appeal gets it liberal supply of financial and human resources along with necessary weapons and ammunition. While the modern world tries to reason with the forces of medievalism, they respond by creating fear globally, disrupting normal life everywhere and upsetting civic life globally. Nations are forced to remain alert all the time, employ armies of security forces for maintaining internal security and protect their assets and people on ground, in the air and on water. That is the work of the Satan/ Devil. He will not allow wo/man to live normally in peace and happiness. One of the attributes of the Devil is that he has no ears! He has only fears! He has no values. Can the modern man put the fear of God in to the Satan/Devil? Man's survival depends on the answer only if it is in the affirmative.

More security, more counter terrorism measures, more strikes in terrorist hideouts are not the right answers. It is not about body but the mind that the problem belongs to. It emanates in the name of Islam, whether construed rightly or wrongly. Even the question whether the proponents of this kind of Islam represent the entire community across the globe or not is not very relevant. It is enough for a handful of them to run the show. Even a single suicide bomber can do more damage than a whole army. So, it boils down to freeing the mind of the vulnerable from captivity of the perpetrators and preachers of inhuman acts of barbarity. They need to be dealt with severely rather than the victims of their religion of terrorism which is supervised by the Shaitan (Satan) himself.

The usual grounds like unemployment or marginalization hold no water. These problems afflict all kinds of people, not Muslims alone. But no other section of society indulges in bombing hospitals, metros, airports, planes, buses, schools, theatres, malls or markets. It is a highly profitable business for many people in the world to market all kinds of ideas in the name of secularism, freedom, racism etc. if not communism or capitalism. These are ideas which have flown from the West to the East in modern times, though they were in practice for centuries in these countries a few centuries ago till they suffered loss of their freedom to the medieval barbarism in the name of Islam or Christianity.

Other ideas too have spread from the Western world, which are highly offending to the Easter sensibilities. Terrorist strikes are justified as a fitting reply to the moral decadence promoted by such ideas in the name of Western Culture. Europe and America are targeted for this reason. What has long been known as obnoxious or perverse can't be made popular by the West throughout the world. It is great ideas alone which evoke positive responses from people as human beings universally. Were it not so, the ISIS would have gained popular support across all kinds of people, but it has ended up inviting strongest condemnation. Terrorism and its face like AQ/ISIS are the most hated idea and people of this century!

The Western world has to recognize the danger posed by these terrorist forces as a threat to the whole humanity and not when it alone comes under attack. It is sad that while the whole world has commiserated with New York, London,

Paris, Brussels and Orlando, it has failed to make even a passing reference to the lives lost in countries like India to terror attacks in the past two decades. The West displayed a patently pro Muslim tilt in Bosnia and elsewhere in pursuance of NATO & American foreign policy goals of weakening Russia. If the western countries approach terrorism in this way, they will never be able to deter the ISIS from inflicting more serious injuries to their people or national assets. They have to establish ethical values to inform all affairs of man in this modern world. Values are what distinguish the civilized world from terrorist outfits like the ISIS and their ideology.

Why are the terrorists targeting the West? It is so because the West poses the gravest threat to them. The West has been ferociously pursuing the agenda of democracy everywhere, including the Muslim countries, which practice authoritarian rule. They derive their authority from the Sharia Law contained in the Koran. The democratic concept of the Rule of Law is in conflict with the Sharia in many respects, especially rights of the women and the power of the religious hierarchy over the government. The conflict between the temporal and the spiritual power had existed for centuries in the West before democracy succeeded in establishing its supremacy. But they still have the Institution of the Pope, who can be the rallying point in crisis. The Caliphate had worked the same for the Muslims, which the ISIS has been trying to revive. As modern ideas flow from the west, many of them perverse too, there is a perceived threat to the Muslim idea of Life. There lies the root of the conflict. Whatever be the shape of the conflict, it draws into it the entire humanity. This conflict is doing the same.

# Academic Accountability Audit

The gay abundance with which university professors at the JNU in Delhi had indulged in making patently ill-informed statements on issues of serious national concern have highlighted the need for auditing academic standards, performance and requirements in our universities. As on date, the university professors enjoy maximum autonomy and freedom. They are not answerable to anybody. It is up to them if they take classes or not. Even if a professor does not take a single class in two years' PG program, nobody can question him or her. If the students suffer, it is none of the professor's headache. If he fails to produce even one research paper in ten years or more, he can't be questioned. If he does not guide a single PhD scholar under him, he has no qualms of conscience. For such professors it is more important to indulge in student politics and party politics than performing their duties as professor.

It is more remunerative for such a professor to engage in private tuitions or run some business under cover of an NGO. While running the NGO, such a professor compromises even national interests when he gets foreign funds for the NGO. He might not understand the true objective behind all the allurements like International Awards and become unwittingly an agent of the foreign intelligence agencies. Foreign visits in the name of seminars or conferences cast an irresistible spell on bureaucrats and professors equally. As members/chairpersons of government committees/commissions, professors wield great influence on government and its policies and, thus, easy targets for predatory foreign agencies. They might commit indiscretions like others and act against public interest.

In order to provide high quality, uninterrupted, highly useful professional academic services to the students, there is an urgent need to fix academic and research workload, performance appraisal, accountability and improvement mechanisms for all universities. Professors without adequate academic work rust and indulge in unproductive activities unconnected to their sphere of work. They are paid huge salaries and they have to justify such payments by rendering quality professional services. They must properly guide their students but never misguide them.

The limited time of the students at the university can't cover the study of the syllabus comprehensively and gain mastery in even one topic. Hence it is absolutely necessary for the professors to come to the aid of the students and assist them by teaching them properly. The professors have experience of several years and study in-depth the subject and thus can act as an "extractor" of the relevant information from various books and research journals. Such distilled information, if communicated to the students in a language easily understood by them, can prove genuinely beneficial rather than taking long notes in long hand by spending several days in the university library. The poor students at best have only 9000 hours for study at their disposal during the two years of PG. During this period they have to read, study, understand and analyze the various topics in a comprehensive manner. It may demand every effort to assimilate and absorb information contained in more than 900,000 pages in subjects like law, philosophy, literature, history, political science, sociology, economics, environmental studies, international affairs and others in science and technology.

Can they afford to waste even a minute of their extremely tight schedule? Even selecting the right book or article in a magazine is as challenging as consulting our friendly "Google Pundit". There is a device of extractor to help users to find the appropriate information on the internet without wasting time in perusing hundreds of pages of little relevance. The role of a University Professor should be akin to that extractor device.

Should the professors use the students for their ugly political activities, abusing the trust of a student in his teacher? These professors are expected to have read all these pages during the course of their career, because they have risen to the position of the Professor after years of academic work. It is their bounden duty to share this learning with the students.

If they have no mind for the ethical aspects of their profession, there is need to prescribe it under the law. An institution like National Higher Education Audit Authority of India can fill the gap.

They are doing no charity. They are paid public money for doing this duty. They have to do their duty to earn their salaries and allowances.

Selection to public services is rather tough. Various personality aspects are assessed in addition to physical and mental fitness. Aptitude is also assessed. Public servants are given training prior to actual posting. This mechanism needs to be extended to university teaching appointments. Then alone they will acquire the necessary perspective and widen their horizons. Such teachers will make valuable contribution to nation building.

# Destabilizing the Narendra Modi Government

Now it is no secret. Attempts are regularly afoot to destabilize the Narendra Modi government. Each packet of the program, packed in very attractive packaging, is sent at e-mail speed. The product quality and the script bear the distinct markings of foreign expertise. Its implementation in crude desi hands has so far failed to earn the returns expected. These are sophisticate software programs but the handling is crude. The executioners are crude in skills and handle them crudely, substituting calm handling by violent actions. It all started with a seemingly harmless aggression called tolerance. Introduced in the public discourse silently, it has surprisingly lingered on. So it is the main storyline in some newspapers, their lead articles and commissioned columns. It was followed by tutored show of returning the awards bestowed by the Sahitya Akademi, which earned the derisive sobriquet of Award Wapasi. It was supplemented by engineered "burning/attack" etc. on Churches even as not even one Church in service for some years has been targeted. The Akhalaq murder gave them the handle to whip up communal passions even though it remains a mystery till today as to which political party the victim belonged to, whether he was an active member of any political party, whether he was the victim of a conspiracy by his party to make political capital out of his "lynching" just when the Bihar election battle was gathering traction and needed the fuel of communal passions, whether it was a contract killing and if an honest investigation in the case is available in the public domain. In any case, it has proved a sharp weapon in the hands of all the Jaichands and the Mir Zafars of India to keep the communal fires burning in the name of minority/ lynching /beef. The program continues in the name of Vemula. It has been used to create unrest on the university campuses to attack the PM and his colleagues. JNU has been used to the maximum in this case as the students and the faculty, in collusion with the agents of the ISI of Pakistan and recruiters of the ISIS emerged to raise anti-national and pro-Pakistan slogans. It was sought to give it the color of unrest against Modi (their low levels in addressing the Prime Minister of India and painting a highly uneducated and immature student as one challenging him) and anger of the youth. The JNU students and their professors have been condemned roundly by all sections of the country. Only one newspaper group has been writing encomiums in praise of these people almost regularly in the name of the need to change the laws so that no notice is taken by the law enforcement agencies against these traitors, enemy aliens and persona non grata. The Opposition Parties imagine their decrepit leaders are the "youth".

So far so good. The Opposition can't be expected to sit quiet and the foreign agents are yet to be exposed. The people are aware of terrorists, their activities and supporters in the country. But they are oblivious of the designs on the sovereignty and integrity of the nation.

The underground operations are carried on to damage the federal structure of the nation, since India is a very strong nation as a federation but highly susceptible as a quarrelling geography of several contending states. It need hardly be reiterated that some wise thinker left us the maxim "united we stand, divided we fall". For making the constituents of the republic fight with each other, acts of disrespect to the Rule of Law, Constitution of India, Judiciary and existing laws of the land is being increasingly encouraged. Elected governments and their Chief Ministers express their views which are patently against the constitution of India. They disobey lawful orders of the Supreme Court, use street language to condemn the prime minister and other high dignitaries and generally act "independent". They have absurd notions of "azadi" and "swaraj", which they want to implement. They act dictatorially in running their governments as if they have the authority to operate outside the law which has allowed them to form the government.

Worse still, a calculated program of organized violence has been started recently in Haryana. Now it is planned to throw Punjab in the fires of terrorism of the decade of the 1980s. Water war has begun. The Congress was to start it for regaining power in Punjab after defeating the Akali government in the forthcoming elections to the state assembly. Another political party is inflaming passions to violate the water sharing agreements in violation of the law and the orders of the highest court of the country. It is openly fanning violence in Punjab by promising not to allow the completion of the Sutlej-Yamuna canal which supplies drinking water to Haryana & Delhi in lieu of power to rule Punjab in the forthcoming elections to the state assembly.

Water disputes are politically very sensitive all over the world, including India. The ruling party, Akali Dal, has always cashed these sensitivities. It was, therefore, not surprising at all that it lost no time in passing a bill to de-notify the land for acquisition for constructing the link canal from the Bhakra Dam to the river Yamuna in Haryana. While Punjab didn't implement its responsibility, Haryana has done it. Haryana & Delhi are going to suffer. Delhi will get no water from Haryana, which has threatened to stop Yamuna water flowing into the Munak Canal which brings the water to Delhi. Haryana has advised the Delhi government to construct its own canal from Bhakra Dam to Delhi. The Delhi Chief Minister loves to walk into political disputes of this kind to remain in the news without break. Haryana came into existence after reorganization of Punjab in 1966. In 2004, the Punjab government under the Congress Party was the first to de-notify the land meant for acquisition. It meant violation of the river water sharing agreements with Haryana and Rajasthan. The Supreme Court nullified that move decreeing that the construction of the canal be completed. But the Punjab government passed the law terminating the water sharing pacts. The matter is before the Supreme Court in a Presidential reference and it has not yet been returned to the President with the advice of the Supreme Court.

The enemies of India have a dossier of issues in their possession which can create disturbances in no time in the country. Some of them have been dealt with above, and sharing the rivers waters is another burning issue. The latest legislation of the Punjab government to de-notify the land acquired for canal construction was a quick response from the Akali Dal ruling government to the provocative promise made to not allow the work to continue if voted to power by the Punjab voters. The Supreme Court has ordered all concerned to maintain status quo. It has directed Union Home Secretary and Punjab Chief Secretary and the Director General of Police to take control of the entire stretch of the land in Punjab acquired for construction of SYL canal. The Punjab government has announced that it will defy the Supreme Court order. It has serious repercussions for everyone.

Such conduct on the part of the constituents of the Democratic Republic of India bodes ill for its existence. It negates the very Constitution of India, under which all state governments and the union government function. If one state disobeys the law, the others will follow; if one Chief Minister uses un-parliamentary language in public discourse, others will also do the same; if one state declares its independence/azadi/swaraj from the union of India, others will also do the same. It is for the Delhi voters to see what they can do to their government which is working against their interests and ensuring that the people in Delhi don't get their share of water from the SYL canal.

Attempts are underway to use the Punjab elections to revive the terrorist activities of the decade of the 1980s. The attack on the Pathankot Air Base in Punjab in January 2016 was the signal. Full-fledged operation will start if the Akali-BJP alliance is routed in Punjab. The result of the extremist operation in Punjab last time was the Operation Blue Star and the subsequent assassination of the Prime Minister Smt. Indira Gandhi and the consequential riots following it. The allurement of forming a government is more than enough for traitors who are prepared to work for the enemies of the country even if it ends up in another blue star. They know that it will not be possible for the Modi government to handle such a situation. They also know that if they are able to form the government in Punjab, it would put Modi under tremendous pressure. Their limitation is that they think others can't think as intelligent as they can. They have repeatedly given proof of their mentality. National interest is the last thing on their mind. It will be supported to the hilt by the extremists as it is showing the signs of indulging in populism of elections and will easily play into the hands of the inimical forces pursuing the agenda of destabilization and dethroning of Prime Minister, Narendra Modi. If the foreign forces can destabilize PM Modi and create lawlessness in Punjab again, they can achieve their agenda of destroying the Indian Republic and democracy.

A weak, backward and poor India suits everybody. They create internal disturbances not only in India but other countries, make neighbors fight, sell weapons and ammunition, control the economy and run the government from behind. PM Narendra Modi does not fit into their requirement of a Head of Government as a tolerant and subservient person to serve their interests over those of his people. He is too independent, too strong, too popular, too honest, too patriotic, too nationalist and too loved to ever be of use to them as the previous government of Congress alliance (UPA).

Their operations can be served by a person nurtured by them for quite some years. Such persons are trapped by exploiting their weaknesses and shortcomings. Some of them are power hungry others look for name, fame or glory. International awards are used to inflate their vanity. These awards are given to those who have the propensity to defy the rule of law or the lawful government for all the wrong reasons, but can carry out the patently anti-national orders of these powers. The loss of power for the Akali-BJP alliance will result in these anti-India forces turn Punjab into a disturbed area, forcing the Union of India and PM Modi to take decisive action against them.

These forces are already dreaming of Operation Blue Star-II. The statement of the Prime Minister of Canada that his cabinet has more Sikhs than the Modi cabinet is yet to be fully unraveled. Let us hope it is nothing more than bombast of a politician. A rupture in the Akali-BJP ties will affect the strong alliance of these two at the central level. Even though it poses no threat to the Modi government, it certainly weakens it to some extent. For the Congress it will mean losing Punjab forever. With no clear winner in such a riotous situation, Punjab will suffer another era of extremist violence.

Any Delhi type irresponsible experiment by the Punjab voters in electing their government will turn the state into a disturbed area for decades. Irresponsible or immature representatives of the people of Punjab will not hesitate to demand azadi. Already the anti-national demand was made at the JNU last February for Jammu & Kashmir and other states. It is these elements who are dreaming of forming the next government in Punjab. They were behind the rumpus in the JNU. Disturbances in Punjab will easily be extended to neighboring Haryana, Rajasthan, Delhi, J&K and the entire North Eastern States of Assam and the seven sisters, where insurgency with the active involvement of foreign forces has been causing disturbances for decades. Once mayhem is created in some parts of India, the organized insurgent groups can spread it everywhere. Naxalites, Maoists, communal extremists, religious fundamentalists, reservation agitators and a variety of other incarnations of the people on the wrong side of the law can create homeland security problems in no time. In fact, there are known to be contractors for providing crowds for rallies or creating riots at a few hours' notice.

It is against this background that Punjab occupies the top of the national security scenario and stability of the government of India. At no cost the anarchists and anti-national forces should be allowed to gain roots in Punjab. These agents of foreign powers have no ideology or commitment to serve the nation. They have no faith in the constitution of India. They are autocratic and do not recognize any authority established by the law. Their word is law and others must simply acquiesce.

The Akali Dal should not have openly threatened to disobey the orders of the Supreme Court. It is the nation that ultimately suffers due to acts of such recalcitrance of the constitutional authorities. If they don't mend, the people of Punjab may make them history.

It is not as if there is no remedy for such unlawful actions. The Constitution of India has provisions to effectively deal with such situations. But it is sad to use them in the 69th year of India's Azadi.

The Modi government will not only run its full term but also get another term in 2019. The foreign forces will be defeated in their mission. India will emerge a stronger nation through these travails. Only the people must remain alert and foil all their attempts at creating disturbances or spreading misinformation through press, TV, radio, community radio or social media. People must effectively participate in governance as good and responsible citizens and make positive contribution to nation building.

# Abuse of Freedom of Speech

A variety of opinions, views and acts are the central point of discussion in the name of freedom of speech in India ever since the BJP (Bhartiya Janata Party) came to power at the center. In essence, it was a shock to the vested interests involved in subversive activities against the people and the nation. This government was unlike the Congress government under which exercise of the government authority by a minority of interest groups for their own growth at the cost of the silent and timid majority of the people created the impression that India is a banana republic ready to be grabbed by anybody who could practice deception, corruption, violence, dogma, inducement, allurement, jargon, rhetoric, foreign money, external influence, blackmail, wealth and wine to easily rule India again. They were not wrong as the Congress misrule of more than 50 years only validated their perception. It was the time when the majority of the people suffered the maximum, especially losing faith in the nation, people, civilization, culture, philosophy and beliefs. It created an unequal situation where some people exercised excessive freedom to say or do whatever they wanted, while those exercising minimal freedom of speech were furiously resented in a well-orchestrated manner.

The media has not only played the most irresponsible part in creating such an ugly situation in India but carries on its negative activities unabated. It has never acted as an independent fourth limb of democracy in India. It has always acted partisan, maligning everybody speaking for and on behalf of the people or the nation. Partly it is due to its upbringing in the English environment. They are an anglicized lot. This section lacks in-depth knowledge and interest in Indian languages, texts, thoughts, traditions, customs, mores, taboos or practices. It thrives on some superficial idea about the English culture and tries to superimpose it on the Indian people without thinking even for a moment whether it is appropriate or inappropriate for them. But these media persons are able to speak the English language faster and more fluently than many Englishman. That gives them the easiest way to capture the news market and convert the status of the Fourth Estate into a thriving industry. It has no qualms of conscience in hitting left & right the majority of the people. It promotes hate speakers, jumps to the support of the most pernicious views and speakers, condemns neutral views abusing its monopoly of the media, sermonizes whosoever does not agree with them, interprets ideas like the freedom of speech according to its own convenience, contributes to intellectual confusion and creates anarchy for selling sensational breaking news.

Does freedom of speech mean one can say whatever one wants to? Does freedom of speech mean abusing anybody? Is freedom of speech the sole right of a minority? Does it mean the majority has to suffer the non-stop onslaught of the minority in the name of freedom of speech? Is the freedom of speech of one different from the freedom of speech of another? In a clash between the two groups, who intervenes? Is it right to put in place necessary laws to regulate the freedom of speech? If there is some law in place, is it not the duty of everyone to respect and obey it? Do the professors or students in a university enjoy greater freedom of speech than an ordinary citizen? Is it freedom of speech to act as an agent of an enemy alien? Does it qualify to be freedom of speech to condemn the country for restrictions on anti-national activities at the behest of an enemy country? Can it be called freedom of speech for the intellectuals (real or assumed) to use undignified, intemperate, and vituperative language for the Head of the State, Head of the Government or other organs of the state like the judiciary, army or federal bank?

Unfortunately in India, intellectual abuse of the children, adolescents and the youth has been the prime function of the political parties for furthering their agenda. The newspapers help them in disseminating foul ideas, foul language and foul action plans. Freedom of speech is extensively used by all of them for achieving this goal. This sly approach to impressionable minds makes many of them street children called "urchins" whereas the well-educated well fed well-spoken of the leaders and the elite become gentlemen and ladies to shoulder the onerous responsibilities of "political leaders" for serving the poor, especially street children! How do these politicians change their colors can be gauged from the fact that they talk of the poor before elections but serve only their near ones after forming the government.

In effect, it is an attempt to beguile the young and distract them from seriously pursuing their studies. A half educated person makes a better party worker. Cast in an agitator's mindset, s/he can contribute to instant strikes on university campus, where even imaginary restrictions on freedom of speech can be cited as curtailment of students' rights and be given a spin by the content starved television channels followed by newspapers. The rest can be done by the social media cells of the political parties and their student wings on the campuses all over the country. What more can any political party ask for than lawlessness and chaotic situation in society?

In the name of freedom of speech, the very identity of the nation can be questioned, its constitution condemned, its government threatened and its territorial integrity and sovereignty challenged. Active participation of university professors, domestic and foreign, lends special charm to such agitations and makes hero of the student leaders. None of these students ever reaches the top position in her/his party. The performance of young spokespersons on the television proves only one point that the intellectual integrity of brilliant students gets terribly corrupted so fast in a political party that they seem to have bartered away their freedom of speech forever for that insignificant political office. It makes one cringe to see even women performing that way, because a family or society is doomed if its women lose moorings or integrity.

Freedom of speech is the most valuable aspect of any strong and living culture. India is a country whose citizens have always enjoyed freedom of thought and expression and speech. It lost it when it lost its freedom itself. The Kutub Minar in Delhi, opposite the JNU, is a living testimony to the savage violence to the right to freedom, freedom of speech and freedom of worship when Kutubbudin Aibak, a slave of Mahamud of Gori left behind by him as a regent after defeating Prithviraj Chauhan, the king of Delhi, demolished more than 27 magnificent Hindu and Jain temples and built the minar using the debris. The iron pillar near the Kutub Minar is a marvel of the metallurgical advancement of the Hindu India as it has not rusted even though exposed to elements of nature. It was the grand pillar on which was hoisted the flag of a grand Krishna temple or Shiva temple as the place is near to the famous Kurukshtra. The height of the minar indicates that Kutubbudin was spurred to raise the height of his memorial higher than the temple post. The votaries of freedom of speech can never understand such a barbaric onslaught on freedom of speech and expression in creating magnificent structures in red stone and white marble as those 27 temples demolished by Kutubbudin Aibak to construct in their place such an ugly structure. It demands advance research in architecture and engineering of the temple building in ancient India. The Sun Temple at Konark, The Khajuraho Temples Complex, the Dilwara and Ranakpur jain temples, the temples in south India and the Maurayan creations of Didarganj Yakshi are testimony to Indian achievements in art, culture, architecture and beautiful temple building. History of that barbarity has partially repeated itself to some extent in the barbarity of the ISIS which all of us have silently witnessed without knowing how to end it. Even then, political parties like the Congress and the communists use the ISIS to intimidate the people of India in the name of freedom of speech. In present day India, there is no bar on anybody's freedom of speech. The left parties, however, don't allow other students, professors or visitors from the media or civil society to address the students on university campuses like the JNU, Jadhavpur University in West Bengal or the Hyderabad University. The leftists have promoted the cult of violence in India, especially in universities and colleges. They have been copied by others. Dissent and different points of views are meted violent treatment leading to death or serious disability. But there is justice for the victims of such acts if court of justice is approached. There is not one instance of denial of justice to anybody since 15th August 1947. Those in doubt need to give full details to update their knowledge.

A valid question may be asked: if it is true that there is no bar on freedom of speech in India then why so much is being said about it in the media? As detailed in the foregoing, it is a political agenda after the BJP formed the government and Narendra Modi entered office of the Prime Minister of India. He has upended the functioning style of the previous government of the Congress Party when he declared immediately after taking over as PM that he would neither act corrupt nor allow others to do so. He said it in Hindi and for the impact of the expression it needs to be reproduced here: naa khaaungaa naa khaane doonga, which was just the opposite of khaao aur khaane do (meaning eat and let others eat). He has proved by his subsequent functioning that he really meant it. That has upstaged thousands of agents of forces inimical to India and the majority of its people.

These agents have been indulging in a vilification campaign against the prime minister. Freedom of speech is just one pretext. They started by roping in the literary awards winning writers to return the awards in the name of growing intolerance but licked dust when these so called writers were jeered by the people as those who had either bought these awards or got it as a measure of loyalty to the ruling party. They collected a lot of muck, including their friendly journalists of the press and television. It frustrated them terribly. Then they fell back on their tried methods of student agitations. Thinking that professors enjoyed great social respect and public trust, they made academicians to give statements that there was no freedom of speech in India. Unfortunately for them, they made a grave mistake in choosing the Jawaharlal Nehru University (JNU) professors, who hardly fit into that description. The students they chose have made a mess of their political agenda by overshooting limits of public discourse and intellectual debate. These students, abetted and aided by their incompetent professors, converted the campus into a place in Pakistan by raising anti-India slogans and threatening to dismember the country. The professors displayed utter lack of knowledge and responsibility by making silly comments, thrilled by the presence of the captive audience, which encouraged them to talk like the several anti-India elements making fiery speeches against India from the Pakistani soil. This is not freedom of speech. They do not get paid heavy salaries to make such a fool of themselves publicly. In the privacy of their home, there is no objection to even this kind of madness, as there is no restriction on their remaining unclothed.

How does it matter if one believes in God or not? How is it anybody's concern whether one follows one or the other religion? But nobody has the right to interfere with another person's private affairs. To make it a right to freedom of speech to attack someone's private affairs is not freedom of speech. All those foreign forces who were busy exploiting the freedom earlier now know that their unlawful activities must cease. There is no bar on their lawful activities. Do they enjoy that level of freedom of speech in any other country? Are they enjoying that level of equality in matters of thought, belief and expression anywhere else? They should be thankful to India for that level of equal treatment and freedom.

There is no other society than the Hindu society which is so liberal, open and accommodating in the world. The world must recognize it and contribute to make it stronger. India neither seeks to extend its geographical territories nor increase its numbers by inducing others to join its population. The violence that the world has been witnessing since the First World War is the direct fall out of the unethical ambitions of nations to expand their geographical boundaries or populations.

It is time for the world to appreciate and acknowledge the values of the Panchsheel Doctrine of India so as to make the world a place to live in peace, happiness and harmony like a global family. The choice is of all those votaries of freedom of speech. Nobody should try to intimidate India in the

341

name of freedom of speech. The next wave of attack on India's liberal & open society will come not from one cult but a combination of cults who are mistaken to treat India as a market for all their foul ambitions beneath the veneer of freedom of speech. India is awake and strong enough to defend herself.

# Diagnosing the JNU Rumpus

India has been subjected to the ardhasatya (half-truth) by a political ardhakumbh of the students & professors of the JNU under the influence of a variety of political forces in the country and abroad. Prominent among them are the Congress Party, the Communist Party of India, the Communist Party (Marxist), other left organizations, the Janata Dal and other smaller parties, journalists attached to these parties and their TV channels, newspapers like the Times Of India and the New York Times, foreign professors like Noam Chomsky and Pollock and a group of other American Lobbyists, politicians, lawyers, writers (generally without work) and anarchists who get excited at the dimmest glimpse of political trouble. They are collectively and severally responsible for depriving a student of his peace of mind, academic career and prospect of breaching the chains of mortifying poverty. He has been instigated to act or partner others in seditious activities, without as much as understanding the grave implications of all this. This naturally brought the police into action, which charged him with sedition and detained him. He has secured bail for 6 months, with conditions to behave responsibly, from the court. Immediately on release, he sought to modify his seditious slogan by replacing it with these words: "freedom in India" and not "freedom from India".

The modified version gives away the superficial understanding of this student of anything relating to freedom. Obviously he doesn't understand the depth of the phrase "freedom in India". He has uttered these words as drilled into his head by his manipulators, who had made him raise the slogan "freedom from India" in the first instance. Obviously he is unaware of the loss of his freedom at the hands of these manipulators. The first thing education teaches us is to free our mind to be able to think freely and weigh the pros & cons of each issue so as to arrive at a reasonable conclusion. This student has become a captive to the caprices of the crooked political forces of the country, which are always scouting for recruits to the party, like the religious organizations looking for new faithful to increase their numbers. They hunt for the most vulnerable among the worst poverty stricken, harassed, tortured, frightened and hungry persons in the most backward, undeveloped, uneducated, illiterate sections of society in rural India. In such a situation, the weak have no choice at all. Rather they not only thank their benefactor profusely but feel obliged for life to them. This is called loyalty.

Loyalty of the poor to the benefactors means slavery. The slavery of the body is less exploitative as compared to the slavery of the mind. The religious fundamentalists or the communists, for example, rule the minds of their victims. They don't allow them freedom of thought or independent action. They feed them ideas and expressions which can further their objectives in the name of revolution, a catchy expression. In the name of revolution they give vent to all their bottled up anger. In the village any word against the politician or the criminal results in instant reprisal. In Delhi or Hyderabad or Jadhavpur challenging the authority of the law becomes a means for them to feel free of the fear of the feudal forces in their village.

The student at the JNU is a perfect example of such a game which has been played regularly after WW-II, globally and in India particularly. It used to be a fad for every student and teacher on the campuses in India to make a statement of his "progressive" identity or left leaning. The left had comparatively easier access to the elite in India. The glossary of the Cold War - capitalism represented by America, colonialism represented by the UK and entire Europe excluding the Eastern European countries of the Soviet Block, and dictatorship of the proletariat- dominated all public discourse for decades in India. The proletariat fitted so comfortably with the kisan & mazdoor (farmer & Labor) pair of words in India that it overwhelmed the entire discourse on democracy and economic planning in the country. The student in the JNU, raising the issues of freedom from or in India is as ignorant of these political concepts as was the elite of India till the year 1962. The Chinese aggression delivered the first terrible shock to a smug Indian polity and elite class (The imposition of Emergency in 1975 was the next big shock).

Those in mental captivity of another dominant entity (person or political, religious bureaucracy, drug syndicate, crime mafia) not only remain a slave themselves but also barter away the freedom of their children. India has practiced for long an ugly system of "bonded labor" (Bandhua Mazdoor). It is illegal now. But it goes on surreptitiously in the same way as drug pushing or bootlegging goes on. Under this practice, the labour is under an oral bond between the creditor and the debtor to discharge his loan by rendering unpaid labour to the debtor.

On his death without fully discharging the loan, his children are bound to continue doing so until the entire loan is recovered. Extend this practice to student recruits to political parties and the present disquiet on campuses will become clear.

Students act as agents of political parties on the campuses. Their union elections cost more than a million in JNU and Delhi University (not so much in the neighboring Indian Institute of Technology) because of the involvement of the political parties, who finance the elections of their candidates. That lays the foundation of an educated class which is ever ready to create anarchy on the street on the pretext of non-issues. They look for opportunities to foment trouble on university campuses, goading students to take the extreme steps like suicide to get free publicity. They never dissuade enraged students from taking extreme step; rather they encourage them by showing the media coverage to prove their point.

Professors with political ambitions help the parties to further their agenda. By indulging in politics, these professors betray complete dereliction of their academic duty. They hold back vital information from their students, release information in installments, delay completion of PhD work, demand favors from female students unbecoming of university professors and indulge in outright corruption too. These intellectuals deride anything Indian and eulogize everything American, but they have not published the code in Harvard on professors indulging in physical relations with their students. The exploitation of the immature students and their youthful exuberance and idealism is unethical and sinful. The professors on the campus are exclusively responsible for subverting the academic aspirations of the students in their charge, destroying their careers and diverting them from the education highway to the dusty roads of petty politics. Basically it is due to the professors themselves being unqualified or unprofessional in their jobs. None of them is a Nobel Laureate. Hence, they indulge in cheap politics, which is the easiest to indulge in because their jobs are not at stake and they are not accountable to anybody and their understanding the expressions like freedom of speech includes freedom from India. Their spirits begin to fly high on getting coverage on TV & newspaper space given to their views and photographs. It lends added charm to their success if a Noam Chomsky or a Pollock also enters the campaign or a foreign newspaper like the NYT gives them prominence. How much of India do the foreign newspapers or professors understand? They ought to ponder if it is fair on their part to casually partner with the traitors of India threatening to destroy India and proclaiming Independence.

The misguided JNU student union president, who has modified his seditious slogan to freedom in India, needs to answer a few questions. Who is not free in India? Does freedom not mean freedom from want? Is freedom inclusive of freedom from disease? Freedom in India also means freedom from illiteracy, lack of education, unemployment, backwardness, medievalism, feudalism, exploitation, hunger and poverty. Does he acknowledge them as candidates for freedom in India? Can he demand freedom without contributing anything to achieve it excepting holding demonstrations and raising anti-India slogans as tutored by his half-educated mentors? Is it not his primary responsibility towards his parents to provide them relief by way of extending financial help to them after engaging in gainful employment commensurate with his qualifications so as to return a part of the investment made by them on his education at the cost of going to bed empty stomach many a times in order that he could complete his education? He has dashed all their hopes. Even if his parents say they never expected any help from him, isn't he supposed to contribute to the best of his ability to the reduction of poverty to make India free from it? Is it not his moral responsibility to repay the non-financial support he had received from his friends and village folk, who had extended him emotional support to encourage him to complete his studies so that he could open opportunities for others in the village to gain access to education or employment? If he thinks "moral responsibility" is a bourgeoisie phrase, he should be ready for the villagers to raise slogans to destroy him or his family and get freedom from his hegemony being a highly educated boy from amongst them following his rumpus at the JNU? Family, society, village or the country are structures which have evolved from ages of collective thinking and experiments. The JNU, its faculty and students came into existence only later.

This JNU student, as thousands others distracted like him by his professionally incompetent professors, has proved himself a failure as a responsible citizen of India. He has lost his way. He will contribute nothing to make the people free in India. Had he been honest, he should have chosen to work for the improvement of the economic conditions of the people in his village in Bihar. He has written off Bihar as a state beyond any kind of hope as it suffers the worst form of feudalism of the politician-criminal gangs and Left Wing Extremism, rule of the jungle and Naxalites & Maoists, where freedom of speech is non-existent. People like him only add to the number of the poor in India, who live on alms, loot or doles from the welfare schemes of the government. They are a useless bunch, aptly described as useless fellows incapable of working outside the home or inside to earn a living, and yet enemy of family food grains.

What can he do for Delhi? Will he bring leftist revolution to Delhi? He forgets that all his male & female mentors have not been able to bring any revolution to Delhi in the last 68 years!  He can only help the forces of anarchy and communist violence in the national capital in complicity with the anti-national extremists & terrorist modules operating in India.  He will end up like a political slave to some political party or its leader. He will be bartering away his freedom to these elements for his survival in the rough and tumble of politics, barely able to sustain  his ideas to live with the rhetoric till disillusioned.

Delhi is the biggest mandi (wholesale market) of political commission agents. Here even the foreigners indulge in free market trade. They are uneasy with Prime Minister Narendra Modi's government for not giving them special treatment by exempting them from all Indian Laws. Due to this India is under twin attack: terrorist attacks and soft power offensive. The JNU rumpus is manifestation of it.

# Beware India of Soft Power Offensive

Soft power offensive is deadlier than war. Traitors of peacetime are more dangerous than those in war time. A war is known to every member of the society, but not the soft power offensive. In war soldiers are killed; in soft power offensive a nation is killed. The soft power offensive is mounted in soft style. It relies on the power of the word, visual or music. It camouflages the hideous intent of the enemy in impressive vocabulary. It does not employ an army of millions but just a few people. The few in its employ have the astounding power of multiplication into a hundred and thereafter into thousands and in due course in millions to destroy a strong nation and a strong society. It achieves its goals at a very low cost. Its commanders are the most influential elite of the world, who engage the elite in the target country. These elite are the creamy layer of a nation. They occupy the commanding heights of all centers of power in their country. It includes eminent personalities from political, economic, intellectual, academic, religious, media, scientific, technological, trade, agriculture and other fields, who exercise influence on the people and public opinion.

The game begins with controlling the media. Journalists are enlisted. With their active support, desired stories are planted. Governments are negatively depicted. Short-comings are invented, and if there be any, they are overplayed. Writers are invited to debates on TV and contribute articles to the chosen newspapers. These are regulated so sophisticatedly that the writers turn into mere rubber stamps. Publication in the newspapers or appearance on TV is too tempting to writers and TV participants. It spurs the ambition of the budding writers, who are prepared to do the bidding of the operators for a single opportunity of publishing or telecast even for a short time. The glamour world is too competitive and entry itself is extremely difficult. New participants are not welcome. For ensuring that their name is not deleted from the invitee list of the television or newspaper industry, they are always keen to do their bidding.

The soft power offensive begins here unobtrusively. It gathers momentum in chosen academic institutions where students and faculty, with no world class research or books to their credit, desperately try to attract attention. They are the raw material for the soft power offensive.

They start with just one activity to generate a debate. Slowly, the debate is steered to anti-social activity. Attempts to stop such undesirable activity are turned into controversies skillfully.

The enthusiasm and idealism of the students in universities is exploited to cause nuisance in the full knowledge that it is bound to attract disciplinary action at some stage. Discipline is a concept most disliked by the youth, who are misled in to violent action. Violence, though condemned by the people, turns into media fodder for long.

The soft power takes charge of the situation and portrays the government poorly. The government is compelled to take action, orders police action according to the law and the law takes its own course. The media targets the police. The soft power seeks extra-legal remedy by placing before the government demands difficult to meet; the soft power mounts attack on the government using stretchable words like tolerance or freedom of speech.

So, what the soft power offensive in essence turns out to be is this: turn your eyes away from all anti-national & anti-social activities taking place in the country, on university campuses or in the media and don't punish the traitors of the peacetime.

The aim is to disturb peace, public order and social harmony while the offensive attacks national values, culture, security, sovereignty, territorial integrity, government, parliament and the judiciary.

Should the country remain oblivious of the advancing dangers to its very survival? Unlike in war, there is no ceasefire in soft power offensive. It has the flexibility to quietly withdraw into safe hiding only to resurface at the opportune time and place of its choosing.

Colonies of traitors are quietly raised and nurtured by the soft power offensive countries as a measure of their foreign policy. The divide between developed and developing, or developed and least developed countries is as real as between the rich and the poor or the masses and the classes or the elite and the mediocre in any country.

In situations of poverty, lack of education or health care, unemployment or under-employment or un-employability, even the slightest empowerment is welcome and the beneficiary pledges his/her loyalty for life to the benefactor.

That is how even communists in India locate potential party workers from hungry families, nurture them, finance their education but control their mind. That exactly is how terrorists are produced. Feeding the hungry body is used to feed the mind the language of revolution, jihad, dogma, ideology, hate, revenge, war, killing, terrorism, lawlessness, disorder, indiscipline and conflict.

The soft power offensive exploits language, visuals, art, music, poetry, fiction, drama, films, food & drinks- in fact every soft weapon in its armor to cast the spell to vanquish and take over the reins of a country.

Diversity is the law of Nature. Even in the tightly integrated country, diversity at personal, group or social level will be there. India lives in its diversity. Exploiting that diversity is easy for the soft power marauders, especially when they can easily enlist persons whose minds and tongues are captive to their masters. They do as ordered, exactly as the drug peddlers do. These minds remain captive and enslaved forever as freedom from bondage is unthinkable in this business.

If the Prime Minister Narendra Modi is being subjected to repeated onslaughts from the soft power giants, there is nothing unusual. They never expected him to become the PM of India, certainly not with such a clear mandate. Then he was not expected to last long. He has frustrated his rivals by performing a series of feats after taking over as Prime Minister of India. He has done the most unthinkable: made the President of the USA to be the Chief Guest on the occasion of the Republic Day celebration in Delhi last year and enjoy the proceedings sitting along with the President and the PM of India from the Rajpath in the open! He had been so popular in his interactions with leaders like the Presidents of the USA and China and Prime Minister of Japan and other dignitaries that his rivals went mad. Having failed to check Modi from becoming the Prime Minister of India and proving successful too, they resorted to Soft Power Offensive against him.

So, conflict situations are regularly created in different states. For it they target Modi. Intolerance, freedom of speech, Akhalaq, Rohith, JNU etc. are pretexts to attack Modi.

For many months the rivals failed in their attempts as the state chief ministers were responsible to deal with all those incidents. So, they chose Delhi finally as policing is directly under the government of India in Delhi and Modi could be blamed for everything. These smooth operators, shouting tolerance from every corner of the universe, are so intolerant themselves of the Indian laws and independent judiciary that they seek to overturn them all so that they have a free run to achieve their nefarious goals in the shortest time. They have failed to understand the personality and character of India, which they have mistakenly mixed up with the traitors in their employ.

The offensive mounted from the JNU has proved negative for these elements as they have jumped in to the fray directly. Normally soft power offensive is started covertly, the attackers operating from the wings. In JNU, they had to come out, even though many of them had covered their faces like the terrorists generally do, raised anti-national slogans and vowed to destroy India.

In spite of their agents among the journalists and TV personalities, students and faculty, political parties and leaders, the perpetrators of the strongest soft power assault have licked dust and exposed themselves as traitors, anti-national and anti-people individuals and groups.

Caught on the wrong foot, they now want the sedition law to be changed so that they get away easily. They want all laws to be changed so that they escape the law. They will go on like this for years. But the people have seen their true identity for the first time.

Foreign money and management will keep them alive for long, but without freedom of thought or action. They will have to think, speak and act as ordered. The Devil of the offenders has enormous capacity to cause damage and social upheaval.

Indian people will have to remain watchful. As Modi goes on adding feathers to his cap, these forces will turn more ferocious. They will also enter into big alliance or (mahagathbandan) to cause maximum damage to India or Prime Minister Narendra Modi.

The people should not trust any of the mediocre and paid journalist, newspaper or TV story. Writers, professors, public figures- Indian and foreign- leaders from across countries, and other reputed names are being misused or misconstrued by these forces to sell their program of destabilizing the government of India or even physically harm the PM Narendra Modi.

People should exercise their own wisdom in analyzing developments in political, economic and social life in the country. They should beware of these marauders out to play with the minds of the people by feigning to be fair, neutral or unbiased by publishing contradictory stories in the same issue or other sister publications or TV channels to buy reader/audience loyalty.

It is purely a business for them judging them by their obsession with minority (which for them means Muslims only) and Dalit issues and their addiction to inflate any insignificant news into a mass movement.

They challenge the wisdom of the Indian masses as well as classes.

We are trained to respect (shraddhaa/ aasthaa) the teachers, elderly and other high dignitaries, but today that has become a weak point for all kinds of criminals to exploit. We believe in Satyam Bruyate, they practice Asatyam Bruyate; we respect Truth, they practice lies.

The war is unequal because for the moment there are many on their side without understanding their true intent. But even a limited number of patriots are enough to fight the legions of the traitors.

Only thing is to empower ourselves fast with the best of knowledge. India has always believed that knowledge is of no use unless shared with the people. Knowledge is public property and must be disseminated without reservation.

India has not promoted IPR or Trade Mark culture. Knowledge is not used to establish hegemony over others. What the Super Soft Power intellectuals are doing today is nothing short of attempts to establish their dominance and hegemony on academic centers in countries like India and control through them all significant sources which easily influence public opinion.

These forces inflate a mediocre university like the JNU to the stature of a dominant university, whose views apply to all other universities without question. For them, the mediocre professors, writers, journalists, poets and politicians are the best bait to disturb the smooth functioning of the government as by law sanctioned.

The foreign scholars and intellectuals apply "sanctions" against India and other developing countries. They have been in the business of intellectual sanctions since the days of the Cold War when they used the word "democracy" to fire at the enemy (the USSR and China). History is nothing more than an account of the Soft Power assaults carried out by different forces.

In the modern times, their economic compulsions egg them to seek new markets. For India knowledge is for the sake of knowledge, for them it is lucrative business. They seek new territories, new populations. We have no intentions to capture foreign territories or renegades; they have designs not only on our territory but also people, whom they will convert into slaves to forfeit all their wealth as had been the case in the past. Beware Indians of the Soft Power Offensive against our Nation!

Perversion, diversion, subversion do not qualify for free speech or intellectualism. Nothing is "unlimited', not even freedom of any style & brand, whether thought, speech, expression or action. There is nothing unlimited in the cosmos. Everything is limited wrapped in freedom. Freedom of speech and expression get accordingly limited by the same laws of Nature that grant them.

Everybody enjoys the same rights equally. If the right exercised by one tends to limit the right of the others, it invites regulation in the common interest of society. Call it morals or Law, they have the same effect to impose reasonable restrictions on speech and action in public interest. Unlimited action by individuals becomes anarchy, which threatens to endanger the lives or property of others in society and, thus, qualifies to be curtailed lawfully.

# Part VI

## Challenges Ahead

# Alert for Prime Minister Modi

PM Modi has already spent 24 months out of the 60 he had secured from the citizens of India. He has succeeded in serving the people to the best of his capabilities. In a nut shell, he has worked as a true **Raj Yogi**. The country started well after independence but lost its way somehow after 25 years. Post Emergency public services witnessed a terrible decline in honest delivery. Sadly, honesty became a vice and dishonesty a virtue. One need not go beyond the 15 Point Programme- a sham exercise to fool the people, public servants and the government. Since then the nation has been craving for an honest government. What they got was perhaps the worst government which indulged in open corruption for full 10 years with gay abundance, till the people came to trust Narendra Modi. In between two other governments at the center and several at the states had come, but could not survive their full term or secure public mandate for a second term. The Janata government and the Atal Bihari Vajpayee government were not corrupt but the first one was uprooted in about 3 years and the other was defeated after a very successful first term. <u>And here lies the warning sign for PM Narendra Modi.</u>

The PM has maneuvered his way through the negative forces rather successfully in his first year in office. It was largely due to the Congress Party's shock at its most humiliating defeat and the opposition's total rout. The media, especially the English newspapers and TV channels had been at their hyper-active best fifth column. Fortunately the PM had brought with him the power of the social media- he tweeted before they twisted news or painted it with their own preferred shade of views. PM Modi outpaced them. The people enjoyed it. They followed Modi and abandoned the newspapers and the TV channels. This only added to their frustration.

His party leaders helped them by making irresponsible statements without understanding the complexity of governance. All of them wanted to prove their warriors-of-words worth (shabdveerta). For the opposition and the content starved newspapers/TV channels it was godsend. They exploited it fully. They, who were in terrible fear of Modi, suddenly grew bold to challenge him politically.

The people in India are not aware of the enemies outside India. Pakistan or China are not the only two countries to engage our total attention, there are more powerful and better organized forces with clear plans and designs on India. They are successful in their communications whereas Indians generally end up in cross connections. Just compare the Obama speak "tolerance" and compare with every statement instantly flagged as "controversial" or "disputed" by the media and one will draw the same conclusion. Any statement made by foreign forces working against our national interests carries more value for our media than those made by the Indian leaders.

It happens to be so because the values of the west and the east are in conflict many a times. Our elite opinion makers are intrinsically for western values and criticize whoever takes pride in Indian values. Modi is branded by them "rightist" and hence all criticism directed at the BJP

(Bharatiya Janata Party) is automatically aimed at Modi. Fortunately for Modi, as also for all our politicians, all Indians don't read newspapers, much less the English language newspapers; neither do they like to watch English news or debates on TV. That way the damage is restricted to the urban habitats and the middle class people, who have their own opinions on most topics.

However, their campaign against Modi has only grown in their Goebbellian editorials, student disturbances and disruption of parliament. Modi's tweets alone can't take on all of them. Even if he does not fall into their trap, he will digress to non-action in the remaining tenure.

The fact is it is this latter part of his first term that is crucial for him and his party and most of all to the people of India.

If Modi has survived the non-stop assault on him all these months, it is due to his integrity and plans for public good, which have kept him so much above his opponents that they will never succeed in harming him till 2019.

But that is no policy. Even the Pandavas in the Mahabharat needed the help, support and cooperation of many to survive the 18 day war. Even the Pandavas could not have won their war without their Sarathi (Guide/mentor). In Modi's case, policy should be his guide. Even then, he should try to take the media along rather than suffering a hostile media. He should either clean the media of corruption or discipline them lawfully. It is no easy task because media is a roaring business and source of unlawful power. Our journalists are half-politician and half-intellectuals, who block entry of all those who can express freely and frankly on public issues. They are openly loyal to political parties. Modi should carry on with his direct to home approach and assuage the feelings of the media to some extent. He needs to deliver in the next 24 months before electioneering drowns every good effort in cacophony. What could he do?

Modi has to convince every housewife of his commitment to serve the people of India. Jan Dhan Yojana has no meaning to her so long as Dal (pulses) sells @200/kg. Who else can understand her pain than a chaiwallah even after becoming the Prime Minister of India? Efforts should be made in all sincerity to make available Dal at least @ 60 to 90 rupees/ kg. Price manipulation, artificial shortages, hoarding, black marketing in essential commodities are discredited and yet effective strategies to defeat the opponent in Indian politics when policy or programs can't be matched. It was more than a year ago when Arhar and Urad had touched 190 and 200/ kg that I had sounded a note of caution in my comments in The Economic Times of the consequences. The Food ministry, Finance Ministry and the Consumer Affairs ministry ignored these warnings. If Modi does not understand the public anger at such high prices, who else will? In Mumbai more than 100,000 Tons of Dals were seized in raids but the matter was brushed under the carpet and prices had continued to rise.

In India, if Dal & roti sell at such hellish prices, the opposition cashes it. Next year the UP Assembly election will be held. It will be a giant fight. Voters will be treated to liberal feasts by all parties on an unprecedented level. It means Dal, potato, onion, sugar, edible oil and condiments will be stocked in huge quantities by the parties as soon as the new crop starts arriving in the market around Diwali. The price behavior around the festival season has always played tricks with the consumers. The UP Assembly election as well as elections in other states will lead to shortages. Even though it is the responsibility of the state governments primarily, the central government would not be able to deflect the criticism and may be blamed for price rise. This has to be avoided at all cost. Modi will be left with less than 12 months to control prices before the next general election. It is preferable to pick up the subsidy bill on account of Dal rather than reviving the government of the corrupt as had happened in 1980 and 2004? If it happens, it would be the greatest shock to the people of India, who may not "trust" any leader for decades.

Modi has to understand that he can reach the voter at almost no cost this way rather than all other schemes or advertisement blitz. People must get enough to eat at affordable price, get reliable health facilities and education for children. If they get it, it makes all the difference that no advertisement campaign can ever do.

Modi can't expect the Congress to change even a bit and cooperate in the smooth functioning of the parliament, for it is a matter of survival for them. The media can't close down its business and withdraw to the Himalayas. The foreign forces will only increase their pressure as the economic conditions in the developed countries worsen. Domestic political and social conflicts will take time to end till the new generation completely replaces the old generation. Re-establishing values in society, government and administration will take time. It is no time for Modi to create new enemies on a daily basis by ill-advised government policies like the EPF withdrawals or interest rates, NOC for Doctors and gaps in schemes and their implementation. The intelligentsia may not be on the same page but need not be offended till the BJP produces its own scholars to take on the established ones. They may not make much of a difference in the voting, but influence public opinion. The past can't justify blocking of the present. Modernity is the need of the hour and antiquity the strength of our "collective thought".

Modi's second term will be guaranteed by Indian housewife. LPG cylinder will be of use if she has Dal to cook and chapattis to make. There will be any number of challenges before the Prime Minister in the next 35 months. So far he has overcome every challenge successfully and is likely to go into the next election with a creditable report card to show.

# About the Author

M.L Gupta retired in 2006 as Joint Secretary to the Government of India after having served the nation for more than 35 years in various ministries of the government of India including the sensitive Ministry of Home Affairs, Ministry of Social Justice & Empowerment and Ministry of Industry and represented India globally on numerous occasions as a member of the official delegation of the Government of India.

Prior to that he was in academia for 4 years. He graduated in 1964 from the University of Rajasthan with a Degree in English Literature, Hindi Literature and Political Science and earned his Master's degree in English Literature as well from there. He also studied Law at the University School of Law at Jaipur.

He is a civil society and current affairs analyst and takes special interest in matters pertaining to consumer rights, human rights, constitutional developments, economic policies, social policies, law & justice, urbanization issues, poverty eradication, health care, employment & livelihood, industrialization, pollution, developmental administration, education, anti-corruption programs, peace, philosophy, spirituality and literature. His writings can be found on his blog - www.vaaniyog.com.